D0381452

HOUSE, M.D. VS. REALITY

Most Berkley Boulevard Books are available at special quantity discounts for bulk purchases for sales promotions, premiums, fund-raising, or educational use. Special books, or book excerpts, can also be created to fit specific needs.

For details, write: Special Markets, The Berkley Publishing Group, 375 Hudson Street, New York, New York 10014.

House, M.D. vs. Reality

Fact and Fiction in the Hit Television Series

Andrew Holtz, M.P.H

BERKLEY BOULEVARD, NEW YORK

THE BERKLEY PUBLISHING GROUP
Published by the Penguin Group
Penguin Group (USA) Inc.
375 Hudson Street, New York, New York 10014, USA
Penguin Group (Canada), 90 Eglinton Avenue East, Suite 700, Toronto, Ontario M4P 2Y3, Canada
(a division of Pearson Penguin Canada Inc.)
Penguin Books Ltd., 80 Strand, London WC2R 0RL, England
Penguin Group Ireland, 25 St. Stephen's Green, Dublin 2, Ireland (a division of Penguin Books Ltd.)
Penguin Group (Australia), 250 Camberwell Road, Camberwell, Victoria 3124, Australia
(a division of Pearson Australia Group Pty. Ltd.)
Penguin Books India Pvt. Ltd., 11 Community Centre, Panchsheel Park, New Delhi—110 017, India
Penguin Group (NZ), 67 Apollo Drive, Rosedale, North Shore, 0632, New Zealand
(a division of Pearson New Zealand Ltd.)
Penguin Books (South Africa) (Pty.) Ltd., 24 Sturdee Avenue, Rosebank, Johannesburg 2196,
South Africa

Penguin Books Ltd., Registered Offices: 80 Strand, London WC2R 0RL, England

While the author has made every effort to provide accurate telephone numbers and Internet addresses at the time of publication, neither the publisher nor the author assumes any responsibility for errors, or for changes that occur after publication. Further, the publisher does not have any control over and does not assume any responsibility for author or third-party websites or their content.

This book was not authorized, prepared, approved, licensed, or endorsed by any entity involved in creating or producing the *House M.D.* television series.

Copyright © 2011 by Andrew Holtz
Cover design by George Long

All rights reserved.
No part of this book may be reproduced, scanned, or distributed in any printed or electronic form without permission. Please do not participate in or encourage piracy of copyrighted materials in violation of the author's rights. Purchase only authorized editions.
BERKLEY BOULEVARD and its logo are registered trademarks of Penguin Group (USA) Inc.

PRINTING HISTORY
Berkley Boulevard trade paperback edition / March 2011

Library of Congress Cataloging-in-Publication Data

Holtz, Andrew.
  House, M.D. vs. reality : fact and fiction in the hit television series / Andrew Holtz.—Berkley
Boulevard trade pbk. ed.
    p. cm.
  Includes bibliographical references and index.
  ISBN 978-0-425-23893-6
 1. Medicine on television.   2. House, M. D. (Television program)   I. Title.
  PN1992.8.M43H65 2011
  791.45'72—dc22

                              2010017431

PRINTED IN THE UNITED STATES OF AMERICA

10 9 8 7 6 5 4 3 2 1

To my family

You make it all possible.
You are the reason for it all.

CONTENTS

CONTENTS

AUTHOR'S NOTE

Suggestions for additional reading on the topics discussed, including Web links where available, are listed in the back of the book. These links are also posted at http://holtzreport.com/housemd.

Season Six began with a two-hour episode, "Broken." This book follows the episode numbering convention in which the first hour is episode 6-01 and the second hour is episode 6-02. The following episode, "Epic Fail," is 6-03 and so on.

A small portion of this book originally appeared in the *Oncology Times* "ScriptDoctor" column.

CHARACTERS

Fans of *House* know well the characters who work at "Princeton-Plainsboro Teaching Hospital" in New Jersey. For other readers, here is a brief introduction.

House (Hugh Laurie): Dr. Gregory House is a brilliant physician but seriously flawed person. He runs the Department of Diagnostic Medicine. His specialty is infectious diseases, but he seems to know everything there is to know about every branch of medicine. Basically, he is a medical detective who can figure out cases that befuddle all other physicians. He is not a warm and caring healer. His only interest is defeating the ailment. If the patient gets better as a result, that's nice, too.

Cuddy (Lisa Edelstein): Dr. Lisa Cuddy is the dean of medicine, the administrator of the hospital and its physicians. She is technically House's boss, but she rarely succeeds at exercising her authority.

Wilson (Robert Sean Leonard): Dr. James Wilson is the head of the Oncology Department. He is House's closest friend. He tries in vain to cajole House into abiding by ethical and legal standards.

Foreman (Omar Epps): Dr. Eric Foreman is a neurologist. He was one of the original members of House's staff. At times he has been put in charge of the department.

Cameron (Jennifer Morrison): Dr. Allison Cameron is also one of the original members of House's staff. She has come and gone from the hospital. Although she is a specialist in immunology, for a period of time she ran the hospital's Emergency Department.

Chase (Jesse Spencer): Dr. Robert Chase is the third original member of House's staff. He is a surgeon and specializes in intensive care. Like Foreman and Cameron, Chase has come and gone from House's team.

Thirteen (Olivia Wilde): Dr. Remy Hadley joined House's staff in Season Four. She is called "Thirteen" because that was the number House assigned her when he was evaluating a gaggle of candidates after his original staff members either quit or were fired.

Taub (Peter Jacobson): Dr. Chris Taub is a plastic surgeon who left private practice and then joined House's team at the same time as Thirteen.

Kutner (Kal Penn): Dr. Lawrence Kutner is a sports medicine specialist who came on board along with Thirteen and Taub.

Why We Need More *House*

Life evolves. And so does *House*.

In the beginning, the bizarre medical mystery . . . the circuitous journey in search of the correct diagnosis . . . and the fascinating solution dominated each episode. House himself has been an imposing, even overwhelming, character from the start, but we watched to see how the puzzle would be unraveled . . . marveling at the diagnostic logic and medical thrills that enlivened the ride.

Naturally, over the seasons, the characters and their lives have developed from sketches into more detailed portraits. We have become familiar with them—what they want, what they love, what they fear. It's a necessary process of growth. Otherwise, the stories would become stale. Even the strangest medical oddities would have a hard time capturing our interest and attention week after week, year after year, if all we saw were repetitive patterns of collapse and seizure and false leads and adverse reactions before triumph arrived in the nick of time.

Compare an episode from the first couple of seasons to a more recent story. You will see that in the earlier episode the signs and symptoms, the tests and treatments, loomed large. In recent seasons, episodes still have patients with puzzling ailments, but the focus of attention has shifted. The medical steps toward diagnosis are becoming mere sketches, while the personal lives of the characters flower.

The Medical Science of House, M.D., which was written during the show's second season, examined those medical steps that were in the foreground of the young series. It focused on the process of diagnosis and treatment. This book, *House, M.D. vs. Reality*, follows the development of the series. Rather than merely repeating the format of the first book with new medical details plucked from recent episodes, this book takes a deeper look into the lives of physicians, the work environment of hospitals, and the larger world of health care.

Cuddy became a mother. House embarked on a strange hiring binge. Wilson struggled with how to best help his patients at the end of their lives. Thirteen wrestled with her possible futures; everything depending on a flip of a genetic coin. No one saw Kutner's fate coming. Foreman was brought low by a mistake with fatal consequences. And House got clean. These are just some of the major recent events and developments in *House*, and they are each centered in the world of the physician rather than the diagnosis of a patient.

So let's begin this walk through some of the issues that real doctors encounter, and learn something about how those aspects of the world of health care influence not only their careers but also the lives and health care of the rest of us: their patients.

Still . . . *House* wouldn't be *House* without freakish medical cases, so we'll get to them, in due time.

Enjoy the journey.

One

It's Just a Show

"It's a TV show."

"Honestly, who cares if it's 100 percent real or not? It's just entertainment. People want to be entertained when they watch TV. They don't sit there and worry if it's fake or not."

"OMG, just watch the [expletive] show."

Those are the reactions some *House* fans had to *The Medical Science of House, M.D.*, the book that discussed the first two seasons. Even the character of Greg House himself winked at those who compared his fictional world to reality. He was talking with a star of his favorite soap opera in "Living the Dream" (4-14). The actor couldn't understand why viewers loved his soap, which he considered useless trash.

"How can you watch that stuff?" asks the actor who plays Dr. Brock Sterling on *Prescription: Passion*, the medical show within the medical show *House*.

"Because it's awesome!" House replies.

"It's preposterous. There hasn't been one real moment since I've been on the show."

"As opposed to shows that represent the world exactly the way it is . . . like . . . uh . . . can't think of any," House observes with a shrug.

He was right, of course. TV shows are not reality. Viewers know that prime-time dramas such as *House* are not intended as documentaries. So-called "Reality TV" shows are not really that "real" either; the characters and situations are selected, managed, and edited to enhance drama and conflict. Even true documentaries and news programs leave out the dull parts and usually skip over routine topics, which mean the final programs are (thankfully) more interesting than unedited broadcasts of actual events.

And yet fans of *House* do expect that the plot twists and turns will contain basic elements of real medicine. Trying to guess the ultimate diagnosis wouldn't be much fun if, just before time ran out, House announced that the patient had "Rigelian fever" or some such imaginary ailment. On the contrary, *House* fans trust that the diseases, symptoms, tests, and treatments will contain essential elements of reality.

"By watching *House* and absorbing the info you can really learn a lot," one fan commented online.

"Well, if they weren't at least 90 percent true, the show's credibility would be shot to hell. I mean, House, as a character, is fabulous, but the fact that all they're saying is REAL makes it even better," wrote another fan.

The producers and writers of *House* understand that their viewers expect a certain degree of medical accuracy.

"Absolutely. Otherwise you become a fantasy. Sure, we take liberties, but those liberties are still factually based," producer and writer Lawrence Kaplow told me during an interview for my "ScriptDoctor" magazine column.

Having to navigate around the rocks of medical reality adds to the excitement and tension of the medical detective stories. All of that would be lost if the show invented diseases or cures.

"Well, that would get us out of every single box we have really easily. I could tell any story I wanted. You know, bleeding in the brain causes toe fungus; let's just say that. Or hand rashes cause bleeding from the eye. Then the show is a joke," Kaplow says. "Might as well be a space travel show, set in outer space where I just take a zap gun and fix your liver. The drama goes away."

The dramatic bonus isn't the only reason to be interested in the accuracy of medical information on *House* and similar shows. Even though people know it is fiction and the intent is to entertain, things that viewers see on the show stick in their minds. One survey of viewers of the long-running medical drama *ER* found that about one in three said that information they picked up from watching this fictional show helped them make real health care choices or decisions. About one in seven said they had contacted a doctor because of something they saw in the show.

Lawrence Kaplow hears from people who have ailments like those shown on *House*.

"There are a lot of people who have these actual illnesses. When they watch the show and they hear about these illnesses, they are grateful, because they understand and they can identify with the symptoms. They say, 'That happened to me.'"

The power of *House* was shown by the reaction to a single comment about research on brain tumors. In "Half-Wit" (3-15), House's assistants, Dr. Eric Foreman, Dr. Robert Chase, and Dr. Allison Cameron, believe House may have a brain tumor. As they cast about for potential treatments, Chase says, "They've got another trial going on at Duke. Fifteen percent extend their lives beyond five years. If you are positive for protein PHF . . ." Although Chase didn't even finish describing the research, viewers went looking for information on an experimental treatment being tested at Duke University in Durham, North Carolina.

John Sampson, M.D., a brain tumor researcher at Duke, didn't see the *House* episode when it first aired, but he soon heard all about it.

"The next morning people started calling me up and saying, 'They mentioned your vaccine study on *House*.' Actually, they didn't specifically say it was a vaccine, but I guess that's what the majority of people took it to mean," Dr. Sampson says.

Colleagues and friends called and e-mailed their congratulations that his work was recognized on a hugely popular TV show. Patients and their families wanted to know if they could get the treatment. It wasn't the first brush with media attention for Sampson's team. Their investigations into a growth factor protein seen in about a third of glioblastoma tumors had been featured in *Newsweek* magazine and then highlighted on the *CBS Evening News*.

"That was sort of the biggest thing of late. That story created quite a stir as well, but really about equal to the *House* story, if not less," Dr. Sampson says.

So a vague reference on *House* that didn't even mention the treatment by name got as much of a response as a series on the evening news that included interviews with him and others involved in the clinical trials? "Yeah, I would say so," Dr. Sampson says.

In addition to such anecdotes about the real-world impact of make-believe medicine on TV, there is also scientific evidence. The educational effect of medical TV shows has been documented in a number of experiments in which prime-time TV viewers were unwitting guinea pigs of a sort. At least twice during the long run of *ER*, health education researchers worked with the show's writers to insert relatively unknown medical facts into the plots. National surveys before and after the episodes aired demonstrated the power of popular entertainment. In the first study, a subplot included a woman who had unprotected sex and was worried about becoming pregnant. One of the doctor-characters mentioned the so-called "morning after pill" (essentially a higher than normal dose of a birth control drug). Surveys indicated that awareness of this sort of emergency contraception rose from about half of *ER* viewers before the episode aired to two-thirds of them a week after the show.

Researchers saw an even more dramatic response to a minor story line on *ER* about the link between human papilloma virus (HPV) and cervical cancer. This study took place before the approval of HPV vaccines and the ensuing pharmaceutical company marketing campaigns that publicized the cancer risk associated with HPV infection. Before the study episode aired, fewer than one out of five regular viewers of *ER* knew about that link. One week after the show, awareness had tripled to three out of five viewers. Even six weeks later almost two out of five viewers remembered the virus–cancer link.

"And the fact is that in our study, more people had learned about HPV from *ER* than from all news sources combined . . . or medical sources, twice as many," says Victoria Rideout, who was vice president and director of the Program for the Study of Media and Health at the Kaiser Family Foundation when the surveys were conducted.

More recently, they did an experiment in collaboration with *Grey's Anatomy*. This time the subject was the risk of transmitting HIV during pregnancy. The writers introduced a couple that had decided not to have children because the woman was infected with HIV. When she becomes pregnant accidentally, they ask for an abortion because they are convinced the fetus will be infected, too. A character on the show convinces them that with proper treatment there would be a 98 percent chance their baby would be born free of HIV, and that the risk of infection is actually much lower than that of many other health risks facing mother and child.

Before that show aired, barely one out of seven regular *Grey's Anatomy* viewers knew how well treatment could shield a fetus from infection with HIV. After the show aired, the number of viewers who knew the facts had more than quadrupled . . . to almost two out of three. That result means that after one hour of prime-time TV, some eight million Americans had gained a whole new understanding of HIV and childbearing. Six weeks later another survey revealed that while memories had faded a bit, almost half the respondents said that women with HIV had a better than 90 percent chance of delivering an uninfected child. That's triple the baseline survey result.

"And that was just phenomenal to us, because this is an entertainment show. People are not tuning in to it in order to get information on a health issue. They are not thinking of it as being educational or news or informational," Rideout says.

Although the Kaiser team has not done a similar experiment with *House*, there's no reason to think the adventures of Dr. House and the travails of his patients have any less of an educational impact on viewers than *ER* or *Grey's Anatomy*. As Lawrence Kaplow mentioned, the show's writers do feel an obligation to maintain a certain amount of accuracy in their plots. In order to meet that obligation, not only do the writers consult with experts and browse the medical literature for strange and interesting cases, but there are also medical experts on staff, including writer David Foster, M.D.

Dr. Foster says he was introduced to TV writers by another doctor he had become friends with during medical school. Neal Baer, M.D., was then working on *ER*, where he would eventually rise to executive producer. Dr. Baer helped usher in the current era of attention to medical accuracy on prime-time shows, a big change from the freewheeling storytelling of earlier generations of medical dramas.

"And I became more and more interested in writing through that work. People would say, 'Help me with the medicine for this scene.' And then it became, 'Well, would you write the medical parts of this scene?' And then, 'Would you write these scenes?' And then I thought, well, I might as well write the whole script," Foster told me for my "ScriptDoctor" column.

Unlike Greg House, David Foster is a real human being, so even though he is a physician, he doesn't know everything about every disease, test, and treatment. In addition to studying the medical literature and checking with medical colleagues, Foster and the others on the writing team at *House* sometimes turn to a program created just for them and other TV writers in Hollywood. It's called the Hollywood, Health & Society program. The program is based at the University of Southern California's Annenberg Norman Lear Center and is funded by public agencies and foundations, including the Centers for Disease Control and Prevention, the California Endowment, the Bill & Melinda Gates Foundation, the Health Resources and Services Administration's Division of Transplantation, the Office of National Drug Control Policy, and the National Institutes of Health.

"When we are working on new story ideas or people are looking for new things to add to a story they are developing, talking to those people is very helpful and very useful. They may have a story or an experience or a disease that sparks interest and becomes an episode. We do a lot with them that way. Either they bring people here or we call them up and say, 'We're thinking of doing an episode on hepatitis B, is there anybody that we can talk to, an expert on hepatitis B who can talk to us about the show?'" Foster says.

"We work with *House* all the time. They are one of our biggest consumers," says Sandra de Castro Buffington, the director of the

Hollywood, Health & Society program of the USC Annenberg Norman Lear Center. "We have done one hundred and sixty consultations total with *House*."

Buffington says the health experts that the Hollywood, Health & Society program connects with TV writers—experts who may be used to writing for academic journals or speaking to small groups of their colleagues—are sometimes overwhelmed by the potential reach of *House* and other prime-time shows.

"When we prepare the experts to speak with the writers, we always ask them, 'If you could reach up to twenty million people in one hour with up to three messages about your topic, what would they be?' That's a question I always ask them. And they panic. And then we help them sort that through. And it's something that we put in our tip sheets, so that we capture those three messages and we leave those with all of the writers."

The Hollywood, Health & Society program has no control over what the TV writers eventually put in their programs, but Buffington says sometimes what viewers hear is word for word the messages that experts wanted to tell the public.

The long list of topics on which the program has consulted with *House* writers ranges from hospital infections to skin allergies to brain tumors to African sleeping sickness to leprosy to radiation poisoning and, well, on and on. The program also helps provide viewers with information by providing links to online resources from the official *House* Web site. Buffington says that just during Season Five, the program provided 147 links to credible information on the medical conditions, tests, and treatments mentioned on the show.

Viewers use those links. For example, when a link to information on the CDC (Centers for Disease Control and Prevention) Web site is posted, traffic spikes immediately. Then there are smaller Web traffic peaks on following weeks as some of the viewers who go to look up information on the latest episode also check out links from earlier programs. Researchers analyzed visits to the CDC Web site generated from 147 links posted for *House* fans during the 2006–2007 season.

Buffington says the top five searches included four topics in the area of sexual and reproductive health . . . but the fifth was a bit different: ciguatera fish poisoning.

House mentioned it during "Airborne" (3-18) as he and Cuddy tried to determine what had caused a passenger on their flight from Singapore to vomit and collapse during his meal. As viewers who clicked on the link learned from the CDC Web site:

> *Ciguatera fish poisoning (or ciguatera) is an illness caused by eating fish that contain toxins produced by a marine microalgae called* Gambierdiscus toxicus. *People who have ciguatera may experience nausea, vomiting, and neurologic symptoms such as tingling fingers or toes. They also may find that cold things feel hot and hot things feel cold. Ciguatera has no cure. Symptoms usually go away in days or weeks but can last for years. People who have ciguatera can be treated for their symptoms.*

From www.cdc.gov/nceh/ciguatera/?s_cid=nchmTV_HouseSe03_012

"The other thing we learned is that by tracking search engine data from Google, Yahoo!, these kinds of sites, about those topics while the show is airing . . . we find that people are multitasking. They are not waiting until the episode is over or the next day, they are searching during that hour," Buffington says.

"One of the things we love about *House* is that they address some of the more obscure diseases. Sometimes they are actually prevalent in developing countries and not so common here. *House* is always the one show we can count on to address topics that other writers of American television series wouldn't find room for." Buffington says they are studying how the shows teach Americans about diseases that are rare in the United States but cause widespread illness in Africa.

The Hollywood, Health & Society program grew out of the belief of some public health experts that rather than just whining about all the things they thought were inaccurate or misleading in TV shows about health topics, they should reach out to writers in order to help them get things right. Staff at the program understand how Hollywood works. They know that TV writers who call for help with a sticky plot point need answers right away in order to meet brutal production schedules. They take health experts out to TV show production offices to brief writers on health issues and medical research news. And they put out a newsletter that highlights real events and people that might inspire creators of fiction.

UNINSURED HEART

Eric De La Cruz was diagnosed with a weak heart in his early 20's. He needed a heart transplant, but he was a student with no health insurance. Once diagnosed, he was denied insurance because of his pre-existing medical condition. His sister tried to navigate the system, applying for disability, raising money, and using Twitter to solicit support for her brother. He finally obtained coverage, but was too sick by then for a heart transplant.

He died at age 31. His sister is still crusading for the cause, saying if it hadn't been for the delays and denials in the system, her brother would still be alive today.

Real to Reel newsletter, fall 2009

Another recent newsletter told the story of a divorced couple. The ex-husband developed serious kidney disease and needed a transplant. His ex-wife turned out to be a good match. She agreed to donate one of her kidneys. As they recuperated from their operations, they fell back in love and then remarried. Now *that's* a Hollywood ending!

But just as some *House* fans think it is silly to compare a fictional TV show to health care reality, the Hollywood, Health & Society program has taken some hits from critics—not TV critics, but members of Congress, who wanted to yell "Cut!" when the program's budget came up for renewal.

Republican Senator Tom Coburn of Oklahoma issued a report

criticizing a number of CDC programs, including the agency's support of outreach to TV writers.

"A question taxpayers might consider appropriate: should the CDC spend $1.9 million to help Hollywood develop its plotlines?" Senator Coburn's report asked. The $1.9 million figure included all the CDC money spent on the Hollywood, Health & Society program over an eight-year period. Senator Coburn wrote that TV writers should do their own homework: "With the multi-billion dollar television industry, million-dollar-per-episode salaries for TV actors, and millions of dollars of revenue from daytime and prime-time dramas, should it be a priority for taxpayers to have CDC-funded Hollywood liaisons to help producers get the health story lines correct?"

As the issue headed toward a vote, supporters of the Hollywood, Health & Society program rallied, spurred on by the results of studies showing that viewers really do learn health facts from entertainment television.

Well before this budget debate flared up, a spokesman for the National Cancer Institute, which helped support the Hollywood, Health & Society program's early years, compared its impact to that of other kinds of media campaigns on health topics.

"What would be the value of that television program if you bought it yourself, or if you tried to purchase a PSA or an ad?" is one question that the NCI spokesman said the agency asks when it evaluates their Hollywood outreach efforts. "For the $350,000 [NCI] investment, the return is in the tens of millions of dollars," he said. "You can look at the Nielsen [ratings] numbers and see the millions of people you reach, the hundreds of millions of people."

That value equation appears to be carrying the day. A couple of years after critics in Congress tried to eliminate funding for the Hollywood, Health & Society program, the program's second director, Sandra de Castro Buffington, says the program's funding has grown to its highest level.

"I have been traveling and meeting with group after group after group, presenting our results. And people want to be part of this, because they recognize how powerful it is," Buffington says. Eight years after the program began as a project of the CDC, it now has support from several public agencies and large private foundations. United Nations agencies, as well as organizations in Europe and on other continents, are exploring collaborations that would create similar centers around the world.

Of course, the program's work already ripples around the world . . . in every nation where *House* is broadcast and into every home that flips on a TV to watch House and his colleagues match wits with strange diseases.

Two

A Few Zebras from the Herd

Recent seasons of *House* have paid more attention to the lives of the main characters, both in and outside of the hospital. Of course, the strange cases House yearns to investigate keep coming. Strange is an understatement. Here are some real-world reflections on some of the bizarre cases that have rolled into Princeton-Plainsboro Teaching Hospital.

Locked In

"Hey, genius. I think it violates certain ethical laws to rip the organs out of a guy who's still alive. Possibly certain 'law' laws, too."

That's House butting in as an emergency room doctor considers whether a crash victim might be a suitable organ donor. "Locked In" (5-19) opens from the point of view of the man who crashed. Although the ER doctor believes he is brain dead, he is fully conscious, but he cannot move or communicate. The patient is terrified at the prospect that his organs may be harvested for transplant. Viewers hear him shout, "I am alive! I'm here!" But no sound comes from his mouth.

This scene is not set at Princeton-Plainsboro Teaching Hospital and House is not consulting on the case, at least not officially. He's in the ER because he crashed his motorcycle. But House can't leave a strange case alone, so he continues to butt in. Then he gets the man to blink in response to a question, thus demonstrating his brain is very much alive.

Can someone be fully alert and aware, yet from the outside appear to be in a coma or other vegetative state? *House* is not the first series to explore the viewpoint of somebody who is "locked in." A dark comedy series on BBC Radio, *Vent*, explored the thoughts of a man trapped inside what appeared to be a coma. The creator of this series built it on his own actual experiences. Nigel Smith had a brain lesion that prevented him from communicating. He wrote a book about what it was like to live in the hospital while doctors discussed what they believed would be his inevitable decline and death.

Another book, *The Diving Bell and the Butterfly*, recounted the experience of journalist Jean-Dominique Bauby after a stroke left him "locked in." The book was also made into a movie.

"I screamed but there was nothing to hear." That's a quote from a BBC news story in November 2009 that described yet another case that seemed to be very much like the "Locked In" episode of *House*.

Rom Houben was injured in a car crash in 1983. More than two decades later, researchers using brain scanning technology that was not available when Houben was first hurt said they realized that he was conscious.

Speech therapists facilitated communication by moving his fingers over a touch screen keyboard, as described in an Associated Press article:

"Just imagine. You hear, see, feel and think but no one can see that. You undergo things. You cannot participate in life," Houben wrote.

However, skeptics doubted that a man in Houben's condition could communicate so fluently. Three months after the initial flurry of attention to this case, the researchers backtracked. They said Houben was not actually able to communicate. In essence, they agreed with the skeptics that the therapist was controlling the movement of Houben's fingers.

Nonetheless, they stood by their conclusion that Houben, along with at least a small percentage of other similar patients, had more awareness of the outside world than had been thought. The researchers reported the results of MRI scans of fifty-four patients who appeared to be in a vegetative or minimally conscious state. Five of them showed signs of being able to control their brain activity. The brain scans detected different patterns of activity when these patients were asked to imagine either that they were playing tennis or walking around their homes.

The technique has some similarities to the way the patient on *House* was able to indicate yes-or-no answers. On *House*, the patient thought "up" or "down," and electrodes monitoring his brain activity moved a cursor on a display. The real-world researchers reported that one of the patients they tested could answer questions by creating distinct patterns on the MRI images by thinking about either tennis (to indicate yes) or walking (to indicate no). As they wrote in an article in the *New England Journal of Medicine*, "These results show that a small proportion of patients in a vegetative or minimally conscious state have brain activation reflecting some awareness and cognition." They suggested that their technique could be used to answer important clinical questions, such as whether a patient is in pain. And they suggested that someday this sort of technique could slip a key to some "locked in" patients so they could express their thoughts and maybe even control their environment.

A Can of Worms

In "Teamwork" (6-08), the team thinks they have discovered their patient's problem: his liver is crawling with parasitic worms. So of course they give him mebendazole, a standard antiworm therapy. But this being *House*, the treatment backfires. Instead of getting better, the patient gets worse. Thinking he may have leukemia, they prepare to zap his bone marrow with radiation. But just before the treatment begins, Taub and Thirteen figure out that his real problem is Crohn's disease, an autoimmune disorder. Rather than being a problem, the parasitic worms may have been controlling the autoimmune attack on his body. So they have the patient swallow worm eggs in order to restore the infestation.

It's called helminthic therapy. Helminths are parasitic worms, such as roundworms, pinworms, hookworms, tapeworms, flukes, and *Trichinella spiralis*. *Trichinella spiralis* is the parasite that can be found in undercooked pork and is responsible for trichinosis, a serious illness that begins with abdominal pains and diarrhea, but then can progress into muscle aches, itching, fever, chills, and joint pain.

Now, most people would think that one of the great things about modern life in developed nations is that we rarely get infested by parasitic worms. But some scientists think that our lives may have become too clean. They hypothesize that our bodies, including our immune systems, evolved over the eons to coexist with parasites and that by altering the ancient relationship we have caused new problems.

"Diseases like inflammatory bowel disease used to affect 1 in 10,000 people; it's now becoming 1 in every 200 to 250 people. Something's causing it, and it's environmental," Joel Weinstock, M.D., is quoted as saying on a Web page about his research at Tufts-New England Medical Center in Boston, Massachusetts.

In a journal article reviewing helminthic therapy that Weinstock coauthored with David Elliott, M.D., at the University of Iowa in Iowa City, the researchers recapped experiments in mice that showed that worms appeared to provide some protection against conditions similar to colitis, encephalitis, diabetes, and asthma. They also reviewed trials that showed that giving people parasitic worms can reduce symptoms of colitis and Crohn's disease, just as depicted on *House*. Those who are investigating the potential uses of parasitic worms say there appear to be several ways that parasites might have an effect on autoimmune disorders. They may affect how cells in our intestines and other organs act. They may turn down the activity of T cells or other components of the immune system. They may reduce intestinal inflammation. It could be a combination of these effects.

There are a variety of experiments under way or planned that intentionally give people parasitic worms. For example, researchers at the University of Wisconsin–Madison are looking into the effects of parasitic worms on relapsing-remitting multiple sclerosis. Participants in the trial will drink a liquid containing 2,500 parasitic worm eggs every two weeks. MRI scans will look for any changes in lesions that are part of multiple sclerosis. Similar studies are being done at other institutions in the United States and other countries.

Researchers caution that some parasites can interfere with liver function or may cause high blood pressure. There are also signs that the worm infestations might make some vaccines less effective, thus leaving people more vulnerable to serious diseases. A more palatable option might be to develop new medicines intended to produce the same sort of effects on the immune system that have been connected with parasitic infestations. Several pharmaceutical companies are exploring this option.

On a somewhat related note, some people have tried using parasitic worms in hopes that the worms would help them lose weight by consuming food right out of their intestines. A warning from the Hong Kong Health Department said there is no scientific basis for using parasites to help control weight and that "parasite infestation may also be fatal if serious complications such as intestinal, biliary tract or pancreatic duct obstruction arise. The worms may even invade such organs as the lungs."

It's not a new idea. Advertisements from the early 1900s touted "sanitized" tapeworms as a way to fight fat. Maybe just thinking about the worms would be a preferable way of avoiding overeating.

That's Gotta Hurt

"Painless" (5-12) opens with a man attempting suicide. He has been in pain for years and sees no hope of relief. Other doctors have failed to find the cause of the pain. Even powerful painkillers no longer offer relief. The man's suffering is so severe that his young son actually tries to help him commit suicide.

Like the other doctors this man has seen, House cannot find the cause or remedy. Eventually he agrees to discharge the man, knowing he will probably attempt suicide again and likely succeed. But then House notices a plumber scratching his groin. That's his "lightbulb" moment.

"Testicles. What do they make you think of?" House asks the team.

"STDs, testosterone issues, that summer on Fire Island," Taub shoots back.

"Oh, so close. The correct answer is epilepsy."

Foreman objects that epilepsy doesn't cause pain. And Thirteen adds that it would have shown up on an electroencephalogram, or EEG. Of course, House has the explanation for how the signs of epilepsy eluded them.

"Not if the seizures are in a place you can't see on an EEG, a place too deep in the brain, like the area that controls the muscles supporting the . . ." House leaves them hanging.

"Testicles," Taub finishes the sentence.

House then quizzes the patient about how the pain started. He hits pay dirt when he predicts that at first the man's pain felt "like your kidneys were being pulled out through your scrotum."

One description of a somewhat analogous case can be found in a research letter to the *Journal of Neurology, Neurosurgery & Psychiatry*. A boy was brought to the hospital after seven months of mysterious painful attacks. In this case, the source was clearly in the boy's groin, as it was in the earliest occurrences for the patient on *House*. The cause was a mystery. After the boy had been in the hospital three days, doctors witnessed one of the painful attacks.

"The boy, who was playing cheerfully, suddenly started screaming and clutched his scrotum with his hands," the letter reported. "The entire attack lasted about 2½ minutes and this was followed by slow return of the right testis to its normal position within the scrotum." Ten days after admission to the hospital, an EEG "showed random epileptic activity over the left central area." And so the author of the letter advised readers that "scrotal pain associated with testicular jerking is an unusual form of seizure."

There are few other descriptions of such cases in the medical literature, although some textbooks do include epilepsy as one possible cause of pain in the groin and genitourinary system.

Death Cats

"A cat predicted my death," the patient tells House as she pleads for his help in "Here Kitty" (5-18). The woman is a nurse at a nursing home. She is worried because Debbie the cat curled up next to her to sleep.

"She was in the news," the woman explains. "We found her as a kitten. She lives in the nursing home. She only sleeps next to people when they're about to die."

House at first rejected the idea that a cat could predict death. It does seem far-fetched; but an essay that appeared in the *New England Journal of Medicine* titled "A Day in the Life of Oscar the Cat" included this: "A nurse walks into the room to check on her patient. She pauses to note Oscar's presence. Concerned, she hurriedly leaves the room and returns to her desk. She grabs Mrs. K.'s chart off the medical-records rack and begins to make phone calls."

The phone calls were to alert family members that their loved one might die very soon. The article about Oscar the Cat was written by Providence, Rhode Island, geriatrician David M. Dosa, M.D.

"He's remarkably accurate. He really doesn't miss. What's interesting about Oscar is that he is not particularly friendly most of the time. He really doesn't hang out with patients or other people on the unit. He keeps to himself and does his cat thing. But when somebody is near the end, he seemingly becomes comfortable with people and spends a lot of time holding these vigils," Dosa says.

Oscar the Cat has lived at the Steere House Nursing and Rehabilitation Center in Providence since 2005. He's on a floor devoted to caring for people with advanced dementia, mostly Alzheimer's disease. Dosa, who also works at Rhode Island Hospital and teaches at the Warren Alpert Medical School of Brown University, says that for most of the patients this unit is the last stop.

Although other animals have lived at the unit, it soon became clear that Oscar was special.

"About a year after Oscar arrived, people started to talk about this cat that would hold vigils for patients at the end of life. It started with some of the hospice nurses, and then some of the patients' families, who would be with the dying patient at the end of life, would start chiming in about how Oscar had come to visit right before their loved one would pass on," he says. "Initially we were all somewhat skeptical about this, but he repeatedly seemed to be at the bedside as each individual patient would pass on."

In fact, Oscar is not unique. There are other cases in the medical literature of animals that behave in a particular way shortly before someone dies. Dosa recalls that his medical journal essay sparked a flurry of media attention, including jokes on late-night shows, along the lines of "If Oscar's on the bed, you're dead." Nevertheless, Dosa says most families seem to welcome Oscar's presence. After all, he notes, the unit Oscar calls home is devoted to the care of people who are very near the end of their lives.

"It's not a place where death is surprising; in fact, it's expected. Because of that, I think people take comfort from the idea of having an animal there to share the experience with," he says.

And while the staff relies on their clinical expertise and experience to advise families when it appears that a person on the unit is near death, Oscar's input is valued.

"You certainly don't want to cry wolf about something like that; so, yes, having him there sometimes does allow us to be a little more deliberate with calling family members in or getting clergy to come to the bedside or calling a family member in from the opposite coast. It's been helpful."

In the "Here Kitty" episode, House's "eureka moment" comes when Debbie the Cat sits on his laptop. It's warm. He concludes that the cat is attracted to patients with fever or who have heating blankets. Dosa doesn't buy that explanation.

"The working hypothesis is that Oscar responds to pheromones or

perhaps ketones that are released from human cells as they are in star-
vation states or dying, but ultimately it's a matter of speculation as to
why he does what he does," he says.

Biological Liar

We've all heard the legend that when a young George Washington was
asked by his father if he knew who had chopped down a cherry tree, he
declared, "I can't tell a lie, Pa; you know I can't tell a lie. I did cut it with
my hatchet." Historians generally doubt the incident really happened,
but that's not the point here. The matter at hand is an episode of *House*
that offered just the opposite proposition: that a patient was unable to
avoid telling lies because of a physical disorder.

In "Known Unknowns" (6-07), a young patient slings accusations
that a man she met at a hotel drugged and abused her. But her story
doesn't check out. Foreman says her fabrications are involuntary: "She
can't control it. A bleed in her brain is affecting her thalamus, causing
her to lie."

Rather than calling it lying, a more precise term for the phenomenon would be confabulation.

"Confabulation is making up things when you don't know what the
right answer is," explains Bruce L. Miller, M.D., professor of neurology at the University of California, San Francisco.

Miller says that some patients with problems that disrupt memory
may fill in the gaps with invented stories.

"We see that with a lot of neurologic diseases. We see it with a lot
of memory disorders. Alzheimer's patients can confabulate. The clas-
sic example where we see it is something called Korsakoff's syndrome,
which is alcohol-related injury to the thalamus where there is a memory disorder. These patients make up stories around what they don't
remember," Miller says.

While the problem Foreman described is different, the thalamus is
a part of the brain that plays a key role in memory. Miller says that if
a patient like the one in this episode of *House* came to him, he would

first do a simple memory test. If the patient were not only making up stories but also acting inappropriately, he would begin to suspect that the problem might lie in the brain's frontal lobes, rather than in the thalamus.

Several years ago, Miller and his colleagues wrote a journal article about a patient with Korsakoff's Syndrome. "We thought that the memory problem was due to injury to the thalamus, but the confabulation was due to loss of the connections between the thalamus and the frontal lobes. So when the connections restored themselves, even though the thalamus didn't work, the confabulation disappeared. We argued that this is the frontal lobes, not the thalamus, causing the confabulatory problem," Miller says.

Confabulation is more common among older patients, but it may be seen in younger people who have suffered a major head trauma, stroke, or other brain damage. Miller says that patients with this sort of memory disorder aren't trying to deceive those around them; the stories they make up are just their way of trying to fill in the disturbing gaps in their memories.

Premature Autopsy

It was surprising enough to make House shout and Foreman scream. A man thought to be dead suddenly woke up with a yell just as Foreman began an autopsy.

Earlier in the episode, "Brave Heart" (6-06), the case comes to House's attention because the man is certain he would suddenly die of heart problems at age forty just like his father, grandfather, and great-grandfather. When the team doesn't find anything suspicious, House discharges the man. Hours later, House learns that the man has suddenly collapsed and was declared dead. Miffed that he apparently missed something lethal, House wants to help with an autopsy to find out what killed the man.

In the morgue, Foreman takes a power saw and begins to cut into the body. He stops cutting. "That's odd," he says. "It almost looks like he's bleeding." House and Foreman peer closely at the small pool of blood at the base of the incision in the man's chest. Then the patient wakes up with a scream. "I think the autopsy's gonna have to wait a little bit," a stunned House says.

Occasionally, people are indeed declared dead prematurely. Before electrocardiograms and other modern vital sign monitoring equipment were developed, errors of this sort were common enough that the prospect of being buried alive haunted writer Edgar Allen Poe.

It may be asserted, without hesitation, that no event is so terribly well adapted to inspire the supremeness of bodily and of mental distress, as is burial before death. The unendurable oppression of the lungs—the stifling fumes from the damp earth—the clinging to the death garments—the rigid embrace of the narrow house—the blackness of the absolute Night—the silence like a sea that overwhelms—the unseen but palpable presence of the Conqueror Worm.

From E. A. Poe, "The Premature Burial," 1850

Though rare, errors in declaring death still happen.

Michael Baden, M.D., a forensic pathologist with extensive experience as the former chief medical examiner in New York City and as director of services for the New York State Police Medicolegal Investigation Unit, says two scenarios capture most of the cases he has heard about. First, an elderly patient whose death was expected: "Usually they don't do EKGs to find out if somebody's heart is beating if they are elderly and they have a disease. So these things happen," he says. Second, a victim at a car crash or other hectic trauma scene: "That's because, if somebody looks dead, somebody has an injury, doesn't appear to be breathing, it's too easy to make a mistake outside of a hospital, on a scene where there is a lot of commotion.

"When a body comes to a morgue, there is a presumption of death. The person doing the embalming or preparation for autopsy would look at the body, feel the body. If the skin is warm, that would be a clue that they'd want to look further. There is no checklist, but there is common sense," Baden says.

Baden recalls a case in Albany, New York, in which an elderly woman was sent to the morgue. As newspaper accounts of the incident recount, the woman had been found on the floor of her home. She was cold and motionless. Paramedics found no signs of life and a coroner declared her dead. The body was placed in a cooler for over an hour. Then when a morgue technician took the woman's body out to transfer her to a funeral home, he noticed the body bag moving, as if the body were breathing. It was. The woman was unconscious, but not dead at all. She was taken to a hospital, but died about a week later. A newspaper article reports that this time doctors confirmed that her heart had stopped beating.

Other news reports tell of children and adults waking up in coffins. The family of a man declared dead prematurely after a car crash in North Carolina in 2005 tried to sue the medical examiner. The family contended that because of the error the man did not receive medical care that could have prevented permanent injuries. A judge ruled that the family could not sue the medical examiner. However, according to news reports, they did reach a settlement with the county government to pay for the man's twenty-four-hour medical care.

Another news report, this one from Caracas, Venezuela, tells of a case similar to the one depicted on *House*. According to the Reuters news agency, thirty-three-year-old Carlos Camejo was declared dead after a highway crash in September 2007. "Examiners began an autopsy only to realize something was amiss when he started bleeding," the news report says.

Dr. Baden says actually bleeding is routine during autopsies. "The body constantly bleeds during an autopsy, because as you cut through blood vessels, blood leaks out, like a garden hose full of water after the spigot has been turned off and you cut it. It leaks whatever is already in the hose," he says. Still, there is a difference between the way live patients and dead bodies bleed. "It wouldn't be 'There's bleeding, therefore he is alive.' It would be 'There's more active bleeding than usual, therefore he might be alive.'

"Ninety-nine percent of forensic pathologists will never see one of these cases," Baden says. Nevertheless, based on his casual viewing of some episodes, he says he has a generally favorable view of the plausibility of the scenarios on *House*. "I find that *House* is much more accurate than the forensic science shows, like *CSI*."

Three

Professional Opinions

What Do Doctors Think?

As far as other doctors on the show are concerned, it seems that with the exception of Wilson, Cuddy, and House's fellows, Greg House is not very popular.

In "5 to 9" (6-14), House has the temperature in an operating room turned way down, so that the surgeon using it will hurry up and clear the room for House's patient. The surgeon complains to Cuddy.

"I took care of it," she responds.

"It's not an 'it.' It's a 'him' you need to take care of. You've got the entire staff catering to House's every whim," the surgeon says. He threatens to resign unless Cuddy does a better job of controlling House.

There are plenty of doctors in real life who frown at House.

"I can't stand to watch House. It just makes me crazy. I want to teach him doctor-patient communication and respect for persons and autonomy. I want his colleagues to deal with an impaired provider," says one.

Others enjoy a cathartic release watching House say and do things they know they can't . . . and shouldn't.

"I know House is an ass. And I like that he's an ass most of the time because it's amusing. I know that in real life, I can't be an ass when it comes to dealing with patients" is how one put it in a blog post.

And then there are physicians who just love House.

"I think he's terrific," says a doctor who admits that watching the show is a guilty pleasure that many colleagues don't understand. This doctor admires the way House's mind operates. "He's actually figured out the concept of objectivity in making a good decision, so I actually like him."

Physician and ethicist Kathy Neely, M.D., wrote about physicians' views of their fictional colleague in an article for the magazine of the Northwestern Medical Humanities & Bioethics Program.

"Unlike Dr. House himself, his physician fans I've encountered are usually some of the most sensitive, caring people I know. They typically laugh, a bit embarrassed, and admit House is sort of shocking, but—well—fun."

Even though Neely writes that she enjoys the show, she's not the only medical expert who talks back to the TV at times.

"'Outrageous!' I shouted from the couch when a doctor and surrogate collude to perform the very amputation the patient had clearly refused. 'Impossible!' I scoffed when Dr. House lies to get his patient first on the transplant list. 'No way!' I snorted when Dr. House comments to his boss about her 'fun bags,'" she wrote. She worries about the lessons the show may teach not only average viewers, but also medical students, perhaps subconsciously shaping what they consider to be acceptable and normal behavior by physicians.

House 101

Four out of five medical and nursing students watch television medical dramas. Researchers surveyed students at Johns Hopkins University about viewing of ER, Nip/Tuck, Scrubs, Grey's Anatomy, and House in 2008. House was the most popular show among the medical students, slightly edging out Grey's Anatomy, 76 percent to 73 percent.

Among nursing students, *Grey's Anatomy* beat *House* 80 percent to 65 percent. And as you may be guessing, even though more women are studying to be M.D.s and more men are learning how to be RNs, the difference between medical and nursing student viewing habits may have something to do with the proportions of men and women in the programs; *House* was more popular among men and *Grey's Anatomy* ranked number one among women.

The survey results were presented in an issue of the *American Journal of Bioethics* that included several articles about the lessons in ethics students may be picking up from television shows. The survey found that most students watched the shows, including *House*, with their friends. The researchers speculated that the conversations among viewers may help shape opinions about the best way to respond to situations like those depicted on the televisions shows. The group experience and conversation may help students decide what responses are "normal" among their peers. The students said that as far as their education about medical ethics goes, the TV shows played an insignificant role, that they paid the most heed to what they learned in school, with family, friends, medical journals, and other sources also being more important than TV medical dramas. Despite those self-assessments, the researchers said the question of how much influence TV shows have on medical and nursing students should be studied further. They wondered if the students might be underestimating the influence of the stories on shaping views about how things work, or should work, in medicine.

The researchers did note that older students had a lower opinion of the TV shows, perhaps indicating that they had gained a better understanding of the gap between TV and reality as they gained more direct clinical experience. Of course, most viewers have no medical training at all, so the survey results could be interpreted as suggesting that average viewers may be less skeptical about the TV stories than those who have firsthand experience with how health care is provided.

This study was not designed to establish the actual effects of televised medical dramas on the bioethics-related attitudes and practices of students in the health professions. However, given how popular these shows are with students and how frequently students recalled portrayals of the ethical issues the shows address, future research should try to assess these effects.

From M. J. Czarny, R. R. Faden, M. T. Nolan, E. Bodensiek, and J. Sugarman, "Medical and Nursing Students' Television Viewing Habits: Potential Implications for Bioethics," *American Journal of Bioethics* 8, no. 12 (December 2008): 1–8

In a recent update to this line of investigation, Czarny and his colleagues reviewed all of the episodes from the second season of *House* as well as the second season of *Grey's Anatomy*. This study, like their earlier one, did not seek to gauge the effects of the portrayals of ethical quandaries, but it did catalogue their variety and context. The authors also wrote that the "viewer frequently gets the feeling that Dr. House's actions are ethically problematic but ultimately acceptable given his enviable single-minded pursuit of the appropriate diagnosis and treatment." In other words, the ends justify the means.

The unresolved and vexing nature of some of the ethical issues portrayed, as well as the complex depictions of professionalism, may be more likely to engage viewers in moral reflection than to shape their opinions in any particular direction.

From M. J. Czarny, R. R. Faden, and J. Sugarman, "Bioethics and Professionalism in Popular Television Medical Dramas," *Journal of Medical Ethics* 36, no. 4 (April 2010): 203–206

The *American Journal of Bioethics* issue from 2008 also included comments from some experts who teach classes for medical students along with other duties. Mark Wicclair, Ph.D., is a professor of philosophy and an adjunct professor of community medicine at West Virginia University in Morgantown, and he also works at the University of Pittsburgh's Center for Bioethics and Health Law. "I really love the show," he says. And he sees value in examining the world of health care according to House.

> *Is it worrisome that medical students appear to enjoy watching a series that features such an unethical physician? It would be if one assumed that they look at House as a positive role model. However, this may be an unwarranted assumption.*
>
> From M. R. Wicclair, "The Pedagogical Value of House, M.D.—Can a Fictional Unethical Physician Be Used to Teach Ethics?" *American Journal of Bioethics* 8, no. 12 (December 2008): 16–17

One reason Wicclair sometimes uses episodes of *House* in his classes is a very practical one: as the survey documented, students like the show.

"It's not that easy to teach ethics to medical students," he says. "They are focused on science and clinical issues. So one way to get their interest is to latch onto something they already have an interest in. And a lot of students watch the show, and love it."

House displays medical brilliance that any student (or experienced professional) can only dream of. But that's not the full explanation for the appeal of the show to those in health care. Medical students, just like other viewers, are attracted to House not because he is so good, but because he is so bad . . . so deliciously bad.

"House is the anti-ideal, if you will, the paradigm of the physician who does everything contrary to the accepted norms in bioethics. I thought that that was a marvelous way of actually getting students to think and reflect about why these standards and norms that we do accept are justified," Wicclair says. "One way of teaching is just to show people the positive role models and say, 'See, this is how it's done. Do it this way.' Shows like *ER* have very sensitive physicians and nurses, good role models. But I'm a philosopher and so I like to not only get people to accept things, I like for people to understand the justification for various standards and norms. One of the standard norms in medical ethics is informed consent, and if you see somebody like House, who flagrantly violates that rule, but it seems to work out really well all the time, it's a great way to get students to reflect and ask, 'Why is it important to get a patient's informed consent?' "

Just as House's behavior toward patients and colleagues is unrealistically bad, so too is his medical skill unrealistically good.

"It all works out marvelously well. Generally, House finds out what the condition is, diagnoses it, comes up with the treatment, and at the end of the show patients are very grateful. You know, that's not the way the world really works. If physicians were to act that way in the real world, chances are that they wouldn't find the proper diagnosis, or even if they did, the treatment would have some horrible side effect and the patient would get sick and wouldn't be terribly grateful," Wicclair points out.

And that's where he finds the instructional value in these fictional stories. Students may start rooting for House and cheering his success, but as they look closer, cracks in the façade become noticeable. The disparity between the neat story lines on TV and the messy reality they witness during clinical rotations is illuminated. And the lesson "Don't be like House" sinks in.

Howard Trachtman, M.D., likes to watch TV. Here's how he began the article he wrote for the *American Journal of Bioethics*:

> *I have to make a confession at the very beginning of this commentary. Many nights after dinner, I have been observed to sink into the den couch only to resurface an hour or two later after watching reruns of* Law & Order *for the umpteenth time. I could not be bothered by anyone while watching* The Wire. *I thought the last episode of* Six Feet Under *was the most original hour of television I have ever seen.*
>
> From H. Trachtman, "The Medium Is Not the Message,"
> *American Journal of Bioethics* 8, no. 12 (December 2008): 9–11.

Trachtman's commentary was juxtaposed with the other articles in the *American Journal of Bioethics* about the popularity of TV medical shows among medical and nursing students. Trachtman argued in his commentary that even when *House* is held up as an example of the wrong way to treat patients, he had concerns about elevating this show and others to the status of teaching tools in medical school classrooms.

> *It is said that children learn more on the bus going to elementary school than they do during the school. That may be so, but I would not use that fact to sanction inclusion of the discussions in the back-seat into a grade-school educational syllabus.*

From H. Trachtman, "The Medium Is Not the Message,"
American Journal of Bioethics 8, no. 12 (December 2008): 9–11.

And so Trachtman doesn't want TV characters confused with real people. After all, they don't even look like real people.

"The thing I find funny about these shows is that they are always stunning people to look at," he says. Of course, looking at pretty people is part of the attraction of entertainment TV. "Most of the doctors I know are pretty schlumpy-looking. We don't look half as good as the people on TV. Our calls go unanswered. We spend a lot of our time doing administrative stuff that you never see on TV."

Besides the obvious contrast in the physical attractiveness of carefully groomed and cosmetically transformed TV stars compared to real health care practitioners, Trachtman says there are other important distinctions between TV and reality that viewers may not be aware of.

"Because of the intense competition for viewers and sponsors and the short attention span of the audience at home, there is strong incentive for network television to depict extreme cases that push the limits of healthcare and ethical deliberation. This leads to a strong tendency for the media to sensationalize problems and to focus on trendy issues rather than on mundane problems in order to attract as many viewers as possible," he wrote in his article. "Gregory House will be forced to decide whether to transplant the heart from the victim of a drive-by shooting into a 5-year-old child with cardiac anomalies or a 30-year-old poet with acute cardiomyopathy. Neither will be seen debating the requirements of how much care she must provide to a blue-collar family with limited financial resources but whose members are ineligible for federally funded medical assistance," he wrote.

It's that chasm between the exciting cases of TV patients and the mundane, but real, people doctors deal with that Trachtman sees warping our expectations of real doctors and nurses and health care institutions. He says he even sees the effects of media role models in some of his students.

"I always joke about a certain kind of medical student or resident who I think presents to me as if they are playing to the camera, talking like people on TV," he says.

And just as TV characters are prettier than real people, they also tend to be much smarter. Each week, Dr. Gregory House's superhuman intellect slices through a Gordian knot of signs and symptoms, while doctors in the real world muddle through.

"We are there to make the patient get better, not so much to be brilliant. The shows emphasize the cognitive 'Ah, ha!' moment, like Sherlock Holmes, rather than what medicine really is." Trachtman says he likes smart doctors and smart patients, but that he rarely sees anyone solve a medical problem with a flash of insight that ties up all the loose ends. Instead, doctors mostly hope to stumble onto an effective strategy. Of course, House and his colleagues rely on a trial-and-error approach to most of their medical mysteries . . . with their fingers crossed that they cure the patient before killing him or her. But the stark contrasts in outcomes and high-stakes gambles are what really set TV medicine apart from what Trachtman sees every day. Of course, how interesting would it be if Foreman tried a treatment, and then when House asked, "Did it work?" Foreman almost always replied, "I don't know. We'll see." But that's what doctors actually have to accept: that they rarely know for sure that they are doing the right thing, they almost never know the full effects right away, and when the results are known, they are almost always in-between; that is, neither a clear victory nor an absolute defeat, unlike on TV.

"It's always predicated on a clear-cut black-or-white outcome. Most of the time, for myself in pediatric nephrology [kidney disease in children], it's rare for children to die in my subspecialty. I win, I lose. It's all in very subtle gradations," Trachtman says.

But every now and then, things do happen quickly: a patient declines quickly and deeply.

"The slope of her illness is so steep. It almost does remind me a little bit of a TV show. But that is so exceptional. They make it the rule. I find it to be the exception. Most of my encounters with patients are very, very evolutionary in nature. And most of what I do is a mixed blessing."

He hopes to do more good than harm working in a world painted in shades of gray. The point of entertainment shows is to be more colorful and exciting than real life, but Trachtman worries about viewers being distracted from the real issues society faces as we try to improve health care. He says people should understand that the greatest improvements in health come from small changes in dealing with common things that affect a lot of people, not the bizarre, though exciting, cases that House takes week after week, cases that are far more rare than lightning striking a person.

"The TV shows are about the lightning strikes. They are interesting. And they are fun. And they are engaging. And they are exciting. And they make us all feel better."

But the steady diet of "lightning strike" cases may lead viewers to overestimate just how much they need to worry about being struck by lightning, in the medical sense. And so the desire to have a health care system of heroic doctors available to rescue them from freak occurrences may trump their interest in supporting basic, routine care.

"We have to teach people to get down into the trenches and spend the time. And they do. The fact is that good doctors always have. I think this [health care] system is skewed, and the TV shows augment that skew by downgrading the long hours that are taken to give people insight into their illness, to gain control of their disease, to integrate their families, their work, their lifestyle, to make healthy choices so that they live good and healthy and productive lives. That's where medicine should be heading," Trachtman says. "That's never covered on TV, never covered on TV. The inordinate amount of time that it takes to teach people to modify their diet and check their urine, and look at their blood pressure, and do all the things for diabetes, and nutrition; these are long, long difficult battles that good, competent doctors are fighting every day."

Getting back to his commentary in the *American Journal of Bioethics*, Trachtman asked readers to understand that he wasn't arguing against shows like *House*, but just asking that the entertaining fictions be kept in the proper perspective.

> *I fear that I have come across as a stuffed shirt, an almost dead white male. I am not arguing for canceling medical dramas from television. I hope people watch them and enjoy them as much as they like. I am only advocating basing the teaching of bioethics to health professionals in training on vehicles that will stand the test of time and which focus on physician education rather than the Nielsen ratings.*
>
> From H. Trachtman, "The Medium Is Not the Message,"
> *American Journal of Bioethics* 8, no. 12 (December 2008): 9–11.

In conversation, he notes that the article was intended to be part of a point-counterpoint exchange, and that actually he thinks *House* and other shows can be used effectively in educating medical and nursing students about bioethics and other areas of medicine.

"Good teachers can use anything. You can always flip anything and make it into a valuable teaching tool," he says. "There is so little time and so much to learn, so anything that they can use that would make students assimilate more information in a quick way, well, all the power to them."

But as the survey of student TV viewing pointed out, attitudes about the shows tend to be more negative among more senior students, suggesting that the more a person knows about the real world of health care, the more troubled that person may be about the dramatic license taken by TV writers. Older students simply know better. By contrast, the average viewer has little or no direct experience that could counterbalance the media images.

Trachtman doesn't say that any shows about medicine need to be factual documentaries. Indeed, he underscores the value of storytelling; specifically using stories to help people understand how illness fits in the total experience of patients. A common complaint about modern medicine is that it can reduce people to a set of lab values and patient chart notations, obscuring the humanity of the patient. Stories about illness and healing can provide richer context to see the whole person. But Trachtman says good stories can't be rushed.

"Illness occurs in the context of a story. The story has plot and character and backdrop. But that conveys a commitment. You have to read through a novel. You have to spend time with it," he says.

His commentary gave several examples of powerful medical storytelling.

Literature and other humanities provide rich alternative sources of information that can foster a genuine appreciation of bioethics by medical and nursing students. Novels such as The Plague *and* Arrowsmith, *memoirs such as* My Own Country *by Abraham Verghese, essays such as "Illness as Metaphor" by Susan Sontag, plays such as* Ghosts *and* Wit, *and music and paintings composed during bouts of illness are part of a rich tradition that has helped physicians, nurses, and patients confront and grapple with the pain of disease, the impact of illness on personal identity, and the responsibility of physicians to each other and their patients.*

From H. Trachtman, "The Medium Is Not the Message," *American Journal of Bioethics* 8, no. 12 (December 2008): 9–11.

As wonderfully entertaining as *House* is for TV viewers, it certainly doesn't pretend to be a timeless work of art on a level with the masterpieces Trachtman points out. That sort of artistic achievement simply may not fit into an hour . . . minus commercials.

"There's something about TV shows that makes me smile, with a chagrined smile. It's just too fast," he says.

Of course, a zippy pace is part of the attraction. And it's not just students who like *House*. In a journal article about medical paternalism, that is, health care providers who push their own views and judgments onto patients, Mark Wicclair speculated that the reasons some physicians disdain *House* are the same ones that entice many others.

> *Those who dislike it often cite the series' lack of realism. Paradoxically, this feature may help to explain its appeal as well. In the world of the series, House is able to decide what is best for patients, and, in the end, his decisions appear to have been right. He has discovered the diagnosis and the treatment, he is hailed for his brilliant clinical skills, and his paternalism is tolerated, excused or even endorsed. He repeatedly flaunts ethical, legal and institutional rules and challenges the authority of Cuddy, the hospital administrator, but because of his clinical brilliance (his repeated success in diagnosing and treating illnesses), his "bad behavior" generally is tolerated, if not encouraged. Until the third season, the most severe "punishment" he faced was to be required to spend more time seeing clinic patients. Fiction, perhaps, but this unrealistic world may have considerable appeal as a fantasy to physicians who may desire to be right all or most of the time and who may be frustrated by the real-world constraints, obstacles and disappointments that they confront.*
>
> From M. R. Wicclair, "Medical Paternalism in *House M.D.*,"
> *Medical Humanities* 34 (2008): 93–99

House gets away with all sorts of things real doctors can't, and he exudes a confidence and certainty few real doctors would dare to.

"In terms of medical professionals and students, I think it's really kind of a fantasy world for them," Wicclair says, "where they see somebody talking back to patients and family members, treating them quite brusquely, and they get away with it. I think that's one of the reasons students enjoy it so much, besides the fact that it's just good entertainment, I think every medical student has had a situation where they would have just loved to tell a family where to go, like House does, so it's a bit of a fantasy for them."

The fact that House gets away with things real doctors can't may delight many, but it repels others. A real doctor who practiced the way House does would doubtless cause great harm to many patients. That may be part of the reason some doctors don't like his character, but perhaps there is another reason. Maybe they are jealous.

"It is either hate or love," Wicclair says. "The ones who aren't very attracted to that fantasy and can't see the humor in it, they just say it's unrealistic. Of course it is. That's the point. But there are some people who really get into that fantasy."

Rights and Wrongs

House is always right . . . At least that's the face he puts on things, though in recent seasons his expression has revealed some self-doubt that wasn't there in the early episodes of the series. Nevertheless he quickly recovers from those moments when he seems almost ready to concede that someone else might be right.

In the study of bioethics and professionalism by Matthew Czarny and his colleagues that was mentioned earlier, the researchers counted up all the instances of events in these realms that appeared during the second season of the series. The most frequent bioethics issue to appear in *House* was consent. That doesn't mean that House always ignored his obligation to get his patients' voluntary consent before performing tests or treatments. Sometimes a scene will illustrate appropriate consent procedures; but it is not hard to locate plenty of examples of ethical and legal violations.

In "The Itch" (5-07), the team is working with a man who has severe agoraphobia. He not only fears going out in the world, he doesn't want anyone coming into his world. But House sees that when the man is anxious he exhibits symptoms that may offer useful clues. So in direct violation of the man's wishes, House brings a troop of gawkers into the apartment to trigger an attack.

The second most common type of bioethics issue seen by the researchers studying *House* was "ethically questionable departures from standard practice. Most of these incidents depicted physicians endangering patients unnecessarily or acting unethically in their pursuit of a favorable outcome for a patient," the study authors wrote. Not surprising to any regular *House* viewer. The most common issues related to professionalism that were documented by the researchers involved respect (in House's case the lack of respect) for other professionals and even for patients. By the way, the study also analyzed the second season of *Grey's Anatomy*. The most common professionalism (or lack of professionalism) issue noted was (make a guess) . . . sexual misconduct.

Mark Wicclair points out that House often bulldozes through the valid reasons that patients may have for not wanting to do what House thinks is best for them. One problem is that House almost always sees decisions as black-or-white, live-or-die. He overlooks the (less dramatic) middle road or third option.

"House says that if the patient doesn't agree to be on a respirator, he's going to die in a very painful, suffering way by choking to death," Wicclair offers as an example. "That's a no-no in the real world. If a patient decides not to be put on a ventilator, then she is given sedation and palliative care so that she doesn't suffer. It's a third way. You can go on a ventilator, you can not go on a ventilator and choke to death, or we can make you comfortable. But House always presents things in a way that paints one of the options as being very rosy and the other as being completely bleak. In the real world it's often not quite that way: both options aren't great and there's maybe two or three others that aren't that great either, so you are choosing among a variety of options, none of which is a clear winner. That's more the real-world situation."

Wicclair also sees examples of House equating disagreement with stupidity and of House rejecting any goal other than maximum survival . . . though there are a few exceptions. At one point in "Painless" (5-12), House was willing to allow a patient in unrelenting agony to leave the hospital, even though he knew the man was planning to commit suicide. In "Son of Coma Guy" (3-07), he even instructed a man on how to commit suicide in a way that would leave his organs in good condition for transplantation. But in this case, House knew that the man who would die was about to drop back into an irreversible coma. Meanwhile, the man's son would likely die without a heart transplant. So even though House helped a man die, that man's awareness was about to flicker out anyway, and the solution maximized the chances of survival for the son.

Wicclair understands how the black-or-white choices make for entertaining drama and that House's choices, though seemingly rude and uncaring, are also easily seen as being in the best interests of the patients.

"If you have appendicitis, there is a clear decision. But in many cases, if you have some condition, let's say there are three or four options, each one is going to have disadvantages and advantages, and sometimes there is no really clear winner. And you never see that on *House*. It's always, 'We're going for the Big Kahuna!' And usually he gets it," he says. "And that's probably one of the reasons besides the fact that it's entertaining—I can't stress enough the fact that it is an entertaining show, but I think one of the reasons it is appealing to the general public is that he really looks like, despite his gruffness, despite his disrespect for people, he's doing good for them. He's a real champion, even when patients don't want it."

House also violently ignores a person's right to refuse treatment when he kidnaps an actor who plays a character on his favorite soap opera in "Living the Dream" (4-14). House thought he saw signs of a serious disease when he watched the man on TV. So even though he trampled the man's rights, he was doing it for the patient's benefit. It works on the show, because it almost always works out for the best on the show, but the logic is not as compelling in the real world, where it is not always easy to be sure which choice will lead to the best outcome for the patient.

"In the program, it looks like the doctor knows best. And that's one of the things that one has to fight in medicine, is the idea that doctors do know best. They may know medicine best, but they may not know what's best for patients, because patients have all sorts of priorities and preferences and values. And it is not necessarily maximum length of life or maximum health," Wicclair points out.

The Hospital Is a Mean World

One of the reasons that many real doctors and others who work in health care often have a different opinion about House's behavior than do fans of the show is simple: different amounts of firsthand experience with the world of hospitals and clinics.

How often do you hang out in a hospital or doctor's office? Not often, unless that's where you work, right? What if I pointed out that you probably see the inside of a clinic or hospital ward or even an operating room almost every day? Of course, you see it on TV, not with your own eyes. This sort of media experience is not firsthand experience, but it still has an effect on how you view the real world around you.

Amir Hetsroni, Ph.D., sees firsthand how TV shows fill gaps in our personal experience. He does research and teaches classes on communication. At the beginning of a term he will often quiz his new students.

"I ask, 'How many of you have ever been in an operating room, not as an anesthetized patient?' In a class of thirty or forty students maybe one raises his or her hand, usually not even one. And then I ask the following question, 'How many of you think you can describe to me what an operating room looks like?' All of a sudden half of the students are able to describe it, sometimes more than half. How do they know about it? They've never been there. It's from television," Hetsroni says. "It's unconscious. They don't even know that's where they're getting the information."

Medical dramas make us feel like we know something about a world, the world of medicine, with which most of us have little direct experience. Beyond learning the basic layout of an operating room— that the anesthesiologist usually works near the patient's head, for example—viewers absorb other recurring themes from TV hospitals. They see patients who are younger, thinner, and prettier than the average hospital patient.

Hetsroni and his colleagues did a census of TV patients. Less than 4 percent of them appeared to be over age sixty-five, while the share of the U.S. population that is at least sixty-five is three times greater than that. And the average age of hospital patients is even older, not surprisingly, since diseases creep up on all of us as we age. But, hey, entertainment of all sorts is dominated by people who are younger, thinner, and prettier than the rest of us.

The most important question for any patient (and the patient's loved ones) is "Will I get out of here alive?" The likely answer is far different on TV than in the real world. But rather than being filled with unrealistically happy endings, the wards of today's TV hospitals are deadlier than the real thing. And not just a little deadlier. According to Hetsroni's analysis of the outcomes of hundreds of TV cases, the death rate of fictional patients is nearly nine times that of real hospital patients.

Hetsroni's analysis of what happens to hospital patients on TV included complete seasons of *ER*, *Chicago Hope*, and *Grey's Anatomy*. He says he did not include *House* because the show focuses on wildly bizarre cases, while the other shows give the impression that their patients are closer to the mainstream. It wouldn't be surprising to find that a similar analysis of patients treated by Dr. House showed that his patients actually fare better on average than patients in the real world who have similarly rare afflictions. Nevertheless, it is certainly the case that even when House ultimately saves patients, their hospital stays are filled with one terrifying crisis after another. That kind of life-or-death roller-coaster experience is definitely not what you want to go through if you or someone you know has to go into the hospital.

Getting back to Hetsroni's survey of TV hospitals . . . The finding that TV patients are far more likely to die than real patients is the opposite of what most people believe. After all, a "Hollywood ending" is supposed to mean that the characters surmount monumental challenges, that they succeed against all odds, and that everyone lives happily ever after. Even communication researchers have long accepted that view.

"This is what you are raised on when you study communication at a university, for instance, that TV is a very, very 'Goody Two Shoes' place, a very, very nice world where nothing bad happens, nothing that cannot be resolved within a forty-five-minute episode. And currently the situation is pretty different," Hetsroni says.

It is generally thought that audiences want to see happy endings with the good guys beating the bad guys and all the young, pretty heroes and heroines smiling and celebrating as the closing credits roll.

"And that raises the question of what attracts people to view the shows, because usually researchers have been thinking that people watch television because they want to run away from a tough life and find a safe garden in these nice dramas, very, very hopeful dramas. Indeed, the situation is pretty different," Hetsroni says.

The prognosis for TV patients wasn't always so gloomy . . . not in the days of *Marcus Welby, M.D., Dr. Kildare, Emergency!,* and other medical shows from earlier eras. When Hetsroni started his study, that's the kind of TV health care he expected to find.

"I was quite surprised, honestly, to come across the finding that hospitals in medical dramas are very, very scary places. I was raised on more traditional medical dramas in the 1970s in which most of the diseases were cured in thirty or forty minutes. And the biggest diseases were something like a problem with your tonsils," he says. "All of a sudden, when we come to the modern medical dramas, like *ER* and *Chicago Hope*, we come to a very nihilistic surrounding, where actually the survival rate is much, much lower than the survival rate in real hospitals. It's a very scary place."

He thinks the turn toward a darker, grittier portrayal of life—and more frequently death—in medical shows was part of a larger course change by the major broadcast television networks as they tried to adapt to the growth of cable television. HBO and other cable-only networks not only did not have to abide by the constraints of regulatory standards on acceptable speech and other content, they weren't trying to please the mainstream. Instead of devising programs acceptable to almost everyone, cable channels consciously sought out viewers willing to pay extra in order to watch the kind of programs not available on free, broadcast channels.

"Showing more controversial drama, more sordid drama, more morbid scenes." That's the content Hetsroni says the cable channels started creating. And the shift that started on cable spread as broadcast networks fought to compete—and it entered the television hospitals. "For instance, more scenes that portray gore, that portray operations very explicitly. When you look at the medical dramas from the 1970s, even when you look at shows like *M*A*S*H*, you will never see so many scenes where you have close-up shots of an operation in progress."

Whew. That's good news that your odds of surviving a hospital stay are far better in reality than on TV. Good to know that if you or someone you know has to go into a hospital, the stay almost certainly won't be as nail-biting as the typical TV case. But the constant exposure to all this calamity may still have a negative effect on viewers.

"You see it week after week, show after show, on and on and on. Eventually, you become frightened. It's not a conscious process, where you become frightened because you say, 'In *ER* they didn't manage to save that person's life, so that will also happen to me.' Instead, it's totally unconscious. But there are studies which clearly document this process, which we call 'cultivation.' In other words, you think that the way life is portrayed on television is equal to your surrounding life," Hetsroni says.

He says the effect is small. For most people, most of the time, it may not make a measureable difference in attitudes or beliefs about the risks of going to the hospital. But Hetsroni notes that even if very few viewers change their health care decisions because of the effect of TV shows, it all adds up. There are more than 300 million people in the United States, almost all of whom watch TV at least sometimes. So even if more than ninety-nine out of a hundred aren't affected, the number who are could still reach into the millions.

In the world of prime-time television, hospitals aren't the only scary places; based on the events in a typical TV drama of almost any genre, it's a mean, mean world out there. The most closely studied area of potential media influence on viewers is the depiction of violence.

"It's one of the very few cases where there is very consistent evidence of an effect, starting in the 1960s and continuing to this day," Hetsroni says. "It's called the Mean World Syndrome."

The Mean World Index was developed by communication researcher George Gerbner. Gerbner compared media habits of study participants with their answers to a questionnaire that included questions such as:

"Do you think most people would try to take advantage of you if they got a chance or would they try to be fair?"

"Would you say that most of the time people try to be helpful or that they are mostly just looking out for themselves?"

"Generally speaking, would you say that most people can be trusted or that you can't be too careful in dealing with people?"

What's interesting is that fear of crime appears to correlate more closely with the level of crime on TV than it does to actual rates of crime reported by law enforcement agencies. It appears to be an international phenomenon. For example, a survey in Belgium asked people whether they or anyone they knew had been mugged or their house burgled, how frightened they were of crime, and their amount, frequency, and type of TV viewing.

This study included measures of direct and indirect experience of crime. There was no significant relationship between experience of crime and either watching crime on television or (more surprisingly) being afraid of crime. It appears, then, that in a sample of the general population mediated experience (i.e. watching television) is a better predictor of fear of crime than actual experience of crime.

From J. Van den Bulck, "The Relationship Between Television
Fiction and Fear of Crime," *European Journal of Communication*
19, no. 2 (June 2004): 239–248

In the United States, too, there seems to be a disconnect between fear of crime and actual rates of crime. The Gallup polling organization reported in October 2009 that "Gallup's annual Crime poll finds 74% of Americans saying there is more crime in the United States than there was a year ago, the highest measured since the early 1990s." By contrast, statistics collected by the FBI indicated just the opposite: that rates of serious crimes were dropping across the board.

Crime Rates in the United States

TYPE OF CRIME	CHANGE FROM 2008 TO 2009
Violent crime	down 6.1%
Murder	down 8.1%
Forcible rape	down 3.5%
Robbery	down 8.8%
Aggravated assault	down 5.0%
Property crime	down 5.5%
Burglary	down 2.2%
Larceny-theft	down 4.8%
Motor vehicle theft	down 17.8%

From www2.fbi.gov/ucr/cius2009/data/table_01a.html

While perceptions of health and health care and their relationship to media portrayals have not been tracked as carefully as crime and the fear of crime, it appears that the issues share many similarities. And so even though personal experience is the most powerful influence on our beliefs about how things work, media depictions fill in gaps in our experience. The consequences can be quite real. Hype and hysteria about "stranger danger" have prompted well-meaning parents to be fearful of letting their children roam and play in the neighborhood, and led them to drive students to school instead of letting them walk or bike, thus stealing away opportunities for physical activity and perhaps even reinforcing trends that contribute to growing obesity among children. And so depictions of hospitals and doctors on TV can warp our expectations of our health care institutions and professionals.

Lighten Up

That's the reaction to all the attention paid to the influence of media portrayals of medicine by a physician who is also quite familiar with the media world . . . and law as well.

"I see those shows not as tools to teach patients what medicine is like, those shows are soap operas and dramas that happen to be set in my profession. I think it's great that people realize that there is so much to what we do that it is compelling to tell stories," says Anthony Mazzarelli, M.D., J.D., M.B.E.

That alphabet following his name means that in addition to his medical degree, he also has a law degree and a master's degree in bioethics. He uses all of the degrees, practicing emergency medicine and law in New Jersey, as well as teaching. There's one more set of letters that goes with his media experience: WPHT-AM. That's the radio station in Philadelphia where Mazzarelli hosts a weekly talk show.

Mazzarelli says he knows that people pick things up from TV shows. He works in an emergency room, and especially when *ER* was on the prime-time schedule, he would hear patients tell him that he wasn't doing things the way they do on TV. And he offers a more recent example of the power of pop culture: "Now when you tell a patient, 'We're going to give you procedural sedation, so you don't feel this procedure we are doing, and the drug we're going to give you is called propofol,' they actually know that drug, because that's what killed Michael Jackson."

He admits that many of his colleagues don't keep up with pop culture and may not always be familiar with the events and images that are shaping their patients' perceptions. Still, he is confident that gap can be bridged.

"I think a physician can form a bond without necessarily having to have the same TiVo schedule as their patients," he says.

Mazzarelli even sees a silver lining to medical shows and all the other shows that use health care scenarios to make dramatic points. He thinks the topics and issues the shows raise can spark useful dialogues between patients and professionals. To those who get upset about unrealistic portrayals of doctors and other health care professionals, Mazzarelli says there is a simple way to overcome them.

"TV can portray physicians and medicine in a certain way, but the most important driving factor is the interaction people have with the doctors they interact with. I think the bonds you form with patients will carry through any of these stereotypes on TV. I'd hate to see us give them more credit than they deserve or more blame than really should be given to them. The most important thing we can do is take good care of patients and have good relationships with patients."

Four

Show Within a Show

This book is about a show about medicine. "Ugly" (4-07) adds another layer. It is a show . . . about a show about medicine.

The beginning of the episode is in black-and-white to denote that the images are coming from the camera of a documentary video crew. The video crew is following a teenage boy with a massive deformity marring his face. He is on his way to Princeton-Plainsboro Teaching Hospital to have a complex surgical procedure to remove a frontonasal encephalocele. Encephaloceles are neural tube defects. Brain tissue protrudes through a defect in the skull. They occur in about one in five thousand births, and surgeons usually repair them before a child reaches kindergarten. As usual, the case featured on *House* is far more extensive and complex than typical.

Just as *House* uses elements of real medicine in shaping the basic elements of the plots, this episode adapts some real-world examples of media coverage of health care. Certainly, health care is a popular subject of news and documentary television programs, for the same reasons hospitals are the settings of so many dramas: the life-and-death stakes involved in extreme cases.

Many programs are created by following real patients through their treatment. But part of the premise of this episode is that the camera crew is guaranteed full access to the patient's care because the documentary makers are paying for the surgery. Most news organizations forbid payments to sources, including patients, because of concerns that the sources might say what they think interviewers want to hear, rather than what they actually think, in order not to jeopardize their payday. However, some shows have paid patients for access. In 2004, the Discovery Channel reportedly paid for surgery to remove a massive tumor from a Romanian woman who couldn't get treatment at home. The surgery became a special titled *200 Pound Tumor.* According to news reports, the woman's family said they had tried to raise money for the operation but hadn't succeeded until the documentary deal came along. They said the tumor was so large that the woman couldn't get out of bed. The surgery was called a success at the time.

On *House,* Cuddy allows the video crew into the hospital because she thinks it will be good publicity. Indeed, most hospitals have news offices that are devoted to attracting positive media attention to their hospitals . . . as well as managing responses to news stories that are not always so positive. Giving video crews access to a hospital (or any business, for that matter) is taking a chance. Somebody may say or do the wrong thing on camera. In order to escape the camera, House leads his team into an MRI suite, where metal objects are forbidden. (See the first volume, *The Medical Science of House, M.D.,* for a discussion of the hazards created when the powerful magnets of MRI machines grab items of metal that can be magnetized.) Actually, video cameras simply won't work near an MRI machine because the powerful magnets distort the video signal.

Before the planned surgery, Chase is interviewed by the video crew. He comes off as stiff, speaking in clumsy jargon. That portrayal is certainly an accurate depiction of many doctors or other experts, who either naturally rely on jargon or become tongue-tied by nerves when they are interviewed. The documentary producer becomes frustrated. "We need a sound bite," she says to her videographer. Then she turns back to Chase. "Would you say he'll be ready for the junior prom?" she asks. "Yeah, yeah, that's probably true," Chase replies. "No, I mean I need you to say it," she tells him. She is putting quotes into his mouth . . . a no-no at respectable news and documentary operations, but something that does indeed happen. More typically, interviewers will simply instruct people to answer in complete sentences. Good interviewers also ask questions in ways that can't be answered with a simple yes-or-no reply.

Whether interview subjects are coached to give specific answers may depend on whether the program is being done by journalists from a news organization or producers from an entertainment department. The two may work at the same company but answer to different bosses and different ethical standards. Indeed, it is often painfully obvious that the comments from people on so-called reality shows are scripted, even on networks where telling an interview subject what to say could get a news producer fired for unethical behavior.

Concerns about having a video crew inside a hospital involve more than just the image of the hospital. Any reporter working on health care stories has to navigate federal and state laws and regulations, as well as ethical standards, that are intended to protect patient privacy. The legal landscape of patient privacy changed dramatically when the rules known as HIPAA took effect. HIPAA stands for the Health Insurance Portability and Accountability Act of 1996. The law changed a number of rules governing health care in the United States. The "Portability" part of the name comes from changes that allowed more people to keep their health care insurance in effect when changing jobs under certain conditions.

In April 2003, almost seven years after HIPAA was passed, sweeping new medical privacy rules authorized by the law finally went into effect. The tougher standards were prompted in part by stories of people being fired from jobs or facing other discrimination in the early years of the AIDS epidemic because of leaks from hospitals or doctor's offices that revealed HIV test results or treatment. The HIPAA privacy rules constitute an incredibly complex document. The version posted on the Web site of the U.S. Department of Health and Human Services runs more than one hundred pages including front matter. It carries the unintentionally ironic title of "HIPAA Administrative Simplification." The complexity and the heavy potential penalties for violations have spawned a "HIPAA-compliance" industry of lawyers and others who advise health care providers and institutions on how to follow the intricate rules. Almost all missteps have been handled with warning letters and corrective actions, but federal law allows for fines of up to $1.5 million dollars. Jail time is even possible for knowingly disclosing protected health information. So hospital administrators take the rules very seriously.

Before HIPAA, video crews often could shoot stories in hospitals using a sort of "shoot first, get releases later" system. Producers would agree not to use any footage that might identify a patient unless they obtained permission from the patient or family, depending on the circumstances. This sort of arrangement allowed reporting on emergency medicine, for example. After all, when reporting about heart attack treatment or car crashes, it is impossible to get an advance release from a person before the event, and when patients arrive at the hospital they are often in no shape to give permission to be videotaped. But HIPAA largely ended the practice of getting permission after shooting footage. Now when video crews enter a hospital, a hospital representative gets permission from the patient or family before letting the cameras roll.

In "Ugly," the documentary video crew clearly had the patient's permission in advance, so HIPAA would not have barred the scenario in the episode. However, it is worth asking whether the family gave permission freely . . . or whether the boy was essentially forced into surrendering his privacy, since without the money from the video company, he would not have been able to afford the surgery he so desperately wanted.

But the show appeared to include at least one possible HIPAA violation. The crew goes to interview Cameron as she is working in the emergency department. There is no indication that the patient Cameron is treating when the crew arrives (and other patients visible in the background) gave permission in advance to have the video crew take their pictures. And it's not just a matter of when the camera started rolling. According to HIPAA, people observing care have to be part of the health care team or have some other permitted purpose for being present. Technically, it could be a violation for the producer to see who was in the ER even if the camera never rolled.

Interestingly, even if the producer and her camera crew grossly violated the provisions of HIPAA, she and her team would not face any penalties under the federal rule. The regulation applies only to health care providers and other specific "covered entities." In other words, if a patient or family member filed a complaint with the Office for Civil Rights of the U.S. Department of Health and Human Services, it would be Cuddy who could be in trouble for allowing the crew to have improper access to patients.

There is another odd aspect of HIPAA. While it has made it much, much more difficult for news organizations to witness how our health care institutions and personnel do their jobs, it allows doctors, nurses, and others to write almost anything they want about their patients as long as they get release forms or disguise the cases. That is because the doctors and other health care providers have a legitimate reason for observing the care . . . because they are providing it. So a perverse effect of the privacy rule is that hospitals and providers can use carefully selected or disguised cases as raw material for articles or books that present their views of the kind of care they are providing. But if journalists or other independent observers want to see for themselves what's going on inside hospitals and clinics, well then HIPAA can be used as an almost impenetrable shield to block access.

Of course, not all the writing about health care by doctors and others is positive. Indeed, there are many books and articles authored by health care professionals that are as sharply critical as anything a skeptical journalist would produce. Also, many, many hospitals and providers go to great effort to find ways to allow independent observers to at least glimpse the inner workings of health care without violating the privacy rights of patients.

HIPAA isn't the only document that guides how reporters, documentary producers, or others ensure respect for the rights of patients, including their right to privacy. Many news organizations have codes of ethics and other corporate policies that attempt to balance the rights of patients with the interests of the public to know what happens inside our health care institutions. Professional organizations like the Association of Health Care Journalists have voluntary standards that help define the ethical practice of journalism. After all, patients are not like public officials or political candidates. The point of the stories is to inform the public, not to scrutinize or exploit patients.

One last aspect of the "Ugly" episode that rings true . . . sort of: when House sees the final program, he is surprised (and upset) to see that he is portrayed as a caring and pleasant person. While it may be more common for subjects of news reports or documentaries to be unpleasantly surprised by portrayals that they believe are too *negative*, the key point is that the general practice of news organizations is to not give subjects any authority to preview or approve the final product. In certain cases, a filmmaker or writer may show subjects portions of drafts in order to check the material for accuracy, but the standard practice is for the writer or journalist to have the final say about what stays in and what gets changed or cut, whether or not the subjects like it. That's really the only way to make sure the final report reflects what the crew actually saw, instead of just what the hospital would have liked them to see.

Five

House and Health Care Reform

One of the reasons the family in "Ugly" agreed to be followed by a video crew is that they needed money to pay for the boy's surgery. No one in the episode questions why the United States, which spends far more per person on health care than any other country, has had a uniquely difficult time figuring out how to provide necessary medical care to everyone.

What would House think of health care reform?

Regardless of your political leanings, health care is a big deal. Poll after poll puts the issue near the top of our concerns. For example, a national telephone survey in early 2010 reported that four out of five Americans say health care is extremely or very important. Add in those who rated health care as moderately important and the total jumps to 90 percent of Americans (Associated Press/Gfk Roper Public Affairs & Media poll, January 2010). A Gallup poll conducted in the fall of 2009 also produced a result that won't shock anyone: health care costs were the second most often mentioned financial problem facing families, ahead of owning a home, college expenses, retirement savings, and other burdens. The only item mentioned more often was a lack of money or low wages.

But once you look beyond that broad agreement on the importance of health care and the ever-growing burden of health care costs, well, things quickly get as complicated as health care itself. And it doesn't appear that people are getting much help from the news. A summary of analyses of news coverage of health care reform reported that instead of informing the public, much of it added to confusion. That conclusion isn't really surprising, since most of the coverage is about the political horse race rather than the contents of any legislation . . . and the stories are full of politicians trying to summarize bills running well over a thousand pages in punchy ten-second sound bites. Indeed, surveys by the Kaiser Family Foundation found that a lot of people changed their minds about health care reform proposals when they heard some of the details of what was actually in the legislation, indicating that despite the flood of news coverage, many people weren't very well informed about the proposals. Another report commissioned by that foundation, well before the last round of political battles over reforming the U.S. health care system, made the point that when it comes to influencing people's deepest desires and fears, the most important media arena is probably prime-time entertainment, not the news.

Dramatic Reform

Certainly TV dramas reach a much wider audience than most news programs. Beyond the size of their audience, some media scholars argue that entertainment TV's impact can be even more powerful than news in subtly shaping the public's impressions of key societal institutions. The messages are more engaging, often playing out in compelling human dramas involving characters the audience cares about. Viewers are taken behind the scenes to see the hidden forces affecting whether there's a happy ending or a sad one. There are good guys and bad guys, heroes and villains and innocent bystanders.

*Instead of bill numbers and budget figures, policy issues are por-
trayed through the lives of "real" human beings, often in life-and-
death situations.*

From J. Turow and R. Gans, *As Seen on TV: Health Policy Issues in TV's
Medical Dramas*, a report to the Kaiser Family Foundation, July 2002

We're not here to debate the specifics of health care reform legislation, either the bills passed by the U.S. Congress in early 2010 or the
many legislative proposals yet to come. House doesn't bring it up, that's
for sure. And that's the point here: House is unconcerned about health
care insurance coverage or costs, unless they get in his way. (See the
discussion of insurance company negotiations in the "Showdown" sec-
tion that follows.) To be fair, House does take only extreme cases, and
even in the real world, costs are less likely to be discussed in the middle
of a health crisis. Nevertheless, many doctors strongly believe that caring for patients can include consideration of the financial burden of
health care.

A recent survey published in the journal *Health Affairs* found that
most cancer doctors consider the cost of treatment when choosing what
to recommend to their patients. And when it comes to deductibles,
copays, and other expenses that patients have to pay out of their own
pockets, four out of five of the doctors surveyed said yes, that does
influence their recommendations. That response doesn't mean they recommend less effective treatment just to save money, but that often there
are a variety of treatment options and so cost is something to consider.
The authors of the study wrote, "Physicians struggle with their professional roles to balance the needed care and the limited resources of their
patients and society."

House doesn't bother to struggle with that balance at all. Indeed,
he seems to operate in a world without any budget constraints, where
every drug and every service is fully paid for (with only rare exceptions). Oh, sure, Cuddy will complain and roll her eyes at some extraordinary expense, but House brushes aside her concerns with a witty and

sarcastic quip and steams full speed ahead. One of the most fundamental themes of *House* is that salvation for patients is achieved by finding that one special, brilliant physician who will employ every cutting-edge drug, device, and procedure in unswerving pursuit of victory over the disease.

It's a popular tenet. After all, doesn't everyone want to be rescued from death by a heroic doctor? But the attitude portrayed on *House* and other medical dramas—a fervent belief in medical miracles—also plays out in the real world, as politicians and policy makers try to figure out how to fix our health care system.

"I think that what most people believe and have believed, because they've been raised over generations to believe it, is that miracles are always possible. It starts with miracles. And that can be a small 'm' or a capital 'M' depending on your faith background. And then you add to that that everybody knows that we are constantly inventing something new and different and better, presumably, because they read about it all the time," says former U.S. Senator David Durenberger. Senator Durenberger represented Minnesota from 1978 to 1995. He was involved in health care policy as a Republican member of one of the committees in the U.S. Senate that deals with health issues. After leaving the Senate, he founded the National Institute of Health Policy in Minneapolis, Minnesota.

That desire for medical miracles can be seen in how voters think about how to spend public money. While it is easy to find vocal opponents of expanding public subsidies or regulation intended to extend health care insurance to more people, when it comes to opening public purse strings to fund "cutting-edge" medical research, it seems voters express a different attitude. Take the case of the restrictions on federal funding of stem cell research that President George W. Bush put in place in 2001.

In reaction to the federal policy, the citizens of California took stem cell research into their own hands: in 2004 voters passed the California Research and Cures Initiative, which amended the state

constitution to make stem cell research a constitutional right and cre-
ated an institution—the California Institute for Regenerative Medi-
cine (CIRM)—to fund, facilitate, and provide oversight for stem cell
research in the state. The initiative provided a mechanism to fund
stem cell research with $3 billion over a decade through the sale of
public bonds, with interest payable from the state's general fund,
amounting to an additional $3 billion.

From J. W. Adelson and J. K. Weinberg, "The California Stem
Cell Initiative: Persuasion, Politics, and Public Science," *American*
Journal of Public Health 100, no. 3 (March 2010): 446–451

People may say they are reluctant to throw billions of dollars at a
problem or create entirely new bureaucracies, both of which this ballot initiative did, but when California voters went to the polls, they
approved it by a three-to-two margin. It seems the promise of medical
miracles is an alluring argument.

Most health care reform proposals are far less enticing. And rather
than dangling the hope of new cures, reform proposals are often seen as
potentially putting some limits on medical decision making. Although
House would certainly heap his scorn equally upon politicians of both
political parties, it seems likely he would lean toward those who say
they want to defend a physician's ability to prescribe any test or treatment he or she thinks might benefit a patient . . . cost be damned. He
would probably have little patience with advocates of reform who stress
the need to "bend the cost curve" in order to prevent rising health care
costs from drowning family budgets, business budgets, even the federal
budget.

Some observers say this tension between freedom and cost control
is how the real public debate over health care reform is shaping up.
Shortly before Congress passed bills that promise to reduce the number
of Americans who lack health care insurance coverage, Larry Wallack,
Dr.P.H., dean of the College of Urban and Public Affairs at Portland
State University in Portland, Oregon, wrote that a focus on controlling
costs is unlikely to rally people to the side of health care reform.

Opponents of reform are occupied with an entirely different question: Are we willing to give up our freedom? John Boehner, the House minority leader, said recently, "This bill is the greatest threat to freedom that I have seen in the 19 years I have been here in Washington. . . . It's going to lead to a government takeover of our health care system, with tens of thousands of new bureaucrats right down the street, making these decisions [choose your doctor, buy your own health insurance] for you."

From L. Wallack, "Health Care Reform: Asking the Right Questions," *Portland Oregonian*, January 29, 2010

Wallack argued that reformers haven't effectively dealt with concerns about freedom, and he pointed out that the real debate is about much more than the cost issues that many health policy wonks focus on; rather it is about basic human values. Some of the responses to the column posted online applauded Wallack's analysis of the health care reform debate. There were also comments that made exactly the sort of critiques of reformers that he had highlighted.

"Individuals need the choice of how they participate," wrote one person.

"America has the best health care system in the world," said another.

And then there was a comment that had a biting tone . . . maybe like something House might say: "The government screws up everything it touches. Anyone wanting government to be in charge of health care is a complete fool." Not that House would accuse only the government of screwing things up; he would likely level the same accusation against corporations and anyone else who disagreed with him about what medical resources to use and how.

A recent analysis of prime-time TV shows found that six out of ten episodes included some sort of health topic as part of the major story line. That means health issues appear on many shows beyond those considered to be medical dramas, like *House*. Despite that widespread use of health themes in entertainment programming, most studies of the media and how they may influence public attitudes on health policy topics focus on news programs; so the report mentioned earlier, *As Seen on TV: Health Policy Issues in TV's Medical Dramas*, stands out as one of the few that look at the policy messages woven into the shows we watch just for fun. The study was done before *House* debuted; researchers analyzed the content of seventy-four episodes of *ER*, *Gideon's Crossing*, *City of Angels*, and *Strong Medicine*. Unlike other studies, which have looked at medical accuracy and other features of how such shows portray clinical care, this analysis examined how the characters and story lines depicted debates over health policy issues, such as HMOs and rules about access to care; Medicare reimbursement; ethics; confidentiality; the right to refuse treatment; and end-of-life care.

> *Hospital dramas provide an opportunity for viewers to learn specifically what goes on at the center of high intensity medicine. The dramas' fictional presentations open curtains on relationships between doctors and nurses, specialists and generalists. In ways that news reports cannot, they play out various assumptions about how health care ought to be delivered, about what conflicts arise that affect health care, and about how those conflicts should be resolved and why. Doing that, hospital dramas represent an important part of viewers' curriculum on the problems and possibilities of health care in America.*
>
> From J. Turow and R. Gans, *As Seen on TV: Health Policy Issues in TV's Medical Dramas*, a report to the Kaiser Family Foundation, July 2002

Despite the wide range of policy issues considered, one issue stood out in the report: malpractice. There were a variety of flavors of the topic, including malpractice lawsuits and threats of suits, fines for malpractice, and aspects of cost containment that affected malpractice suits and threats of suits. Added together, debates over medical malpractice accounted for about a third of all the policy debates the researchers found in the prime-time medical dramas. That was almost three times as many debates as concerned either patient rights or end-of-life care, with other contentious issues trailing far behind. Maybe the prominence of malpractice on these shows reflects and/or reinforces popular notions that malpractice suits and costs are at the heart of the problems facing the U.S. health care system, even though health care economists say malpractice insurance and lawsuits account for just a tiny fraction of what the country spends on health care. Fear of being sued may well increase the use of some tests and treatments, but experts say other forces, including aging and the availability of new drugs and devices have a far greater impact on health care spending.

> *The programs may help to stimulate thought and discussion by show-ing people how health policy issues might play out in "real" people's lives. While these features of the programs may have stimulated dis-cussion, our data suggest that other aspects of the health care policy scenes may have worked against public knowledge and action. Con-sider the low visibility of resource considerations to the programs' health policy issues. An integral part of so much contemporary pub-lic health policy debate, these arguments about cost came up in only 23% of the programs' health policy interactions.*

> From J. Turow and R. Gans, *As Seen on TV: Health Policy Issues in TV's Medical Dramas*, a report to the Kaiser Family Foundation, July 2002

The researchers found that when controversial topics are raised in prime-time medical dramas, the shows generally don't take sides, pre-senting a variety of arguments. However, the study authors said they did find a slight tilt against cost-saving measures. Certainly, it seems that a similar analysis of *House* would reach similar conclusions: House does not like "bean counters."

Of course, people know that TV shows aren't real. And yet some studies suggest that when the information viewers see in fiction doesn't match what they hear from other sources, the fictional portrayal may win out. Researchers at Washington University in St. Louis did an experiment with college students to find out what they remembered when they watched Hollywood movies that portrayed historical events (though not always accurately) and also read accurate accounts of the same events. The students were tested a week after watching a movie and reading about the facts.

Films and Topics Used as Materials
for Both Experiments

FILM	TOPIC
Amadeus (1984)	Wolfgang Amadeus Mozart
Amistad (1997)	Mutiny on the Spanish ship *Amistad*
Eight Men Out (1988)	The Chicago Black Sox scandal
Elizabeth (1998)	Queen Elizabeth I
Glory (1989)	Fifty-fourth Massachusetts Volunteer Infantry
Marie Antoinette (2006)	The French Revolution
The Last Samurai (2003)	The Satsuma Rebellion
Tombstone (1993)	Wyatt Earp and the shoot-out at the O.K. Corral
U-571 (2000)	Deciphering the Nazis' Enigma code

From A. C. Butler, F. M. Zaromb, K. B. Lyle, and H. L. Roediger III, "Using Popular Films to Enhance Classroom Learning: the Good, the Bad, and the Interesting," Psychological Science *20, no. 9 (September 2009): 1161–1168 (epub July 23, 2009, at www.ncbi.nlm.nih.gov/pubmed/19645691, accessed on December 30, 2009.)*

"Watching a film clip increased correct recall of consistent information relative to recall of the same information when subjects did not see the clip. However, when the information in the film contradicted the text, subjects often (falsely) recalled misinformation from the film," the researchers wrote in an article in the journal *Psychological Science*. They wrote that they were surprised that even when the film "blatantly contradicted" the facts, students often remembered the Hollywood version of events as being the "true" version.

Some of the students were given specific warnings about misinformation in the movies and told the correct information. Other students were given just a general warning about inaccuracies in the movies or no warning at all. Students who heard specific warnings about which "facts" in the movies were inaccurate did score better than the students given general warnings or no warning at all. But of course, viewers of *House* and other medical shows aren't told specifically which parts of each episode are faithful to the facts and which are not.

Communication researcher Susan E. Morgan, Ph.D., who has studied how entertainment TV shows, including *House*, affect attitudes about organ donation (see Chapter 9, "Miracle Stuff," on organ donation), says that based on the findings from that research, it would make sense that *House* and other shows also influence people's attitudes about other issues.

"Like insurance, and how hospitals work, and that kind of thing. I'm sure it really screws up people's experiences when they go into hospitals and they expect stuff to happen the way they see it on television and it turns out that's not how things are done," Morgan says.

Morgan recognizes that TV shows are just one source of information that people use to learn about the world, including the world of health and health care reform.

"With health care reform, it's such a big unknown, such a big, scary unknown that hits at the central core values of what it means to be an American." Morgan refers to her father as she talks about how people interpret the information they receive from the media. "My father is an immigrant. He escaped from Communist Hungary. Anytime something sounds like socialism to him, he bangs his fist on the table and wants to reach for a shotgun," she says with a chuckle. "And the thing is, he would benefit from health care reform. It's ironic that all these people who would benefit are against health care reform. It's because it's a big unknown. Anytime something is novel and unknown, we have to rely on the media for information about it. So that's the first place that we get our information from, the media. Then we start thinking about how it meshes with our internal values. And sometimes we don't know how to make sense of that. So then we engage in these interpersonal discussions within our community of people."

It's not just watching a show that influences what we think about the topics we see portrayed on TV; talking about it later has a powerful effect on what we remember and what conclusions we settle on. When we discuss the shows with friends and family, we find out what *they* think . . . and that affects our opinions.

"You end up discussing these things and then you collectively make sense of it, which is why we have all these pockets of people who come out for or against something. And it's how people who are really poor and who don't have health care can be against health care reform. It seems insane to me, but since I studied this stuff, now I understand why," Morgan says.

Personal experience usually wins out over media messages. So when *House* does a show about something we know about firsthand, or that someone we know has been through, the TV portrayals may not change our attitudes. But face it: how many of us have firsthand knowledge of the effects of health care reform? If you have lived in another country or know somebody who has been cared for in another kind of health care system, then those experiences come into play, but most people in the United States know only the system we currently have.

"With health care reform, we have nothing to rely on except the media. We have nobody to talk to who has had experience with the type of health care reform that is being proposed. It's a big unknown," Morgan says.

A lot of the discussion about how the media portray health care reform focuses on news programs. It's natural to assume that when people want to learn about political debates and public policy issues, they turn to the news for facts. But when it comes to actually deciding what we think about an important issue, entertainment programs may have a more powerful influence than the news. That's because shows like *House* tell emotionally powerful stories. We may watch the news, and stick some of the facts we see into the rational parts of our minds, but we *feel* the trauma and fears, the successes and joys, of well-written characters on our favorite shows. For that matter, even with news programs, we are most likely to remember the human interest anecdotes, rather than the points made by experts interviewed for the reports.

"The factual stuff, [viewers] are not remembering, they are not retaining. They are being presented with facts, but it's very dry. It doesn't have the same kind of holistic impact on people's attitudes and their ultimate behaviors," Morgan says.

There's one more impression that every medical show, including *House*, gives viewers, no matter what efforts are made to ensure the accuracy of the medical care or the portrayals of health policy issues. That unavoidable impression is that health care has an overwhelming influence on our health. However, the fact is, medicine often has little to do with health. Think about it. How much time do you spend with doctors when you are healthy? Not much, right? Medical care focuses on managing illness.

Other than vaccinations, health care actually has little to do with promoting health. Even screening tests don't keep us healthy; they just detect signs of sickness earlier. Many estimates of the improvement in health and life expectancy over the last century conclude that medicine can claim credit for about 10 percent of the gains. What's more, if medicine really was the most important factor in preserving health and extending life, then the United States, which spends far more on health care per person than any other country, wouldn't be steadily falling behind other nations on international measures of health.

Medical rescues are dramatic, and so they make for entertaining TV. But education, social factors, food policies, and even things as mundane as zoning and transportation planning have much more of an impact on how healthy we are than even a doctor as brilliant as House. But then, *House, Urban Planner* probably wouldn't be a ratings hit, would it?

Showdown

For most people, most of the time, most big health care bills are paid for by insurance or public programs. Well, actually, we pay all the costs; but most of the money is paid in premiums and taxes that then flows through insurance companies and government agencies, rather than being paid directly by patients to providers. Health care costs are built into everything we buy, and rising premiums have sucked up much of the money that employers otherwise could have paid out in bigger raises over the last few decades.

House almost never mentions health care costs or insurance. But one episode, "5 to 9" (6-14), did revolve around negotiations between Princeton-Plainsboro Teaching Hospital and an insurance company over the rates the hospital would be paid when caring for the insurance company's customers. When Cuddy meets with insurance company executive Eli Morgan, she demands a 12 percent increase in reimbursements. Morgan's company has offered just 4 percent, and he says Cuddy has no chance of getting what she wants. "There's a lesson every good poker player learns: don't get emotional. You don't have the cards. The sooner you realize that, the sooner a reasonable contract will get signed," Morgan tells her.

But is that really how the cards are dealt?

Robert Berenson, M.D., recently coauthored an article based on research into the relative negotiating power of hospitals and insurance companies (also known as health plans) in California.

"What we were arguing is that the hospitals hold most of the trump cards. If the health plan isn't willing to tell the hospital to get lost, that we can go without you, it doesn't have a serious hole card. It really can't threaten very much. If the hospital knows that the health plan can't do business without it, then it's got the advantage. And that seems to be the way markets have evolved over the last decade," Berenson says.

Although Berenson and colleagues at the Center for Studying Health System Change looked specifically at the health care market in California, he says similar trends are occurring across the country.

The portrayal of insurance company bullying on *House* is closer to the way things were in the 1990s. Many health plans held a hard line in negotiations, and any doctor or clinic or hospital that wanted more money risked being cut out of the network. At the time, HMOs were on the rise, and as an issue brief written by others at the Center for Studying Health System Change put it, "Forced on the defensive by plans, providers often agreed to steep discounts in exchange for promises of higher volume."

Naturally, people didn't like to get notices saying the doctor or hospital they'd been going to for years was being cut from their network and wouldn't be covered anymore. There was a strong public backlash. The health plans began to see that people were more interested in broad access to providers than in slowing the rise of health care insurance premiums. The hospitals and doctors also took steps to bolster their leverage. The balance of power began to shift.

"There were showdowns all over the place. And then I think the health plans basically blinked and said, 'Why are we doing this? We get a black eye with the public, then in the end we come back and put our heads between our knees and say will you please sign up with us, we will give you what you wanted. What's the point?' They can pass it on in higher premiums," Berenson says.

Hospitals merged and consolidated their market shares. As part of that consolidation, they made sure there weren't a lot of extra hospital beds open.

"Even if the health plan was willing to have a narrower network and exclude the hospital, if they don't have other hospitals that can absorb their members, it's an idle threat," Berenson says. So rather than the insurance company having the power to deprive a hospital of patients, as was depicted on *House*, the hospitals could say to insurers, "Where will your customers get care?"

In the episode, the insurance executive tells Cuddy that Princeton-Plainsboro is too small to have any clout. So maybe he thinks his company could find enough beds at other hospitals in the area for their customers. Although not disputing that her hospital might be the smallest in that market, Cuddy retorts, "We are also the best." The insurance executive says that doesn't matter. Berenson says actually some hospitals do claim "must-have" status; in other words, their reputation is strong enough that insurers need to be able to include them in the network in order to sell policies. For example, he points to Cedars-Sinai Medical Center in Los Angeles, familiar for treating many Hollywood celebrities, as a "must-have" hospital for health plans in that market. But as with so many things in health care and in life in general, that status may have more to do with word of mouth than with any objective measure of quality, according to Berenson.

"It's really the brokers in a community, the consultants to the large employers; they are the ones that decide that Cedars-Sinai is a 'must-have' hospital. It doesn't matter what any objective measure of quality is, it is about reputation," he says.

Berenson also points out that some smaller hospitals offer special expertise or resources in specific areas, say trauma or neonatal care, that a health plan wants to include in its network. That can give a hospital a powerful card: you can't have access to the service you want unless you make a deal to cover everything we offer.

In a desperate move during "5 to 9," Cuddy finds out where the insurance company CEO has lunch and confronts him in the middle of the restaurant. She tells him that Princeton-Plainsboro Teaching Hospital has the highest-rated ER in the state and the most advanced ICU (though it does seem strange that the smallest hospital would have the most advanced Intensive Care Unit). Then she adds that her hospital has "the most innovative diagnostic medicine department in the entire country." In other words, she's got House.

So is House the ultimate "must-have" feature of Princeton-Plainsboro? Maybe part of the business case for tolerating House's often outrageous behavior and giving him an extraordinary budget to hire his assistants is that he is the unique resource Princeton-Plainsboro can claim in order to stand up to insurance companies and rival hospitals.

But the insurance company CEO does not appear to be swayed. So Cuddy threatens to go to the news media and try to embarrass the insurance company. She says the insurer's marketing budget is bigger than the budgets of the hospital's Pediatric Intensive Care Unit and Transplant Unit combined, that they spend more on golf tournament sponsorships than the hospital spends on the walk-in clinic, and that the fuel for the company's private jets could keep the air ambulance flying for years. Although Cuddy says she would rather not point out to the press how selective the company seems to be when cutting costs, it's clear she wouldn't hesitate if it could help her get more money for the hospital. And actually, her threat is to do exactly what health care providers often really do when reimbursement battles go public.

"And then they both want to use public pressure. For the most part, certainly now, providers are seen as more sympathetic than the health plans are. You certainly see that the health plans are being beaten up politically, while the hospitals and the doctors aren't being beaten up," Berenson notes.

In 2010, one of the most prominent cases was the intense public scrutiny of premium hikes of up to 39 percent proposed by Anthem Blue Cross in California. Even President Barack Obama singled out the company in a weekly address to the nation.

> *The other week, men and women across California opened up their mailboxes to find a letter from Anthem Blue Cross. The news inside was jaw-dropping. Anthem was alerting almost a million of its customers that it would be raising premiums by an average of 25 percent, with about a quarter of folks likely to see their rates go up by anywhere from 35 to 39 percent.*
>
> From "Weekly Address: President Obama Says It Is Time to Move Forward on Health Care Reform," February 20, 2010 (transcript available online at www.whitehouse.gov/the-press-office/ weekly-address-president-obama-says-it-time-move -forward-health-care-reform, accessed on March 3, 2010)

Anthem Blue Cross executives were called to testify before committees in the California legislature and the U.S. Congress. Their explanation for such dramatic premium hikes? In large part, they said they were just passing along price increases imposed by hospitals and other health care providers. In other words, it's really Cuddy's fault.

In a story in that appeared in the *Los Angeles Times*, the president of Anthem Blue Cross, Leslie Margolin, was quoted as telling a state legislative committee that people were picking on the wrong target. Reporter Duke Helfand wrote:

> *In Sacramento, Anthem's president, Leslie Margolin, told the committee that much of the public frustration over the rate hikes was misdirected and should be aimed at the nation's healthcare system.*
>
> *"This debate and this inquiry cannot and should not be just about the insurance industry or the delivery system or regulators or legislators or customers or brokers," Margolin said.*
>
> *"We have wasted precious time and precious resources doing battle with each other," she added. "We must come together collaboratively and strategically to address the distressing symptoms of our troubled system—rising premiums, for example—and to address the fundamental underlying causes of our collective failure."*
>
> From "Anthem Blue Cross Plans to Go Ahead with Rate Hikes
in California," Los Angeles Times, February 24, 2010 (available
online at http://articles.latimes.com/2010/feb/24/business/
la-fi-insure24-2010feb24, accessed on March 3, 2010)

A statement from another executive at Anthem Blue Cross said part of the reason rates for individual insurance policies (as distinct from the premiums charged for people who get their health care benefits from large employers) is that more healthy people are dropping their coverage. With a smaller pool of people, who are on average sicker and using more health care each, the average cost per person goes up.

And then in a hearing before a committee of the U.S. Congress, Angela Braly, president and chief executive officer of WellPoint, Inc., the parent company of Anthem Blue Cross, testified that the premium increases merely reflected rising prices charged by health care providers, as well as the effects of healthy people dropping coverage and losses on certain types of health care insurance. Braly said that even though rates on some policies shot up, their overall after-tax profit margin in California was just 1.5 percent.

She added that hospitals make higher profits, quoting from data compiled by independent sources that indicate that community hospitals were making margins of almost 7 percent in 2007 and those profits had almost doubled since 2001. However, there are several ways to calculate profits at hospitals. Reports from the American Hospital Association noted that hospital margins dropped in 2008 as the financial markets and investment income took a nosedive. The AHA also points out that if hospitals had to get by only on the money paid by patients (and their insurance companies or public health care programs), they would be losing money. Hospitals rely on investments, contributions, and other income to cover the gap between what they collect from hospital bills and what it actually costs to run their hospitals.

But to get back to the negotiations between Cuddy and the insurance company . . . She kept arguing that Princeton-Plainsboro deserved the increased payments based on the type and quality of care they provided . . . and the fact that they had House. But a recent report from the attorney general of Massachusetts found that the prices hospitals charged did not seem to have any clear connection with the type of care they provided.

> *Although our investigation is ongoing, our preliminary analysis indicates that current contracting practices by health insurance companies and health care providers have resulted in significant differences in compensation rates among hospitals and physicians that do not appear to be based on the complexity or quality of the care provided.*
>
> From *Investigation of Health Care Cost Trends and Cost Drivers*,
> Office of Attorney General Martha Coakley, Boston,
> Massachusetts, January 2010

The report found that prices vary widely and do not seem to relate to quality of care, how sick the average patients are, or the proportion of Medicare or Medicaid patients (who generally bring in less money than privately insured patients). Hospitals that invest in research and in training medical students and residents often say those duties put extra costs on them, but the Massachusetts report did not see a connection between such programs and the prices charged. There were also wide variations in the prices charged for similar services at different hospitals.

The explanation for how hospitals set prices, according to this report, is not so much the underlying costs of providing health care, but rather market leverage—that is, who holds the better cards in insurer-provider negotiations.

Some states have started posting certain hospital prices online (see below). Indeed, there are often big differences in the prices charged for similar services. It's just one more example of how the health care system appears to defy common sense or the kinds of rules that shape prices and practices in other businesses.

In "5 to 9," Cuddy follows through on her threat to drop the insurance company. She announces to the hospital staff that starting the next day no new patients covered by the company will be admitted and that current patients will be allowed only thirty days more. Actually, state regulations generally have "continuity of care" rules that require longer grace periods and other restrictions on cutting off coverage, but when insurance networks change, patients are indeed often stuck with the choice of changing doctors or paying higher "out of network" prices.

Although throughout most of the episode it seemed that the insurance company held the most cards and that Cuddy was probably going to lose the contract—and probably her job—in the end, the insurance company gives in. That's actually how most of these showdowns have turned out in recent years.

The Massachusetts report said that price increases by health care providers accounted for most of the increase in health care costs in that state in recent years. Other reports have concluded that while price increases by providers are responsible for a big part of increasing health care costs, other factors, including the increasing amount of medical care we each use as more drugs and devices are developed, may account for at least as much medical cost inflation.

But whether more of the blame goes to price hikes or to all the new tricks and toys that House and his colleagues deploy, there was likely one immediate consequence of Cuddy's victory over the insurance company . . . something the episode didn't show: the insurance company probably turned around and bumped up premiums in order to pass the higher costs along to customers. And since other insurance companies are dealing with the same costs, those customers are stuck with a choice of paying more or dropping their coverage and facing an even greater risk of bankruptcy due to medical costs.

Although in recent years the health care industry (including both providers and health plans) has generally decided that it is easier to boost prices than to control costs, Robert Berenson is among those who wonder whether that dynamic will soon change. Recent health care reform legislation may provide subsidies to some people and spread the burden around a bit more broadly, but in general the overall costs of health care and health care insurance in the United States are likely to continue rising faster than wages. At what point do insurance premiums get so terribly expensive that consumers decide maybe a bit more control might not be so bad after all?

What's All This Gonna Cost?

It seems like a simple question to answer: just how much would it cost to be treated by House? Just write down the cost of each test and treatment ordered in an episode, add them up, look at the total . . . and hope the patient's insurance company has a sound balance sheet.

But it's not that simple.

The first challenge is figuring out exactly what House and his team really ordered. Was that MRI scan done with or without a contrast agent? Exactly how much of the patient's body was scanned? As explained in *The Medical Science of House, M.D.*, when they order a "tox screen," they could be asking for a standard panel of tests or a much, much larger number of tests for less common substances. Were they testing the patient's blood or urine or hair or other tissues? Each of those questions must be answered in order to know what to bill.

Medical bills usually include codes known as CPT codes. CPT stands for current procedural terminology. The term is a registered trademark of the American Medical Association. Health care providers purchase access to the CPT codes. There are a lot of them—more than eight thousand different codes to describe medical procedures and services, so that providers and payers know precisely what they are talking about. And the list keeps growing and changing to keep pace with health care practice.

But even if you could assign a CPT code to something mentioned on *House*, the search for a price would really only have begun. Not only do different hospitals charge different prices for the same item, they charge different prices for the same item depending on who is paying for it. Each insurance company negotiates contracts with providers. And then public programs also set different (typically lower) reimbursement rates.

Then there is the trend toward bundling services or paying one price for treating a patient with a certain diagnosis, regardless of what specific services were provided to that individual patient. In most cases, it's a straightforward matter to document the diagnosis of a patient in a hospital. But it's hard to say exactly how the billing department of Princeton-Plainsboro Teaching Hospital would handle House's cases, in which the diagnosis changes again and again and again.

The infamous murkiness of health care pricing is so extreme that often doctors don't know what they will be paid until after they submit their bill and they receive those "Explanation of Benefits" statements.

But don't give up. Health care pricing is getting slightly less foggy. A growing number of hospitals, insurance companies, and states are offering information on typical charges for common procedures and services.

The New Jersey Hospital Association offers NJ Hospital Price Compare at www.njhospitalpricecompare.com. The site displays information on typical hospital "charges," which are the list prices before insurance discounts or other adjustments. As the Web site points out, the patients most likely to pay the prices shown are those without insurance; in other words, patients who probably have the least ability to pay are billed at the highest rates, although most hospitals will negotiate to a certain extent.

A number of large insurance companies now offer their customers price estimator Web sites that can be used by people who have been given a diagnosis and want to know approximately how much they will have to pay based on which insurance plan they have.

Someday it may be easy find out in advance what a certain health care procedure or service will cost you . . . and perhaps even get the kind of pricing transparency in the health care market that we routinely expect with almost everything else we buy. But that's not the way things are now. Still, let's take a stab at a doing a price check on a few items.

In "Ignorance Is Bliss" (6-09), the suspected diagnoses and the tests and treatments House and his team pursued to track down the culprit included the following:

SYMPTOMS: ATAXIA (LACK OF COORDINATION), ANEMIA, MILD COUGH

Initial tests included: CT, tox screen

Possible diagnosis: TTP (thrombotic thrombocytopenic purpura)

Test: Blood smear, ADAMTS13 antibody test (The maker of this test estimates a seven- to ten-day turnaround time.)

Quiz about mental health history

SYMPTOM: SCHISTOCYTES (FRAGMENTED RED BLOOD CELLS ARE SEEN)

Procedure: Spleen removed

Event: Stroke

Procedure: Catheterization to remove clot

Test: More tox screens

Possible diagnosis: Alcoholism

Tests: Liver biopsy, blood panel that includes measuring albumin level, kidney function tests

Possible diagnosis: Goodpasture syndrome

Treatment: Immunosuppressive drugs and kidney dialysis

Diagnosis: Dextromethorphan (cough syrup) abuse

Treatment: Whole bowel lavage and activated charcoal to clear toxins

SYMPTOM: LOSS OF FEELING IN LEGS

Test: ANA (antinuclear antibody test) (No, it's not lupus.)

Test: MRI scan with ferrous oxide contrast

Diagnosis: Accessory spleens causing TTP (thrombotic thrombocytopenic purpura)

Treatment: Multiple splenectomy

Using NJ Hospital Price Compare to look at charges in the Princeton area shows that a typical case of ataxia involves four days in the hospital and a total charge of around $41,000. A splenectomy involves several days in the hospital and charges of around $50,000. (Who knows what a hospital would charge for removing sixteen accessory spleens.) A stroke is listed as involving six days in the hospital and a charge of $57,000. Drug abuse treatment is listed as five days in the hospital and $50,000.

Separately, one insurance company price estimator showed that a liver biopsy might cost somewhere between $8,000 and $11,000. However, it is impossible to say if that price estimate is for the same kind of liver biopsy referred to in the episode.

The next episode, "Wilson" (6-10), included treatment for acute lymphoblastic leukemia and then a living liver transplant necessary because the cancer chemotherapy destroyed the patient's liver. Estimated charges for treating acute leukemia are somewhere around $60,000 according to the NJ Hospital Price Compare Web site. A liver transplant can easily cost more than $200,000 according to an insurance industry expert. However, since the liver transplant was necessary to treat a problem caused by aggressive chemotherapy, there is always the chance that the insurance company might try to argue that the hospital should take responsibility and absorb the cost of the transplant.

These examples show just how difficult it is to calculate the costs of the tests and treatments that House and his team order in rapid-fire fashion. The next time you or someone you know goes to the hospital for treatment of a straightforward health problem, start counting the pages of estimated charges, adjusted charges, explanations of benefits, bills from the institution, bills from the providers, bills from people you didn't even know were working on your case. Of course, counting the pages might take a long time, so you might prefer to just weigh the paperwork. Then think about what some of House's patients would face. They would probably need to buy a bigger mailbox.

Although there are a number of pundits who argue that people should take more personal responsibility for their health care spending and that more "shopping" would help control medical inflation, the fact is that for now at least it is almost impossible to compare prices, services, and more importantly . . . quality of health care.

Six

To Test or Not to Test

The cost of a test is not always measured in dollars and cents. Indeed, the information a test delivers may carry a toll of its own. Often one test leads to another or to treatments that may or may not bring clear benefits to the patient. Nevertheless, it seems that Dr. Gregory House has never met a test he didn't like . . . or a fact he didn't want to know. That drive to know everything pointed him on a collision course with "Thirteen," as the character of Dr. Remy Hadley is usually called.

In Season Four, it was revealed that Thirteen's mother had Huntington's disease. The disease has devastating physical and emotional effects. Those affected often develop symptoms and die in middle age. In 1993, scientists identified a gene that can cause a protein called huntingtin to be malformed. In affected people, the gene includes excessive repeats of a DNA sequence. While most people have eleven to twenty-nine repeats of the key sequence, in those who have the abnormal gene, this sequence repeats forty to eighty times or more.

The misshapen proteins created by the abnormal genetic instructions can clump around and kill nerve cells. Typically, the symptoms of Huntington's disease begin with involuntary muscle movements. The ability to walk, to talk, even to swallow eventually is lost. Lost also is the ability to control emotions. Violent outbursts of angry words or even physical aggression traumatize both Huntington's patients and those close to them.

The gene variant that causes the disease is dominant, which means that if you inherit one copy from a parent, you will develop the disease, even if the gene from the other parent is fine. (By contrast, a recessive trait is one that has to be inherited from both parents in order to have an effect.) That means if a parent has the disease, then his or her child faces a fifty-fifty chance of inheriting the disease gene. Although some genetic abnormalities cause problems from the beginning of life, people who have the gene that causes Huntington's disease typically are healthy until well into adulthood . . . but then their lives are cut short.

It's a genetic time bomb without a cure. The question that faces anyone with an affected parent is when or whether to be tested . . . to know in advance what fate holds in store or wait for symptoms to appear that signal that time is short.

Thirteen chooses not to be tested. In "You Don't Want to Know" (4-08), House can't fathom why she doesn't want to know whether or not she is probably going to die from the same terrible disease that took her mother. He is so obsessed with knowing everything that he takes a cup that Thirteen was drinking from and has the DNA in her saliva tested. When Thirteen gets an envelope that apparently contains genetic test results, she confronts House about violating her privacy and tosses the unopened envelope into a trash bin. At least House resists looking for himself. Still, it's obvious that he simply cannot figure out why Thirteen does not want to know her likely future.

Many people share House's attitude. They say if there were a test that could tell them how they would die and perhaps about how long they were likely to live, they would want to know.

"You know, that is what people say," says genetic counselor Michelle Fox. But then she adds that's because usually no one has explained to them the implications of this sort of genetic testing. "The way we relate it to the general population is, think about this: we are all at risk for something. So everybody has a parent or other family member with either diabetes, heart disease or cancer."

But most of the common types of heart disease or cancer, or other diseases that are among the leading causes of death, have complex causes that involve multiple genes, environment, lifestyle, accidents, and other factors, so there are no simple genetic tests that can offer black-or-white answers. But as more genes are identified and understood, the number of people facing genetic testing choices is growing. For example, genes that can dramatically alter a woman's risk of developing breast or ovarian cancer were identified just a couple of years after the Huntington's disease gene was isolated.

"If you just ask populations that are at risk, would you take the test? They all say, of course they would. But then, when you really drill down to see if they are really going to call, do they really want to test, what are they going to do with the information, then most of those people will not come forward," Fox says.

She says that when news of a Huntington's disease test first came out, it seemed that everyone in affected families said they were going to get tested. But as it turned out, most did not.

So when someone knows he or she has a fifty-fifty chance of developing Huntington's disease because one parent had the disease, what usually prompts the person to get a test? Fox says often it is because not knowing becomes too much to bear.

"That's the main motivator that I see. People are fixated on the 'not knowing.' That's why people say they would be tested, because they know that the 'not knowing' is going to drive them crazy eventually."

When people come to her before actually getting tested, Fox (unlike House) doesn't try to steer them one way or the other about testing. She says the job of a genetic counselor is to help people understand the various scenarios that often play out after a new piece of genetic information is revealed, so that they know in advance what they may be in for.

She usually starts counseling sessions with a question.

"It's a very simple question: tell us what you're going to do if you test positive for this gene and tell us what you're going to do if you test negative," Fox says. "That's the bottom line: what is this going to do for you?"

Many times couples come in when they are thinking about getting married or before they start having children. If one of them has a parent with Huntington's disease, they want to know if they could pass it on to their children. Then there is the question of what an unaffected spouse may be in for. Will he or she have to care for an ill partner in middle age, decades earlier than most couples have to think about long-term care?

"So people come in sometimes with very, very concrete ideas of what they are going to do if they test positive. Sometimes they haven't thought about it much, but most of the people, by the time you come in and you've spent some money to talk to us, you've generally thought about it a little bit."

Fox says it seems most people do have a pretty good idea how they'll react to the test results, whether they are positive (meaning they have the abnormal gene and will develop the disease) or negative (meaning they don't and won't develop Huntington's disease).

"They actually do," she says. "This is an interesting thing: we thought that people, when they tested negative, would just be jumping up and down for joy and be so happy, even beyond happy. But, you know, they are not, because this is a family disease; so even though they are negative, they are sometimes still caring for a parent, still caring for a sibling that is affected. It affects everybody.

"And then sometimes you have survivor guilt. That's a real thing," Fox says.

A person who tests negative may feel guilty that he or she doesn't share the same fate as family members who tested positive or are already experiencing symptoms of the disease.

Some people say they want to be tested so that they can do financial planning for themselves and their families. Fox says some younger adults want to know if they should pace themselves, or should they try to live quickly because the Huntington's gene is shadowing them? She recalls one person who tested positive and then got busy doing all the things he had dreamed of.

"We had one in particular, this person always wanted to learn French and to travel, and he made it his business to do that in the next five years of his life. That was his goal. He put off some of the other things, such as career advancement, because he just figured, 'I want to do this stuff now. I don't have time to wait,'" Fox says. "Some people have decided to adopt a child, because they don't want to face any risk of having a kid who is affected. And they want to have a kid right now, if they can, because they want to be fairly healthy in the formative years of this kid's life."

On the other hand, some people grow up believing that they will develop the disease, just as one of their parents did. Finding out that they don't have the disease gene, and so are likely to live a long, long time, can be a shock.

"We had this one really dramatic case of this guy who is a high risk behavior kind of guy. He raced cars. He jumped out of airplanes. He did all this crazy, crazy stuff; because he thought he was positive [for the Huntington's disease gene]. Then he finds out he is negative and he has to grow up and be like a real person. He was most unhappy. Because he had lived his whole life on the edge. That's an extreme example, but it happens."

Fox says she's met other people who had stuck with an unhappy marriage or a job they really didn't like because they believed they were going to get sick in middle age and would need family support or insurance and other job benefits. Then the negative test results turn their expectations upside down.

Eventually, as Season Four drew to a close, Thirteen decided to do the test, reversing her adamant opposition to House's badgering about getting tested. At the end of "Wilson's Heart" (4-16), she learns that the result is positive. She will develop the disease that destroyed her mother. In real life, too, people change their minds about testing. Fox remembers one man who came in, got tested, but didn't want to hear the results . . . until two years later.

"This just about killed me, because we knew he was negative. But he had told us explicitly that he did not want to be contacted, and when he was ready to come in he would let us know. And that's exactly what happened. Two years later he was engaged. He came in with his fiancée to get the results. Think about that. That just about killed me, that I could not pick up the phone and call this guy and tell him to come in," Fox says. "That's the thing about patient autonomy. We are really here to serve the patient and do whatever it is that they want to do."

Patient autonomy. That's a concept House always has trouble with. In the case of Thirteen and Huntington's disease testing, House once again pushed his "Doctor Knows Best" attitude at her.

"It's so sending the wrong message. In the real world these things are so complex. And every person is so complex and brings so much to this situation. Even in families, we ask family members not to pressure other family members to be tested," Fox says.

But of course, House is famous for doing the wrong thing when it comes to dealing with people, whether they are friends, coworkers, or patients. So, in a way, by trying to pressure Thirteen to get tested, House demonstrated what's wrong with that attitude.

Although Thirteen tends to mask her emotions, it seems the genetic test results may be having a powerful effect on her in "Lucky Thirteen" (5-05). She's having one-night stands. She's using drugs. The risk-taking ratchets up to a dangerous level.

"That does happen. What happens more frequently is that for the first couple of weeks after finding out, people do get depressed. If they drink a little, they drink a little more, for example. And then they tend to come back to baseline. That's what usually happens. One person that we had did have an extreme reaction and had to be hospitalized."

And so the portrayal of Thirteen's reaction does fit what Fox has seen in her genetic counseling clients: that the impact of the test may push the person's natural tendencies into overdrive. Thirteen's character always had some edginess and risk-taking to it, so it isn't surprising that the test results amplified that behavior.

"She was presented as having some of these issues anyway. And that's probably what this does to you," Fox says.

A review of research into the psychological effects of this sort of test concluded that the long-term effects depend more on the person than the test result. Indeed, over the long run, there appears to be little difference in psychological adjustment between those who tested positive and those who tested negative. The best predictors of future depression or hopelessness after testing are the levels of depression or hopelessness before testing . . . not the result of the test. Fox says that is what she sees, that people don't react to test results in a vacuum. They bring with them all the psychological baggage they carried before the test. If there is a history of depression, then the results (either way) may increase the risk of another episode. But Fox also stresses that depression is common and there is no evidence that it has anything specifically to do with Huntington's disease.

Genetic counselors and others involved with managing the effects of a Huntington's disease diagnosis often ask tough, probing questions in advance in order to find out how a particular person may react to test results. They will ask about any history of depression. They'll ask if the person has ever been hospitalized for psychiatric issues. Fox recalls one client who seemed to have what's called a flat affect; that is, a very low level of emotional response. A flat affect may be related to depression or other mental health issues, so it is something genetic counselors watch for. When this person's test results came back positive for the Huntington's disease gene, Fox says her colleague asked the client a pointed question.

"She asked him flat out, 'Do you own a gun?' Now I almost fell off my chair, but of course that was an appropriate question, because he was coming across as severely depressed."

Comprehensive programs, such as the medical genetics program at the University of California, Los Angeles that Fox works with, have psychologists and others on hand to help people through any rough spots after testing. They have to be ready for all sorts of reactions, including the possibility of a suicide attempt. According to one estimate of the responses of people at risk for Huntington's disease, as many as one in three may consider suicide at some point. The risk is higher among those who test positive for the abnormal gene, but even people who are told they don't have the Huntington's gene appear to have a higher than average risk of suicide.

Thirteen was among those taken hostage by a desperate patient in "Last Resort" (5-09). Her act of volunteering to be a sort of guinea pig, testing medications before the hostage taker would use them, appeared to be, in part, almost a willingness to die, as though the positive test for Huntington's disease had led her to conclude there wasn't much point in struggling ahead with life. Eventually, she decides she doesn't really want to die. She straightens out her life.

In "Last Resort," Foreman promises Thirteen that the experimental drug he is helping to test in a clinical trial is showing "real results," though he doesn't explain what sort of results . . . or how he knows the results when the trial is still under way. Perhaps he is referring to results from some earlier trials. We never hear Foreman explain that such a trial cannot promise any benefit to participants. Indeed, if researchers have convincing evidence that a treatment is better than a placebo, it would be unethical to put people into a trial where they might not receive the treatment. Of course, every trial is done in the hope that the treatment will be better than available therapies, but when trials start there is still uncertainty about whether the treatment is actually better. In fact, in many clinical trials the participants who were given standard therapy or a placebo end up doing as well or even better than those who received the active experimental treatment. That's why the tests are done, to find out which is really better.

There are a number of clinical trials actually going on that involve people who have or are at risk for Huntington's disease. In addition, there are also studies that observe people in order to learn more about the disease and its effects. Much of this research is coordinated through the Huntington Study Group, which helps coordinate the work of scientists in the United States, Canada, Europe, Australia, New Zealand, and South America.

Trials and Studies Listed by the
Huntington Study Group in Early 2010

The clinical trials currently in progress are:

- 2CARE (coenzyme Q10, compound naturally made by the body that helps protect cells)
- CREST-E (creatine, naturally produced by the kidneys and liver and used in muscles)
- DIMOND (Dimebon [latrepirdine], a drug developed as an antihistamine in Russia that may help thinking, although recent results with Alzheimer's patients were disappointing)
- HART (ACR16, a dopamine stabilizer that may improve motor control)
- HORIZON (Dimebon)
- PREQUEL (coenzyme Q10)

The observational studies currently in progress are:

- COHORT (Cooperative Huntington's Observational Research Trial)
- PHAROS (Prospective Huntington At Risk Observational Study)
- PREDICT-HD (Neurobiological Predictors of Huntington Disease)
- RESPOND-HD (An Examination of Responses to Potential Discrimination from Individuals at Risk for Huntington Disease)

Available online from the Huntington Study Group at www.huntington-study-group.org, accessed on February 2, 2010.

ClinicalTrials.gov also lists many more clinical trials related to Huntington's disease, as well as every other type of condition. The registry includes both publicly and privately financed trials in the United States and in other countries, including contact information for those who might want to participate or get other information.

"A lot of the clinical trials now are really aimed at delaying the onset or slowing the progression of the disease. The things that are really coming down the pipeline and being tested in patients now are relatively benign supplements," says Yvette M. Bordelon, M.D., Ph.D. Dr. Bordelon is an assistant professor in the Department of Neurology at the David Geffen School of Medicine at the University of California, Los Angeles.

Those supplements include coenzyme Q10 and creatine, which are widely available over the counter. They are widely touted for having a variety of (mostly unproven) benefits for average people or athletes. Some people who have Huntington's disease or are at risk for it already take these and other supplements, even though the potential benefits and harms are still being examined.

The interest in these substances is based on animal experiments in which the supplements showed benefits in conditions that are similar, but not exactly the same as, Huntington's disease. (For a more extensive discussion of the strengths and weaknesses of animal experiments, see the first volume, *The Medical Science of House, M.D.*) Bordelon says that based on what is known about how Huntington's disease interferes with the function of cells, it makes sense that some of these supplements might have benefits.

"It's the mechanism of Huntington's. We know that energy supplies go down; there's mitochondrial dysfunction, mitochondria being the powerhouse of the cell. We know that's affected," she says.

Supplements are not cures. The hope is that they might help people resist the effects of the disease a little longer. Other experiments are testing treatments intended to help ease symptoms, such as motor control, emotional, and psychological effects of the nerve and brain cell damage. They might not alter the course of the disease, but they might make it a bit easier to live with.

A similar strategy is behind the Alzheimer's disease drug donepezil (brand name Aricept). The drug boosts levels of neurotransmitters in the brain and thus helps some people with early signs of dementia to think somewhat more clearly. However, the drug does not alter the course of the disease itself.

There are also more ambitious attempts to harness genetic knowledge and tools to try to attack the source of Huntington's disease: the abnormal gene and the malformed protein it produces.

"There's a lot of study going on that looks very upstream at turning off the mutant protein with gene therapy," Bordelon says. "These gene silencing techniques are really the hottest new research. It's headed toward clinical trials soon. There are different mechanisms for doing it. One is with RNA interference. The other is with antisense oligonucleotides, or ASO."

These strategies are based on the fact that each one of us inherits a set of genes from each parent. That means that even if one Huntington's gene is abnormal, the other one is probably fine. Find a way to block the function of the bad gene or the malformed proteins it produces, and the good gene and the normal huntingtin protein might be able to keep the person healthy.

"Huntington's is an ideal disorder in which to try to implement this," Bordelon says, "because it's one gene mutation, it's dominant. They are finding ways of turning off only the mutant protein, because we need normal huntingtin in the body."

That's one of the challenges. If a treatment isn't specific enough, it could shut down all huntingtin protein production, good and bad. In animal trials, when researchers eliminated the gene entirely from animal embryos, the embryos did not survive. As an alternative to finding a very specific treatment that would affect only the abnormal gene or protein, it might be possible for people to survive with a reduced level of huntingtin protein production, perhaps slowing, if not stopping, the damaging effects of the accumulation of mutant protein.

"Those are really attractive [strategies], because that goes all the way upstream to the source of the problem, rather than dealing with the downstream consequences," Bordelon says.

But even as researchers are excited by the prospects of such genetic approaches, they have seen grand hopes dashed before. For example, in 1989 researchers identified the gene responsible for cystic fibrosis. The disease interferes with how the lungs, intestines, and other organs function. Patients are susceptible to infections, and eventually the damage may be severe enough that they need a lung transplant to stay alive. When the CF gene was first identified, many people expected a dramatic new treatment to soon follow. However, although the new knowledge of the genetic source of the condition has led to the development of new treatments that have helped CF patients live longer than ever before, the disease has not been "cured."

Even as she works to make scientific progress on Huntington's disease, Bordelon knows to be realistic.

"It's a long process. Honestly, in the end it's probably going to be a combination of approaches, most likely. Even if we are able to knock down the mutant gene, there's still probably going to be some issues that we have to deal with, downstream consequences. So it might be a cocktail treatment. I've tried to move away from using the word 'cure,' " she says. And she keeps in mind the value of incremental advances. "If you have adequate treatments, then that's quite an accomplishment. To actually cure the disease, we need to know a lot more about what it's doing. There's still a lot that we don't know. It's not going to happen next year. The clinical trials might be happening in the next few years, though."

Thirteen eventually decides she does want to enter Foreman's clinical trial. And while the show does not go into details about the experimental drug, in "The Greater Good" (5-14) Thirteen suddenly develops a tumor at the point where the optic nerves from her eyes cross as they enter her brain. Fortunately for her character, the tumor that so suddenly appeared then disappears just as rapidly once the drug treatment is stopped. Optic nerve tumors are not among the known side effects of the leading experimental therapies currently being tested in people at risk for Huntington's disease. However, some of the drugs that are being tested may expose trial participants to increased risks of depression, suicide, Parkinson's disease, and other side effects.

Like most TV shows, *House* both speeds up time (as in the example of the suddenly appearing and disappearing tumor) and collapses the roles of many people into just a few characters. That may be part of the explanation for why the clinical trial story line involved Foreman and

Thirteen, rather than introducing a new character. Why would a new character be needed for this story line? Because in real research institutions, investigators are not allowed to slip friends into their clinical trials.

At UCLA, for example, could Dr. Bordelon enroll a coworker into a trial she was running?

"No, no," she insists. "You go to extremes to make sure it is as unbiased as possible."

Having a coworker as a trial participant, not to mention someone an investigator is dating, just creates too much temptation to stray from impartial objectivity. Bordelon points out that in many studies, physicians cannot include their regular patients in research trials that they are managing. One reason is that the physician may know things about the patient's medical history, personal background, and other factors that could influence how he or she evaluates the effects of an experimental treatment, possibly giving the treatment either too much or too little credit for changes in the patient's status.

Just as House's badgering of Thirteen to get tested for the Huntington's disease gene showed some of the reasons why it is wrong to pressure people into getting predictive tests, this clinical trial story line provides many examples of how things can go badly wrong when the rules of human experimentation and the scientific process are violated. Foreman leans on Thirteen to enter the trial, waving around the promise of "real results" without also being clear about the uncertainties and risks of experimental treatment. He switches her medication from what was probably the placebo to the active drug because he allows his emotional involvement to bulldoze his obedience to the scientific process. Ultimately, he narrowly escapes career-ending consequences.

The co-investigator in "Joy to the World" (5-11) may appear to be inhumanly cold when she says trial participants are not "people" but just "numbers." Indeed, good scientists do (and must) care about the well-being of the people they enroll in their trials. But a certain level of that detachment would have helped protect Foreman from committing the violations of procedures, regulations, and laws that ended up hurting him, hurting Thirteen, and possibly hurting the other researchers and participants in the tainted trial.

Thirteen befriended a fellow participant in the clinical trial, a woman with more advanced symptoms of Huntington's disease. As the woman pointed out, the trial drug probably wouldn't do her any good. Like many real clinical trial participants, she was helping those who would come later . . . probably much later, given the phenomenal amount of research needed to make significant advances against human diseases. The Huntington's disease gene was identified almost two decades ago, and experts know many more years of hard work lie ahead.

"We're hoping for targeted drug therapies, but it's not going to be a cure. It may put off the onset of disease. It may ameliorate the symptoms. But I think curing it, gene therapy or some gene cure, is way down the road, probably not in my lifetime," says genetic counselor Michelle Fox.

For now, those affected by Huntington's disease must face dark prospects and terrible choices. Surveys suggest that as many as a third of people at risk consider committing suicide rather than allowing the disease to run its course. While suicide is often seen as a result of depression or other mental illness, some people with Huntington's disease see it as a way to take control of the final chapter of their life. Even as counselors like Fox and others work to support patients, including helping them deal with suicidal thoughts, she knows that she won't be able to prevent every suicide.

Fox remembers one patient. Symptoms had begun to affect him. From watching the disease attack his father and his brother and others, he knew where his life was headed. One day that seemed just like any other day, he said good-bye to his wife and children, but instead of going to work he drove out into the desert and ended his life. His suicide wasn't a complete surprise. His father had committed suicide. His brother had committed suicide. Huntington's disease is a family disease. Suicide was part of how this family responded. The story is not unique. Then again, that family's story is not typical either. Each family finds its own way.

The depiction of Thirteen's last memories of her mother rings true to those who have seen Huntington's disease up close. In "Let Them Eat Cake" (5-10), Thirteen flashes back to her childhood, to watching her mother's body spasm uncontrollably, to hating her mother for the screaming abuse the disease spewed out of her damaged brain, to hiding in her room when her father was taking her mother away to an institution because they could no longer care for her at home, to watching from her window as her mother sat in the car about to leave forever, to the flood of hate and regret and guilt that Huntington's disease had poured into her young life.

Fox says it is not unusual for a child (or even an adult) to be traumatized by what the disease does to the person he or she loved. Even though the rational part of the mind knows that the psychological disruption and verbal or even physical abuse the person with the disease may unleash on others is caused by a physical disease, it is still impossible to avoid being emotionally injured.

"Even if you understand it is biological, you are still abused, you still have to listen to this going on," Fox points out.

Some couples may separate when the effects of the disease become overwhelming. Sometimes the healthy parent feels that he or she can't protect the couple's children from the other parent's violent outbursts.

"That brings me to a really important point," Fox says. "We try to tell families, 'Please, do not keep this a secret.' Now, telling families that and then what they actually do, those are two different things. But the families that operate in the open are so much better off, I can't even begin to tell you. The families that keep secrets, oh my, it's so convoluted. They are taking up so much energy to keep a secret. They are embarrassed. They are in denial. But the families that are open with the kids, it's remarkable how much better they do."

Speaking of secrets, genetic testing, whether for Huntington's disease or other reasons, sometimes brings surprises that have little to do with medicine. One family was confused when the father began to show odd symptoms. The eventual diagnosis was Huntington's disease. But it didn't make sense. Neither of his parents had had the disease. But a friend of his parents did. Genetic testing revealed that the friend was more than a friend; he was actually the biological father of the man who had suddenly begun to show signs of Huntington's.

When couples come in to talk about genetic testing, Fox says she tries to talk to each person separately, because sometimes key information doesn't come out when the couple is together.

"Moms will come clean. They will tell us that it is a possibility or something like that. They might call us back to say, by the way, you should know that maybe [a pregnancy or child is the product of an affair]."

Of course, it is best if that sort of conversation occurs before the genetic testing.

"We try to do pretest counseling," Fox says. "Pretest counseling means that we go over some of the contingencies. That helps a great deal. That's why we push for genetic counseling to be part of genetic testing, because someone who just does a genetic test doesn't really understand what the ramifications are, by and large."

The possibility of an affair or other secret is just one reason pointed out by genetic counselors that even when it's an individual considering the genetic testing, the results can affect an entire family. Relationship troubles are not the only potential consequence. Sometimes people pay cash for genetic testing and instruct the counselors and others to keep the results out of their regular medical file, in order to keep the information secret from employers, insurance companies, or others who might have some access to their records. Good-quality genetic testing and counseling programs have procedures for keeping test results and other personal information secure, at least when it comes to predictive testing, that is, tests done before any symptoms appear. Once someone has symptoms of a disease, then insurance companies and others may have a right to see certain information.

Individuals did get some additional privacy protection for their genetic information with the enactment of the Genetic Information Non-discrimination Act of 2008 (also known as GINA.) The law is intended to prevent discrimination by employers and insurance companies based on certain kinds of genetic information. Although there is widespread concern about discrimination based on genetic test results, researchers say there are few documented cases of it actually happening. But Fox has encountered cases where people may not have thought about potential consequences . . . such as a person at risk for Huntington's disease who was on a transplant waiting list. A positive Huntington's test might affect the patient's chances of getting a donor organ.

GINA doesn't protect genetic test results from all disclosure. The law exempts life insurance, disability insurance, and long-term care insurance. Companies argued that some people would apply for lots of insurance after getting test results indicating that they would develop a disease like Huntington's . . . without revealing that information on their insurance applications.

The television depictions of Huntington's disease testing and research and treatment are often jarring to professionals who deal with these issues in the real world every day. And yet they also see some value to the prime-time TV attention.

"Huntington's is serving as an example in many different areas of medicine. So it's nice to be able to talk about it more and raise recognition of the disorder and of the approaches like gene therapy that are targeting Huntington's," says Dr. Yvette Bordelon. She uses the story line on *House* to get the attention of young medical and graduate students in her neurology and neuroscience classes.

"I've used that as an example when I teach now about Huntington's, because people know the show, so I start out with that. This has brought Huntington's to the forefront. It brings it into popular knowledge."

And the lessons apply to more than just Huntington's disease, because there are similar issues with Parkinson's disease, Alzheimer's disease, and other conditions.

"That's how I grab their attention and then say that there are issues regarding testing and clinical trials, and we will talk about how it's really done, rather than how it's done on TV," Bordelon says with a chuckle. She adds that she sees the shows have had some educational impact on viewers. "It's interesting that the medical students are asking more insightful questions because of it, particularly in regard to the genetic testing issues."

Naturally, she wants her students, and the public, to clearly understand the difference between TV and reality.

"We're not all like House," she says with a laugh. "We tend to have more compassion and empathy and tact, I think. But at the same time, it's also been a great thing for the research community, by increasing awareness."

Seven

Who's the Boss?

On the Princeton-Plainsboro Teaching Hospital organizational chart, Cuddy is certainly shown as outranking House. But org charts don't always reflect reality. The reality within the show—House constantly dueling with Cuddy for control—is something real-world hospital managers know all too well.

As the third season of *House* drew to a close, Foreman resigned. Then House fired Chase. Finally, Cameron quit. Cuddy told House he is not in charge of hiring and firing staff. "You can't dump your entire department just because you don't know how to deal with an issue," she says in "Human Error" (3-24). House pushes back. "My name on the door. My team. My decisions," he says. "My building. My floor. My people," Cuddy retorts.

"Yeah, now that's a real-life situation," Kevin Donovan says with a chuckle. Donovan is the senior vice president for clinical operations at Elliot Health System, which bills itself as the largest health care provider in southern New Hampshire. He is responsible for the administration of a hospital and multi-specialty group practice of more than two hundred physicians. So when doctors and management don't see eye to eye, he is in the thick of it.

What happens when a senior physician wants her or his assistants to do things one way, but Donovan prefers that those employees do it a different way?

"Yeah, there are definitely situations where there is a rub there," Donovan says with a bit of a sigh. He says even in hospitals where the physicians are employees, who technically have the same legal responsibilities and rights as any other employee, the fact is that physicians often tend to get special treatment. "If the president of the hospital tells me what to do, well guess what, I do it," he says. "But with physicians, it's much more of a negotiation."

In the first episode of the third season ("Meaning," 3-01), Cuddy tells House, "I get what I want, and you don't." Of course, as usual Cuddy's ultimatum doesn't work. Kevin Donovan says that when managing physicians, it helps to use finesse . . . and to give doctors the acknowledgment of their skills, status, and authority that they expect. "That gets back to my point about physicians being employees like everyone else, but they don't necessarily want to be treated as such. So there is much more of a negotiation with a physician, in terms of work expectations, than there is with other types of employees."

By the middle of the fifth season of *House*, Cuddy had become so frustrated with her inability to control House that she turned vengeful. In "The Greater Good" (5-14), she fools him into believing the elevators are out of service so that he has to painfully climb the stairs using his damaged leg. Then she goes further. She steals his cane. Finally, Cuddy brings House down, literally, with a trip wire across his office door. It's not hard to imagine some hospital administrators smiling at the scenes, while fantasizing about retaliating against difficult physicians in their employ, even if they would never actually do anything as outrageous.

A top executive at a nationwide physician recruiting firm says the very nature of the physician-administrator relationship almost guarantees clashes. The doctors know that without them, the hospital can't stay open.

"That is a true tension, because in real life unless you have M.D. or D.O. behind your name you can't admit a patient to a hospital. So they grow up with the mind-set that they are the revenue generators," Brian McCartie, vice president of business development at Cejka Search, Inc., points out. His company helps hospitals and clinics recruit and retain health care professionals. "Whereas the administrator feels [physicians] are employees in the hospital and it's the bricks and mortar that generate the revenue. So there is a link. Neither can do without the other. The hospital needs the physicians, because without them they're not going to capture the patient revenue. The physician needs the hospital, because without it there's nowhere you can look after the patient."

The relationship between House as an employee of a hospital and Cuddy as the top administrator of the hospital (and thus his employer) is increasingly the norm in health care in the United States; but it wasn't always the primary business model. Traditionally, physicians literally "hung out a shingle," meaning they would open a practice and begin attracting patients. When their patients needed hospital care, the physician admitted them and oversaw their care. Under that system, the physician had privileges to admit and treat patients at a hospital, but wasn't an employee of the hospital.

Help Wanted

The changing relationship between hospital administrators and physicians has, of course, affected how doctors find work. For the past decade, Elliot Health System has had a full-time recruiter always looking for physicians who might be enticed to work in their region. In the days when most physicians actually worked for themselves or for small local group practices, the recruiter was not looking to hire doctors, but rather to convince them of the professional and personal benefits of the area . . . and often to be a matchmaker between the doctors and established local group practices. Those days are fading.

"The days of the solo practitioner or small group medical practice are going away. Our recruiter focuses more of her time recruiting to hospital-employed groups," Donovan says. "Like many hospitals or health systems our size, we have a large multi-specialty group practice now that is an arm of the hospital or the health system."

According to a survey of physicians by the Association of American Medical Colleges and the American Medical Association, almost one out of four of those in their late forties is a solo practitioner, but only one in ten doctors in their late thirties is on his or her own. A variety of factors is transforming the work environment of physicians. Medicine and health care regulations and financing are increasingly complex, so it's harder to manage alone. Also, younger doctors are less interested in being on call nights and weekends. Joining a group practice or hospital means someone else is handling a lot of the administrative hassles and there are other doctors to share call with.

Thomas Rundall, Ph.D., Henry J. Kaiser professor of organized health systems at the University of California, Berkeley, says the situations depicted on *House* are extreme, but they reflect real issues.

"I know of no hospital that has the kind of dynamics that you see on *House*; these are exaggerated for dramatic purposes. But the underlying tension that is being blown up out of proportion is in fact there in real life in most hospitals," Rundall says.

Who's right? House or Cuddy? Actually, both are. Rundall says a certain amount of tension is healthy, because you wouldn't want either the physicians or the administrators to always win; a balance of power is good for both patients and the hospital.

"I'm absolutely convinced of that," Rundall says. "It would be disastrous if you didn't have it, because the inclinations of one party or the other would become so dominant that we would either fail individuals in delivering the very best care for their condition or we would fail the larger community and the future patients who might use the hospital, because we unwisely spent the resources available to us in the hospital, then failed and went out of business. It does happen. It does happen and communities are the worse for it."

The final scenes of "Meaning" (3-01) conclude with the Rolling Stones song "You Can't Always Get What You Want" as Cuddy and

Wilson enjoy a rare moment in which they have outmaneuvered House. House thought that a patient confined to a wheelchair with an apparently untreatable condition actually had Addison's disease, which is treatable. Cuddy said he was just guessing. It turns out House was right. But Cuddy was also right that he was going with his gut, not the medical evidence. After Cuddy secretly and (it turns out) successfully begins treating the man for Addison's disease, Wilson urges Cuddy not to tell House about the patient's improvement. They want to take House down a peg, so that maybe he'll be a little less cocky and less convinced that he is always right and that every rule and medical guideline is just impeding him.

"That's a very dangerous attitude to have in many respects," Rundall says of House's extreme self-confidence. "Certainly there are heroic qualities to him: battling against the machine, taking on the uncaring and perhaps stupid or faceless administrators who only care about the budgets and the operation of the system. There is that kind of heroic character throughout American literature and entertainment, but it is also a deeply flawed attitude towards the way in which a complex organization should work, particularly one that is caring for very sick people, and also poses a risk for the very people you are caring for. Bad things can happen to people in hospitals. Bad things are more likely to happen if the policies and procedures and rules—that have been created to prevent those rather adventurous physicians from doing those bad things—are not followed."

Besides the risk to patients posed by an overconfident doctor, there is the fact that House is a jerk to those he works with. In "Here Kitty" (5-18), there is a litter box in the conference room. It belongs to a cat that has a reputation for predicting the deaths of patients. The litter box gets dirty, as litter boxes do. House tells Taub to clean it. Taub refuses and walks out. It's a rare show of defiance in a world where House's fellows almost always do as he asks, no matter how demeaning or absurd the assignments seem to be.

Brian McCartie, the Cejka Search executive, says his firm does occasionally have to work with (and around) difficult bosses when they are trying to attract junior physicians. They try to counsel the difficult senior doctor, while also preparing job candidates by laying out both the positive and negative aspects of the position.

"We're dealing with a lot of egos in this world, so you have got to find a person that has the ability to deal with that," McCartie says. "You would not put a person with House that wants to run the department, that thinks they are more brilliant than House, because that's not going to work. You need to understand the dynamics of the department. That all ties into each and every search, because we are dealing with physicians, so each position will have a personality that ultimately we have to find some compatibility and match. That's the biggest area that we can influence, because if we find the right match, some of the other considerations become less important."

Kevin Donovan also says he has had to figure out a way to work with difficult doctors, though probably none as difficult as House.

"We have, unfortunately, dealt with some people like that before. You deal with those types of people at all levels of jobs, but it is a little bit harder to deal with someone like that who is a physician, because it's hard to put out of your mind [the fact] that it is hard to replace someone like that," Donovan says.

House gets away with his obnoxious behavior because he is so good at what he does. It's true that brilliant jerks may get more leeway than ordinary jerks.

"The answer to that depends on the level of egregiousness of the behavior. If it's something that's not that egregious but more like 'Hey, you're a curmudgeon,' we would do more of the kind of thing of having a friend pointing out that he's a jerk," Donovan says.

He says that usually a friendly word of advice from a colleague makes a difference. If it doesn't, then the case might escalate to formal warnings or more forceful measures. Donovan says dealing with a difficult doctor does not mean always caving in. He says that when things go too far, the medical staff usually will get involved, since typically the doctors in a hospital have their own leadership structure. The dynamic is quite different from that shown by the powerless friend Wilson and the often ineffective leader Cuddy.

"There are times that I can think of that we have fired physicians for behavior issues. And then on the medical staff side of things, there are definitely times that I can think of that we've had their peers sanction physicians because of their behavior. And while that sounds like it's just a slap on the wrist, it actually has a lot of meaning."

It's not only a professional embarrassment to be sanctioned by one's peers, but the record of the discipline would be seen by other potential employers.

Many times House has cajoled his fellows into sticking around (and enduring more abuse) by reminding them of how much they can learn from him and how much cooler his cases are than the routine patients they would otherwise be treating. In "Teamwork" (6-08), Taub has returned to his plastic surgery practice. House tries to entice Taub back by asking whether he really prefers the sort of patient in his waiting room ("A guy who needs two decades' worth of corn chips Hoovered out of his neck") to the sort of exotic case House has ("A guy who can't stand daylight, and whose blood won't clot").

That sort of choice between a comfortable routine and a decidedly less comfortable, but more challenging, practice is a real consideration.

"I'd say that's actually very true." Donovan says candidates for physician jobs weigh multiple factors. "That's the three-step process. It's money, professional satisfaction, work-life balance. As we recruit people, that's the equation that we're always doing a dance with people around in order to make our job more attractive than the job next door. It's very important to physicians how professionally satisfying the job is."

Candidates aren't looking at just the job in front of them, but also the next job they hope to get. Sometimes, moving up in a field requires enduring an apprenticeship under an unpleasant but smart and respected senior physician. If McCartie's search firm were hired to find a physician for a hospital in the Princeton, New Jersey, area, a job that included really interesting referrals and working for a well-known leader in his field, but that senior physician had a reputation for being difficult, what kind of response might he get?

"Good, very good," McCartie says.

Firing Line

The flip side of each arrival, each new hire, is a departure, whether by resignation or firing. At the end of Season Three, House loses his original team of fellows. Foreman and Cameron quit and House fires Chase. In Season Four, he begins building a new team in his own typically unique fashion. As a classroom full of candidates looks on, House strums his guitar and tells them, "This will be the longest job interview of your life. I will test you in ways that you will often consider unfair, demeaning, and illegal. And you will often be right. Look to your left. Now look to your right. By the end of six weeks, one of you will be gone. As will twenty-eight more of you. Wear a cup."

The scenario that plays out over the following episodes bears more of a resemblance to a TV reality show competition than to any hiring techniques seen in real hospitals.

One point: House calls the doctors on his team "fellows," but in medicine, fellows are typically junior doctors who are getting one more year or two of specialty training following the regular residency program. Certainly, Foreman, Chase, and Cameron did not appear to be fresh out of training. But we'll stick with House's terminology here, even though it may confuse people who work in health care.

At New Hampshire's Elliot Health System, Kevin Donovan summarizes how he would go about filling a vacancy.

"If one of my neurologists quits today, we'd sit down and we'd ascertain whether we needed to replace that position, which generally we always do," he says. "We go ahead and post that job on our Web site, but then because physician recruitment is so challenging, we partner with organizations like Cejka Search that have national databases of physicians and are constantly identifying candidates and know of multiple physicians that are looking for specific kinds of things in a job."

Over at Cejka Search, Inc., Brian McCartie picks up the story.

"We would then go to the neurosurgery market with ads and mailers and Internet postings" that describe the job, the institution, the community, everything important to potential candidates. McCartie says that sometimes they manage everything involved in recruiting physicians for clients. With some of their regular clients who are constantly keeping an eye out for good physicians and other key employees, they will post some of their own staff members on-site to coordinate recruiting.

A few of the candidates who applied to work with House appeared to be older, but typically the candidates for junior positions will be younger. McCartie says that these days one of the challenges they face is managing the generation gap between senior physicians and newcomers.

"I have a gastroenterology buddy who was working in the hospital last week and he worked ninety-six hours. That is just a phenomenal amount of work. The younger docs are beginning to say, 'You know what, I'm a physician, but I'm also a father or a mother and a husband or a wife and a soccer coach.' So they are pushing back on a lot of call requirements. They are saying they don't want to be in independent practice anymore, they want to be employed," he says. "You've got physicians now who are subspecializing to such narrow areas that they don't take the bread-and-butter cases anymore. So one will say, 'I'm just a breast surgeon.' Well, a breast surgeon is really a general surgeon, but this surgeon won't do anything but breast surgery. So when an appendix bursts in the middle of the night, that's not a person you can call, because they haven't done a hundred and fifty appendixes in the last year."

Conditions requested by new hires may rankle some members of the old guard.

"Part of the struggle that employers are going to face is when, for example, a younger doctor comes in and says, 'Hey, I don't want to work weekends. And I only want to work one night a week. I don't want to be on three nights a week.' And then the older doctors say, 'Hey, wait a second, I've been doing that for thirty years. What do you mean you're going to hire that person without giving him that responsibility?'" says Edward Salsberg, who studies the health care workforce at the Association of American Medical Colleges. But whether the older doctors like it or not, the growing demand for physicians means the new kids may well have negotiating clout that previous generations of doctors lacked.

Candidates also want to know about the pay, of course. McCartie says physician wages can vary dramatically, not only by specialty, but also by location. Pertinent to House's search for new team members, McCartie says the fictional Princeton-Plainsboro Teaching Hospital would be straddling a line near Princeton, New Jersey, that separates two different physician job markets.

"Physicians south of Princeton tend to be tacked on to the Philadelphia rates, and the Philadelphia rates are very low. Positions north of Princeton get more of the New York rates, and New York rates are a lot higher," he says.

Pay and on-call schedules are fairly straightforward matters. But a good match requires some probing and evaluation of more subjective measures.

"Their résumé is their résumé, where they've trained, what they've done, are they board certified. If they are right out of residency or fellowship, it's easy to pick up the phone and talk to the program director and quickly find out what kind of physician they are. If they've been out [of training] for a while, we spend a lot of time on behavioral interviewing," McCartie says. What does "behavioral interviewing" involve? "Describe the perfect practice. Describe how you dealt with the patient that was unhappy with your skills, or a family member that was belligerent. Their skill set is only part of the mix. Can we get along with this person for the next ten or fifteen years? Can we cover call [on night and weekend shifts] with this person? Do we enjoy this person? You don't have to be best friends with them, but you need to work with them."

Donovan agrees that hiring is not an exact science. It starts with the basics, and eventually there will be face-to-face meetings where employee and employer can get a better feel for each other.

"This is what the job is. This is what our culture is like. This is the schedule we think you'll work. This is the type of patients you'll see. All to make sure that at least from that first-blush analysis that there is a good fit there. And then we bring people in and go that traditional route," Donovan says. "We will have this person come in and we'll take them out to dinner. And then a series of meetings all day long with all kinds people, trying to ascertain from both sides whether it's a good fit or not. If that all goes well, then typically there's a second visit. They'll bring their family back."

Doctors may be comparing several potential job offers, and sometimes it's neither the pay nor the basic nature of the job that makes the difference, but the local schools and neighborhoods, the culture of the institution and the community. It seems that it would be helpful to have a trial period where doctor and hospital could try each other out for size. But McCartie says that's usually not possible. "No, they would not be covered under the hospital's insurance," he points out.

However, when it comes down to the last candidate or two for an important job, a senior physician from the hiring hospital might shadow a candidate at his or her current job; if, that is, the candidate's current boss knows about the potential job offer.

"For high-end positions, what we do is we will often send our surgeon to the facility to scrub in with the person and see how that person interacts in their own environment. So we are able to assess their skill set on their home turf," McCartie says.

In earlier decades, physicians tended to stay in one place. Changing jobs might have raised questions about whether there was some problem that prompted the doctor to move on. Also, in the days when most doctors were solo practitioners, moving to a new town meant starting over to build a new patient base. It might take a few years for the physician's income to get back to where it was before the move. But now, with more doctors working for hospitals or large group practices, the hiring institution may offer a guaranteed minimum income in order to attract a desired physician.

What if things don't work out? On *House*, doctors seem to come and go almost at will. They are never seen negotiating to get out of a contract. In the real world, if a doctor does want to get out of a job, there may be a signing bonus to repay or other penalties for ending a contract early. Sometimes, not only are feelings hurt when a job doesn't work out, but lawsuits may fly, because hiring a new doctor is not cheap.

"I can tell you, the one thing about physician recruitment: it is not an inexpensive endeavor. Our average cost to recruit a physician, depending on the specialty, runs anywhere from thirty to forty thousand dollars," Donovan says.

I Want My Toys

Just as House doesn't like his hiring and firing decisions to be overruled, he'll use every trick he can think of to avoid being told no when it comes to choosing the medical devices, drugs, or other items that he thinks are best. He is not unique.

> In every occupational setting since time immemorial, practitioners of various professions have had tools they have preferred above all others for practicing their trade:
>
> The famed golfer Bobby Jones named his favored putter "Calamity Jane" and would use no other implement for the task.
>
> Roy Hobbs, "The Natural," clubbed his prodigious blasts using his magical bat "Wonderboy."
>
> And who can forget legendary blues singer B.B. King and his beloved guitar "Lucille."
>
> So it is with medicine.
>
> From Wasting Millions by Making Purchases Based Solely on Physician Preference? ECRI Institute. Plymouth Meeting, Pennsylvania, 2009

Those lines open a report by ECRI Institute on "physician preference items." Those are devices or other hospital supplies that are selected by physicians rather than by the hospital's purchasing department. As a guitar player, House would certainly connect with the example of B.B. King's "Lucille."

There is a long history of physicians choosing their instruments (medical rather than musical). Although increasing numbers of doctors are, like House, employed directly by hospitals, traditionally they worked independently (and even now most hospital patients get separate bills from the hospital and the doctors that treated them). That independence tied in with physicians' desire to choose the tools of their trade. Even those physicians who are employed by hospitals may be courted by competing hospitals, which then gives them the negotiating power to maintain control over what brands and models of medical items they can use.

It boils down to a basic mind-set that "I'm the doctor. I know what's best."

"Feeding into this is this sense that 'I am an "artist." I should be able to do whatever I want. Why do you bother me with these conversations about money and how much these things cost?'" says Jeffrey Lerner, president of ECRI Institute. The report from his organization outlined some of the problems created when physicians have unfettered choices over medical items . . . and offered some solutions.

Typically, when hospitals decide to buy a big piece of medical equipment, such as an MRI scanner that can cost millions of dollars, a committee that includes the physicians that will use the machine will evaluate the devices available and make recommendations to the hospital administration. But often there is no such organized process for choosing smaller items, even though these smaller items can be quite expensive. For example, implantable defibrillators, which can shock the heart back into normal rhythm, can cost more than $35,000. That is just the price of the device and doesn't include the surgery or other equipment or care.

The issue isn't just complex medical devices with hefty price tags. Lerner says he heard from one hospital that they spent several years wrangling with surgeons over standardizing purchases of surgical thread. Each packet doesn't cost much, but it all adds up.

In a journal article about the costs of medical devices, Lerner and his coauthors quoted from letters sent to U.S. Senator Chuck Grassley (R-Iowa), who has looked into these issues as part of writing proposed legislation that would ban medical device makers from requiring hospitals to keep secret the prices they pay for devices.

Many hospitals told the senators that they want price information. A large urban hospital system wrote, "Medical implantable devices make up 40% to 55% of a hospital's total supply expense; in our case implantable devices cost approximately $65 million annually." Similarly, a rural regional medical center reported that "medical device spending here comprises approximately 40% of our total medical supply expense and is nearly $3 million annually."

From J. C. Lerner, D. M. Fox, T. Nelson, and J. B. Reiss, "The Consequence of Secret Prices: The Politics of Physician Preference Items," *Health Affairs* 27, no. 6 (November-December 2008): 1560–1565.

Hospital administrators are paying more attention to the cost of physician preference items because increasingly they are getting lump sum payments to treat cases. It used to be that hospitals just billed for each service and item they used, so if a doctor liked to use a more expensive type of scalpel or stapler, the extra cost was just passed along. But medical reimbursement has been changing. Now it is more often the case that if a hospital chooses more expensive devices or other items, it may not be able to add the additional expense to the final bill.

In the early 1980s, Medicare (the federal program that covers most hospital care and many other medical expenses for people older than sixty-five and certain other patients, such as those who need kidney dialysis treatments) began switching to a type of flat fee arrangement for paying many medical bills, based on the assumption that while the costs of individual cases may vary, over the long run, similar cases cost about the same.

For example, according the Kaiser Family Foundation, payments for the top five elective inpatient hospital procedures in 2006 (the most recent data) generally fell into these ranges for hospitals in New Jersey and for the nation as a whole:

PROCEDURE	NEW JERSEY	U.S. AVERAGE
Hip or Knee Replacement	$11,658 to $13,726	$10,085 to $12,257
Gallbladder Removal by Laparoscope with Complications or Preexisting Conditions	$10,983 to $12,956	$9,474 to $11,378
Insertion of Heart Defibrillator	$36,420 to $41,761	$29,410 to $37,779
Back and Neck Operations Except Back or Neck Fusion	$8,324 to $9,928	$7,258 to $9,010
Repair of Previous Hip or Knee Replacement	$14,630 to $17,717	$12,763 to $16,228

Source: Kaiser Family Foundation, www.statehealthfacts.org, "Individual State Profiles, Medicare Hospital Payments, Payments for Top Inpatient Procedures"

As spending on medical devices grows, it becomes an ever more important line item in hospital budgets, so shaving the spending by even just a few percent can make a big difference. For example, the ECRI report on physician preference items outlined an example of a hospital with a $500 million annual operating budget. About a fifth of that, $100 million a year, typically goes to buy supplies. The physicians at such a hospital might control almost half of that supply spending. That means that each 1 percent reduction in the cost of physician preference items would save the hospital almost half a million dollars a year.

When a hospital decides to buy a big-ticket item, like a new MRI scanner, administrators usually work with a committee that includes physicians (mostly radiologists in this case) to review the sales pitches from MRI manufacturers and then decide which model best suits the needs and budget of the hospital. This process allows people to discuss the pros and cons and reach a consensus choice. It would seem crazy to let one of the doctors, say the most senior radiologist, make a multimillion-dollar decision without consultation or compromise. But that's exactly what often happens with millions of dollars' worth of purchasing decisions on implant devices, surgical equipment, and other supplies.

It's not easy to rein in doctors who are used to choosing whatever items they want without having to worry about the price. But don't doctors know best? (Certainly, House is always sure that he does.) And wouldn't most patients tell the administrative "bean counters" to back off? After all, it's the patient's health or even life on the line, and if the doctor thinks a certain brand is better, shouldn't administrators stay out of the doctor's way?

"That would definitely be the majority opinion," Lerner notes. "But what it leaves out is that if there were in fact comparisons among these devices, would you be able to show any differences? The few comparisons that exist don't [show significant differences]."

In other words, while many doctors believe that one device or other medical item may be superior to another, in most cases there isn't any real evidence to back up those beliefs. Maybe the surgeon had a bad experience one time with a certain tool and vowed never to use that brand again, when actually the failure rate of the tools the doctor switched to is the same (or maybe even higher).

Not only does higher spending on medical devices pinch hospital budgets, it drives up the cost of health care for the nation.

In total, the United States spends $26 billion [per year] more than expected on medical devices.

> From C. Angrisano, D. Farrell, B. Kocher, M. Laboissier, and
> S. Parker, *Accounting for the Cost of Health Care in the
> United States*, McKinsey Global Institute, January 2007

That McKinsey report also notes that not only do we pay more than expected for medical devices, we use them more, too, which partly explains why the United States spends much more than expected for health care, even though we aren't healthier than people in other countries. Indeed, although life expectancy continues to rise in the United States, it is rising faster in other countries. As a result, each year we slip farther behind on global measures of health.

Basing choices about medical devices on the clinical evidence, rather than the personal preferences of physicians, might help maximize the value we get for our health care dollars. But at the moment, there is very little systematic tracking in the United States of how well medical devices work. (The same lack of systematic tracking of health care outcomes also makes it more difficult to know how well various drugs or procedures actually work.)

Lerner points out that for more than a decade there has been serious talk about creating a national registry of orthopedic devices. If such a registry were in place, every person who had a hip or knee or other bone or joint replaced with an artificial device would have that fact recorded in a central database. The registry would then also track what happened later. How long did the implant last? Was a revision done? (A revision in this case is a second surgery to replace an implant.)

The main purpose of such a registry would be to gather data on the actual experiences of patients so that researchers could use it to understand what works. Regulators could also watch for patterns that might indicate a problem with a specific device or procedure. (Currently, most problems are reported to regulators voluntarily, which means the data are largely incomplete.)

Lerner notes that other countries do have device registries . . . and the information they reveal can have a profound effect on medical practice. He points to the example of whether to use cemented or uncemented implants. In a cemented implant procedure, a fast-curing cement holds the implant in place. With an uncemented implant, patients have a longer recovery because they have to wait for new bone to grow and attach to the surface of the implant, but on the other hand, many surgeons believe that uncemented implants may last longer and reduce problems with pieces of cement breaking off.

"If you look at countries like Sweden, where there is [a registry], they show, for example, if you use uncemented orthopedic implants, as we do in America, you have many, many more revisions of the surgery than in Sweden. These are very big differences. They have about 7 percent. We have about 17 percent," Lerner says. "Revisions are a nightmare. They are obviously bad for the patient. They are very costly. And they are a harder surgery to do than the initial surgery. So that's the part the public would not see. They say, 'Let the surgeon choose.' Well, that's what's happening and it's not good."

Nevertheless, Lerner understands that this point seems obscure and esoteric to many people.

One troubling aspect of the issue: are physicians preferring one medical item over another based just on their medical judgment . . . or do marketing incentives and relationships with device makers or pharmaceutical companies and salespeople influence their decisions?

House doesn't hang out with industry salespeople. Indeed, early in the series he openly criticized the influence of industry on the practice of health care. (See the discussion in the first volume, *The Medical Science of House, M.D.*, about conflicts of interest in health care. It refers to a speech House was asked to make that praised a certain heart drug in "Role Model" [1-17] and then the fling that Foreman had with a pharmaceutical sales representative in "Sports Medicine" [1-12].)

There has been growing attention paid to the influence of money on medicine, and there are now more restrictions on financial ties between companies and doctors. But the problem hasn't gone away.

In situations where a physician wants to use a device or other medical item that costs more—but evidence is lacking to show the choice is likely to provide a greater benefit to patients—why do hospital administrators let physicians get their way? Lerner says it is often easier to give in than to fight.

"The hospital administration doesn't want to go up against its major admitting surgeons, who are more linked to the manufacturer than they are to the hospital. Quite frankly, what hospital administrator would want to get fired over an issue like this?"

After all, the extra money needed to pay for a more expensive device preferred by a physician isn't coming out of the hospital CEO's own pocket. Like Cuddy, real administrators are careful about which battles they really want to fight with their star physicians. Lerner points out that for patients there is a lot at stake when it comes to selecting an implant or other medical device.

"They are highly valued. You see somebody who can't walk; then they put in a new knee and now they can ski. The upside is quite big," he says.

He sees similarities between power struggles over physician preferences for certain medical devices and other issues in modern medicine.

"It is a microcosm for a lot of very troubling cost and quality issues in health care. And in essence it is a microcosm also for how inside players control so much," he says. "You can make the same arguments about guidelines or quality measures or anything that restricts, in a sense, 'freedom.'" But Lerner points out that greater freedom does not always produce higher quality. "Would you rather have a car built on an assembly line or one built by individuals? The truth is you get a better car out of the assembly line."

Eight

Doc, You Don't Look So Good

Physicians are trained to provide care. Frequently they are very bad about receiving care. House long resisted treatment for his Vicodin habit. The personal lives of House and other characters on the show suffer in part because they try to tough things out rather than ask for help. And then there was the sudden death of Kutner; perhaps another example of a doctor unable to admit being overwhelmed.

Kicking the Habit

Vicodin is a brand name for a pill that combines the opiate hydrocodone with acetaminophen, the drug that is in Tylenol and other over-the-counter pain relievers. At times, Vicodin has appeared to be the only thing that House really cares about.

In Season Three, police detective Michael Tritter is treated by House. Tritter notices the doctor popping Vicodin. Tritter also just doesn't like House's (lack of) bedside manner. So the detective starts sniffing around. He tries to coerce House's coworkers into testifying against him by freezing their bank accounts and other tactics. House has stolen prescription forms from Wilson and forged his signature. In "Merry Little Christmas" (3-10), House is so desperate that when he finds out that a cancer patient has just died, he goes to the pharmacy to pick up the dead man's oxycodone pills.

Eventually prescription fraud charges are filed. But in "Words and Deeds" (3-11), a judge decides not to send the case to trial, after Cuddy testifies she had switched bottles in the pharmacy to thwart House, so that he never actually received the oxycodone he sought. Later in the episode, Cuddy yells at House for making her commit perjury to protect him.

At the end of Season Five, the problems worsen. House may be using methadone and/or OxyContin. Cuddy tries to get House through detox in his own apartment, since he refuses to enter a real drug treatment program. (Although later it turns out House may have hallucinated the detox episode.)

At the opening of Season Six, House is in an inpatient psychiatric hospital, along with people who have severe psychiatric issues unrelated to substance abuse. After House completes detox and other treatment for his substance abuse, the medical director says he won't recommend that House's medical license be reinstated unless he completes further treatment for other psychiatric issues (the things that make him such a jerk and an unethical doctor). House eventually satisfies the psychiatrist that he is ready to go home.

House's dependence on Vicodin has been a central theme of the series since the beginning, obvious to almost everyone around him. In the real medical world, common warning signs of addiction to drugs (including alcohol) include missing clinic duty (well, House does that anyway), erratic behavior during surgery or other treatments, and maybe abusive behavior toward colleagues (okay, that's another one that just seems to be House, not the drugs). Doctors, like others who get into trouble with substance abuse, may be found out because of a drunk driving arrest or other legal issue.

When coworkers notice a problem with a physician, the condition is often advanced and has been developing for a very long time.

"We often say that the last thing that falls for the physician with addiction is work. Doctors are clever. We are all smart. We don't go to medical school by being dumb. And denial, which is part of addiction, we also have that. We also don't take care of ourselves, because we are trained to take care of our patients," says Luis Sanchez, M.D.

Sanchez is the director of the Physician Health Services Program of the Massachusetts Medical Society. In cases of suspected impairment or other issues, the program staff will assess a physician and offer support and referrals to treatment if needed. The program also monitors physicians after they return to practice.

The number of physicians who develop substance abuse problems is small, and the rate does not appear to be much different than that seen in the general population. But physicians (as well as pharmacists and nurses and others) do have special access to prescription drugs that may allow them to hide problems longer than some other people. There are many pathways into addiction. Maybe it starts with back pain (or chronic leg pain). What begins as a temporary response to pain may become chronic and growing.

"But nobody knows about it, because we are very good at keeping it secret. It's probably at a very low level for weeks, months, years, until finally it just blows up," Sanchez says.

When coworkers begin to suspect there is a problem, their responsibility to patients should lead them to report those suspicions. But ratting out a colleague—or risking retaliation from a supervisor—is not easy. To give an extra nudge, in Massachusetts and certain other states, reporting suspected impairment of a physician is not only an ethical responsibility, it is a legal mandate.

"I view that as positive. I view that as a stick. The reality is that very few people do it," Sanchez says. "But it's there, and ultimately, like in *House*, if House (or someone like him) refuses to get care, then the physician is obligated to call the [state licensing] board. And that's often a reason that physicians are referred to us [for treatment]. The doctor or the nurse or someone else will say, 'If you don't go to the physician health program, I'm going to report you to the board.'"

That legal mandate in Massachusetts does not require that the suspicions be made public. Sanchez thinks that's the right balance, in order to improve the chances of successful rehabilitation.

House was almost brought down by Tritter, not for being a drug addict per se, but because of prescription fraud. He forged prescriptions on Wilson's forms and diverted pills meant for a patient. Prescription fraud is indeed one of the typical reasons a physician with a drug problem is discovered.

"Yes, absolutely. They can be very manipulative. They can have their secretary go and buy it for them. We had one physician who had his secretary shaking in her boots [about what might happen to her] if she didn't go and buy the medications for him," says Anderson Spickard, M.D., who founded the Vanderbilt Institute for Treatment of Addiction at Vanderbilt University in Nashville, Tennessee, in 1984. He also works with the Center for Professional Health there. The center teaches physicians about issues such as proper prescribing, sexual boundary lines, and disruptive behavior.

"I've had them all, I'll tell you, after forty-five years I could tell you a bunch of stories," Spickard says. In order to protect the confidentiality of patients, however, he can't go into a lot of the details of the many ways he has seen physicians lose their way because of drugs. The treatment center at Vanderbilt has helped many doctors get back on track and back to practice, but not all. Spickard says some cases stick in his mind, including one physician who refused to believe that he needed treatment. The doctor eventually returned to the old ways that got him into trouble and ultimately died.

Doctors are mostly smart and ambitious hard workers, but when it comes to addiction, their stories share many characteristics with those of people in other professions.

"The job is about the last thing that usually falls apart. That was what I observed in my patients, no matter what their profession," says Wilson Compton, M.D. Dr. Compton is the director of the Division of Epidemiology, Services and Prevention Research at the National Institute on Drug Abuse (NIDA), part of the National Institutes of Health.

He also spent many years practicing and teaching psychiatry and addiction treatment in St. Louis, Missouri. "For some reason that's just part of human nature, people will let their finances and then their families fall apart a little earlier, yet somehow they can keep it together for the few hours a day for their employment, perhaps because the time spent at one's job is limited."

By the time the problem becomes a serious issue at work, an addict has usually already done serious damage to the other sectors of his or her life.

House doesn't really have a life outside of work, though. And it's not that people at work did not notice his drug use. They spent many episodes, many years, covering it up and finding excuses for inaction.

In "Finding Judas" (3-09), Detective Tritter confronts Cuddy about the protective web that House's colleagues have wrapped around him.

"Not one of you has told me the truth about Dr. House," Tritter says.

"The pills allow him to cope with the pain," Cuddy replies.

That rationalization makes Tritter angry. "No, the pills distort reality. He is an addict."

Cuddy tries to minimize the problem. "He's not out robbing a liquor store or . . ."

Tritter cuts her off. "Look, he's treating people. He needs to find a different way to cope, before he kills somebody! If he hasn't done that already."

"*If* you're right, he has a medical problem. It should be dealt with by doctors!"

Tritter gets the last word in this exchange. "Well, it's not being dealt with by doctors. Doctors are covering it up." Tritter says Cuddy has failed.

Despite the criminal investigation that documented the lengths that House was going to in order to feed his need for drugs, House's colleagues continue to shield him from consequences. When the case is heard by a judge who will decide whether to refer the charges of prescription fraud to a trial, Cuddy even commits perjury to protect House.

While perjury is certainly an extreme action, covering for colleagues is not mere fiction. Those who work in programs that treat physicians for addiction say it used to be more common.

"Those are the old days. These programs started in the seventies," says Luis Sanchez. "These programs started because when doctors had a problem such as this, nothing would happen to the doctor until some egregious thing happened or a patient got harmed. Then the licensing board would just take the license. We've evolved."

Physicians also know more about the disease of addiction than they did in the old days.

"Most of the people that were out there taking care of physicians had not been trained at all; not only were they not trained in addiction in general, but they were not aware of their own colleagues being addicted," Anderson Spickard says. In order to bring the problem out into the open, he and his colleagues did research on the extent of the substance abuse issues among the faculty at academic medical centers. "We wrote this paper saying, 'Hey, look, these guys are sick out there, get them into treatment.'"

Spickard says they pointed out not just the problem, but also the fact that when physicians got treatment, they could recover and return to practice. Recognizing and intervening with physicians who may be impaired is also vital to protecting patients . . . and hospitals and clinics.

"We have made extreme efforts to keep these physicians that see their colleagues are getting in trouble from just sweeping it under the rug, because if there is a mistake that's made and there has not been treatment initiated for this individual, and everybody knows about [the problem], the Board of Trustees of the institution is at legal risk," Spickard points out.

Although Cuddy, Wilson, and the rest of the team at Princeton-Plainsboro Teaching Hospital seemed to just throw up their hands as House's dependence on Vicodin and other drugs deepened, they should have known what to do. The national organization that accredits health care institutions requires that they have procedures in place to teach all staff about just this sort of situation and how to respond.

In 2001 the Joint Commission on Accreditation of Healthcare Organizations (JCAHO) required that identification and education of impaired physicians be mandated but separate from disciplinary action and that all staff and resident physicians be educated on physician impairment and offered resources for psychiatric or substance abuse concerns and a referral to access these resources, all while maintaining confidentiality. Additionally, JCAHO mandated that patient safety surveillance be in place until physicians complete rehabilitation or necessary treatment. The American Medical Association mandates reporting impaired physicians secondary to substance abuse or mental illness. Annual resident lectures are required continually to address this issue, making it public and open for discussion.

From R. A. Greenup, "The Other Side of the Stethoscope," *Academic Psychiatry* 32, no. 1 (January-February 2008): 1-2

It seems the doctors on *House* didn't read that issue . . . or get any of the memos about hospitals having employee assistance programs available for their employees . . . or hear any of the experts from physician health programs talk about the problems and solutions. Luis Sanchez says he gives thirty to forty lectures a year with the goal of teaching every health provider and medical student how to intervene in order to prevent patient harm . . . and save the physician's career or even his or her life.

The years-long failure to act by House's colleagues left him open to Detective Tritter's investigation. Those who work with impaired physicians say most of the time coworkers or the physician take action before law enforcement gets involved.

"As a rule, I'd say that [law enforcement involvement] would be very rare. It's usually an in-house situation, where the leaders of the institution are scared to death that they are going to have a [patient] death in the emergency room or in the operating room because a guy is addicted. It's taken much more seriously than it used to be," Anderson Spickard says.

Spickard says that in his experience, law enforcement officers usually do not get involved in dealing with impaired physicians unless there has been a particularly egregious event or felony.

"In fact, they don't want to. They are overwhelmed with these kinds of cases in the general population; and if the physicians can take care of themselves and get their colleagues well, have at it."

But forging or diverting prescriptions, as House did, can lead to potential criminal charges. Luis Sanchez offers this scenario.

"If a physician orders five hundred Vicodin on the Internet, the DEA [federal Drug Enforcement Administration] could show up in that doctor's office within a few months and say, 'By the way, Dr. Smith, we noticed that you've ordered five hundred Vicodins. Please give me a list of the patients that are on them.' Often this is during the doctor's busy day, all the patients are waiting in the waiting room, and the state police and the DEA say, 'Oh, you can't show them to me? You're under arrest.' Then they handcuff the doctor and he is taken out through the waiting room."

It happens, but that's not the image that the DEA's public information officer for New Jersey wants to highlight.

"We don't go out on witch hunts for doctors," says Special Agent Douglas Collier. But he says prescription drug abuse is more common than it was ten or twenty years ago and that it ranks second only to marijuana.

"Unfortunately, some doctors get lost in addiction and lose their focus on their Hippocratic oath to their patients," he says, adding that sometimes greed lures doctors into misusing the power of the prescription pad.

The DEA issues an authorization number to each physician, pharmacist, or other person who has a legitimate reason to handle or prescribe controlled substances. The agency tracks prescriptions and other information, watching for unusual patterns. Sometimes tips come from people close to a doctor.

"Employees will advise us of practices not becoming a physician."

For example, Collier says, "Just recently I had a call about a doctor who was using Xanax. It is a benzodiazepine. It can calm you down."

Collier says sometimes people who see signs that a physician is misusing medications will call the DEA for advice about what to do. When the agency receives such a call, Collier says, "we have to do due diligence. We have to make sure the complaint is valid and investigate any criminal improprieties."

The DEA response depends on the circumstances. Prescription drug cases may be either civil or criminal depending on the specific allegations. Although the DEA is a federal agency, it can also bring charges using state laws. Collier says they use whichever statutes appear to be most appropriate for a particular case. Even if a physician who violates prescription drug regulations is not sent to prison, the consequences for the doctor can be serious.

"We can suspend or revoke their DEA number pursuant to an investigation," Collier points out. "If they can't prescribe medications, they are probably going to look for a new profession."

Collier says the DEA puts a high priority on stopping physicians who may be selling prescription medicines to others. He points to one recent case in which a physician in New Jersey was convicted of selling the powerful pain drug oxycodone (also known as OxyContin and other brand names). According to a statement on the DEA Web site, the doctor wrote "illegal prescriptions to her co-conspirators in exchange for money and services rendered. She also directed certain co-conspirators to create false patient files to justify the illegal prescriptions and caused the filing of a false police report that alleged that prescription pads had been stolen from her office, to conceal her issuance of illegal prescriptions." The doctor was sentenced to eleven years in federal prison to be followed by three years of supervised release, along with a fine of $12,500.

Doctors in all corners of the United States (and around the world, for that matter) sometimes step out of bounds and criminally abuse their prescribing privileges. Scanning through DEA reports of recent court cases turns up some examples from New Jersey.

CRIME	PUNISHMENT
Unlawfully prescribing excessive amounts of controlled substances in return for payments from patients.	More than three years in prison followed by three years of supervised release. A fine of $9,000.
Distribution of hydrocodone (one of the components of Vicodin), alprazolam, propoxyphene, and Provigil. As the DEA Web site put it, the doctor worked with others to get supplies of these controlled drugs "by misrepresentation, fraud, deception, and subterfuge."	Almost five years in prison followed by three years of supervised release. A fine of $4,000.
Possession and distribution of oxycodone. According to the DEA Web site, court documents outlined how an undercover detective met with the doctor and purchased multiple prescriptions for OxyContin and Roxicodone. On four separate occasions, without ever doing a physical examination or asking questions about pain or other medical symptoms, the doctor sold the undercover agent a total of nine prescriptions, for which he was paid $8,000. And the meetings took place not in a clinic, but in parking lots.	Almost five years in prison followed by four years of supervised release. A fine of $10,000.

There was also a case listed that had some similarities to the charges that Detective Tritter leveled at House in Season Three. The doctor pleaded guilty in state court to obtaining controlled substances by fraud. He was sentenced to three years probation and fined $3,555.

However, some doctors worry that DEA policies and actions that are intended to protect the public from prescription drug abuse may sometimes go too far. They say that DEA monitoring, paperwork, and investigations can make some physicians reluctant to take full advantage of pain medicines for their patients.

As a statement from the American Pain Foundation put it:

Reluctance to prescribe powerful pain medicine among the medical community for fear of retribution has led to the needless suffering of countless people in pain.

The Department of Justice must "stop the abuse and diversion of prescription medicines without harming access to these medicines for people affected by pain," states Will Rowe, Executive Director, American Pain Foundation, in his commentary. The commentary points to a failure on the part of the DEA in not abiding by its commitment to the pain community to pursue a balance between the war on drugs and the rights of pain patients, and also cites "the failure of those in authority over the DEA to assert the more comprehensive command."

From a news release issued by the American Pain
Foundation on March 17, 2006

The primary responsibility of the DEA is to enforce drug laws. It is not responsible for regulating medical practice. But when a physician gets into trouble with drugs, even if there is no criminal conviction, state licensing boards may still take action . . . because they are charged with ensuring that physicians abide by not only the laws, but also the ethical and professional standards that medicine aspires to and the public expects.

"In Massachusetts, if a physician got caught by the police for prescription fraud, then hired the best lawyer and got off, that would be well and good, but that license is also revoked. Because the licensing boards are completely separate from any criminal case. The licensing boards don't care about what the person's guilt or innocence legally is," says Luis Sanchez.

Courts and juries have to be convinced, beyond a reasonable doubt, that a defendant committed a crime. State medical licensing boards are set up to follow a different standard.

"The licensing boards feel strongly that the physician's license is a privilege, and anything we do to violate that, that license can be quickly removed; because they are protecting the public. Patient safety is paramount to the boards," Sanchez says. He goes on to note that physician health programs like the one he heads also put patient safety first, but then do what they can to support and rehabilitate doctors who have gotten into trouble with drugs.

Despite his concern about fellow physicians, Sanchez says that if the writers were trying to be realistic, House would have lost his license before the end of the first season. He goes further, saying that while state medical licensing boards can restore licenses to physicians who successfully complete treatment and meet monitoring requirements, the evidence of prescription fraud and repeated actions that violate the ethics and rules of medicine would probably cost House any opportunity for a second chance.

"In Massachusetts, he would have a revocation and they would add onto it: 'No chance of getting relicensed,'" Sanchez says. Based on House's record of deceit and mistreatment of both coworkers and patients, Sanchez says he might consider a physician in his position to be too far gone to be worth trying to rescue through their program. "We would probably not even deal with him at a physician health program. He would go straight to the licensing board. What we are interested in is prevention and early intervention, reaching out to physicians before there is patient harm, hospital involvement, and all that."

Sanchez emphasizes that he is speaking only about what he thinks might happen if House were a physician in Massachusetts. Although he has contact with physician health programs across the country and served as president of the Federation of State Physician Health Programs (www.fsphp.org), he stresses the fact that medical licensing is a state responsibility . . . and so is the decision about whether a physician who gets into trouble with alcohol or other drugs will get a second chance.

"There is no national standard. Licensing boards are state boards. Physician health programs are state programs. All the states do it differently, basically similar, but different processes," Sanchez says.

Veteran addiction treatment expert Anderson Spickard says he thinks his home state of Tennessee tends toward the rehabilitation end of the spectrum of states, though he can't say whether House would be allowed to return to practice after so many years of bad behavior.

"Many states are very punitive; in other words, you get one chance to go to treatment and that's it. If you have a relapse, they are going to take your license. In Tennessee and other Southern states I think we are more rehabilitatively oriented," Spickard says.

At the Vanderbilt Institute for Treatment of Addiction they see the full range of problems and local regulatory responses. "We're not just doing addiction work now, we're doing disruptive behavior, improper prescribing of narcotics, and sexual boundary issues. We've done 1,350 physicians over the last ten years from Canada and the United States in those categories. And every one of them has different sanctions by their [medical licensing] boards."

Here's some good news for House:

"In New Jersey there is a unique opportunity for physicians with impairment problems," says Louis E. Baxter, Sr., M.D., FASAM. Baxter is the executive medical director of the Professional Assistance Program of New Jersey. He says his (and House's) home state was the first to have a full-time physician assistance program. It opened in 1982. Baxter is also the president and chairman of the board of the American Society of Addiction Medicine.

"I'm familiar with the pill-taking, wisecracking, eccentric, and brilliant Dr. House," Baxter says. He is also very familiar with the tricks doctors use in order to hide their impairments, and he doesn't think House would have gotten away with it. "With all of those doctors and residents and everyone else seeing him popping pills and dropping pills, taking medications from patients, those things could not happen in real life and certainly not here in New Jersey."

Baxter says that the physician assistance program works closely with the New Jersey State Board of Medical Examiners, the agency that licenses physicians, in order to encourage physicians to seek help.

"They allow us to administer an anonymous treatment track for those physicians that are seeking self-referral for help or those physicians that are referred by colleagues or hospitals that have not committed major crimes."

When a doctor comes forward, the program staff will evaluate his or her situation and develop a treatment plan.

"We administer it, but it's run by the state Board of Medical Examiners Impairment Review Committee. That committee is made up of two members from the state Board of Medical Examiners, two members from the Professional Assistance Program, and one physician that is appointed by the commissioner of health. We also have a representative from the attorney general's office.

A report on each case goes to the state board's Impairment Review Committee. At this stage the doctor's name is not revealed. When a case is reviewed, committee members ask about the circumstances.

"Were any patients hurt? Were there any malpractice cases against this physician? Did they divert the medicine? Did they write prescriptions? Did they use insurance? If all of the answers to all the questions are no, then they allow us to enroll the person into the alternative resolution program," Baxter says, meaning that the doctor will have a chance to get treatment and return to practice without public discipline. "I would say that more than fifty percent are able to take advantage of the alternative resolution program."

But even when physicians complete their initial treatment, things don't just go back to normal.

"We follow them for a period of five years. We do random urine testing on the individual. If they are impaired when we first meet them, we take them out of practice until such time as they undergo detoxification and rehabilitation. We will see them face-to-face on a monthly basis. They have to go to twelve-step recovery meetings and be involved in an after-care program that generally is group therapy and meets weekly for about a year to three years."

Physicians who relapse are reported to the board, and this time their names are revealed. They may face suspension of their licenses and their cases may become public record. Physicians who enter the alternative resolution program agree not to see patients until they get approval, but technically their medical licenses are not suspended or revoked, so as long as they comply with the program, and there is no public record of the case. Baxter says that opportunity to straighten out without a public black mark is an important carrot that encourages physicians to get help.

"Because we've done such a good job, and I say that honestly, because we've done such a good job of educating the physicians, the county medical societies, hospitals, group practices, they know that if they get into difficulty that they have someplace that they can come. Now, if they don't come to us and the board finds out about it, which they ultimately will, then they are going to go through a whole different pathway which could cause them to lose their license temporarily. So we have a lot of physicians that come to us, quote, voluntarily, unquote, when they realize that they have a problem."

In "Teamwork" (6-08), Cuddy hands House an envelope.

"This envelope is oddly medical license–shaped," House says. He's right. The envelope does contain his official reinstatement.

"Congratulations," Cuddy tells him.

Foreman announces, "House is back in charge."

Just a few episodes after House returned from a drug treatment program, it seems everything is back to normal. That's not how things really work.

"Not at all," Baxter says. "He would definitely be involved with us for a minimum of five years, if he was in the alternative resolution program. If he'd been reported to the state board directly by, say, a pharmacist or a patient complaint, he would still have the opportunity to get into the alternative resolution program, but the board may decide to give him a public consent order and suspend his practice until such time that he got well."

And unlike the scenario on *House*, his fitness to return to medical practice would not rest on the decision of the director of the drug treatment program. House would have had to go through a state process of evaluation and monitoring.

Baxter says their system of offering physicians confidential treatment, coupled with long-term close monitoring and the threat of severe consequences for failure, has worked. He says one review of the program's records indicated that more than 96 percent of physicians in the program successfully completed five years of follow-up. Baxter says another indication of progress is that physicians are coming to them for treatment much earlier than they were a decade ago.

"Most of them required long-term residential treatment. And I'm talking three to six months. Because they had waited so long that their disease became pretty virulent. But over the past five or six years, because of the laws and because people know that they can get the help that they need, we actually get these doctors in treatment very early in their illness."

As mentioned earlier, in "Finding Judas" (3-09), Detective Tritter accused House's colleagues of protecting him rather than dealing with his drug use. That's the reason that New Jersey and many other states have mandatory reporting laws.

"In New Jersey, the Medical Practice Act states that any licensed physician who suspects that a colleague is impaired is mandated to report that colleague. They don't have to have evidence, but if they have suspicions, they are required to report that physician," Baxter says. "In situations where everybody knows that a guy is impaired and no one reports him, they can be subject to licensure action themselves."

So Wilson, Cuddy, and the others, by tolerating House, are actually in violation of the rules and laws of New Jersey?

"That's right," Baxter says.

Special Agent Collier stresses that, even for the DEA, when it appears that a physician is addicted to drugs (including alcohol, the most abused drug), the number one goal is treating the disease of addiction.

"The idea is that they need treatment. We try to get it to them so we can get them back to a productive life," he says. "We don't want the DEA arresting them. It's a medical problem."

He says his office sometimes works jointly on cases with the New Jersey State Board of Medical Examiners, which controls the licenses of physicians. Just because an allegation involving prescription drugs is reported to the DEA, Collier says it doesn't always result in federal criminal prosecution. "We will investigate," he says. "But if we deem it appropriate for another organization to handle the case, we can let them do it."

That handoff may be more likely when it appears that a physician was misusing his or her prescribing privileges or access to drugs to feed an addiction . . . and wasn't giving or selling the drugs or prescriptions to others.

Wilson Compton, M.D., at the National Institute on Drug Abuse, says that focusing on treatment and rehabilitation is not being soft on doctors who violate drug laws. He says that not only is it hard to successfully regain a medical license, but more importantly, the public is better served by a system that encourages doctors to come forward (or their colleagues to report them) as early as possible. But he admits that most people don't see it that way at first.

"When I talk to the public, people are horrified that an impaired doctor's license wouldn't be taken away forever. But by providing appropriate health care, combined with very close monitoring, we can make the public safer. If you simply take somebody's license away, that might work for that individual, but it does not encourage anybody else to ever come forward for help," Compton says. "The enforcement [of drug rehabilitation monitoring] is quite strict and many people will not be practicing medicine when they are done with a program. Not everybody succeeds. But by providing a good enforcement approach, combined with health care, we think we can make the public even safer. That's an important perspective, because I think otherwise people get hung up on wondering why we let somebody with an alcohol problem, for example, come back and see patients. We want to encourage people to come for treatment. We also don't want to see all of the training and money invested in getting a medical degree go to waste. If we can assure, to a reasonable degree, the safety and security of these folks, we would want them to continue to see patients. We need doctors out there."

Think how many House fans were pulling for him to return to work rather than get tossed on the trash heap of ex-physicians.

Proponents of treatment over punishment emphasize that addiction is a disease and that physicians often succeed when they are treated. Even physicians with as checkered a history as House.

"We believe that chemical dependency is a medical illness, just like other chronic illnesses, like diabetes or hypertension or epilepsy. As long as the public is adequately protected, physicians should not be punished for having a medical illness," Louis Baxter says. "In fact, our primary goal is to protect public safety and welfare. It is not to protect the physician's license at all costs. I don't think the general public fully understands that. We will report, and we have reported, physicians who are impaired and who refuse to either stop practicing or abide by the treatment plan that we set up for them."

Addiction treatment specialists in other states echo Baxter's view that programs oriented toward treatment, but that include strict, long-term monitoring of physicians, are the best approach for both physicians and their patients.

"He's sick, not bad," Anderson Spickard says of the typical impaired physician he sees in Tennessee. "And not only that, but the data are that eighty percent of physicians [will recover], if they have a single drug or alcohol [problem] and don't have any underlying disease or dual diagnosis."

"We have these very strict monitoring contracts, which are very, very successful," says Luis Sanchez in Massachusetts. "We monitor physicians for three to five years for total abstinence of all substances. There's no other program like that for anybody. Our success rate is high."

Because the success rate of addiction treatment programs for physicians is so high compared to many programs open to the general public, the National Institute on Drug Abuse (NIDA) is looking at physician health programs for lessons on how to improve addiction treatment for everyone.

"We've been interested in research on it as a model for other parts of the addiction field, because the success rate looks quite good and it is a model that much of the addiction field doesn't follow. It's a combined enforcement and help approach. It has both elements in an integrated manner," NIDA's Compton says.

Typical programs have multiple stages and use multiple approaches: residential programs and then outpatient follow-up using individual and group therapy. They combine very close monitoring with extensive clinical care. While the monitoring is tight, Compton says it isn't quite what people usually regard as "zero-tolerance."

"It's not exactly zero-tolerance. Because zero-tolerance would imply that one slip and your license is completely gone and we will never allow you to have any further treatment; we will just wipe our hands of you," he says. "What this kind of zero-tolerance typically means is that they won't let it go by the wayside. There will be immediate consequences, which will be severe; but there is a recognition that this is a complex disease with slips and relapses, and so you have to set up your system to account for that."

And contrary to the depiction on *House*, in every state, as in New Jersey, physician treatment programs don't just pat doctors on the back and let them go back to their practices at the end of the first intensive phase of treatment.

"None of these physician health programs lets somebody go back to work unsupervised for a very, very long time," Compton says.

The long-term follow-up component of addiction treatment programs that work with physicians is one more reminder of the dual mission of the programs, which is also shared by hospital administrators and state licensing boards. They are not just concerned with the recovery of the physician; their first responsibility is to patients. So there is more to it than just giving recovering addicts some random urine tests.

"You have to have a high degree of suspicion. You have to be a good clinician to look for behavioral abnormalities, because frankly people can fool drug tests and they will go to extraordinary lengths to do so sometimes," Compton says.

Just imagine the creative lengths House would go to in order to try to fool a monitoring program. Actually, he would probably try to sabotage the system even if he was completely clean, just so he could proclaim victory over his minders. In real programs, the people who are monitoring physicians keep an eye out for behavioral problems, they talk with coworkers and others, they try to watch for any signs that something might be amiss.

While physicians who go through good quality health programs typically receive comprehensive and ongoing support, average people who complete standard addiction treatment (especially those who were convicted of a drug crime) may not get much assistance after their initial treatment and they may find doors to jobs and other opportunities closed to them . . . making recovery that much tougher. Compton says the physician health program model may offer some tips for improving the success rate of special drug courts around the country. Instead of dangling a medical license as a carrot to motivate recovery, the drug courts can offer to reduce or eliminate jail time as a reward that is contingent on staying clean. That approach is based on the premise that just as society benefits from returning a physician to practice, we also benefit from returning other people to productive work, rather than paying to keep them in jail.

Louis Baxter also says the approach typically offered to people in the general population who have substance abuse problems may produce only temporary results.

"Some sort of intervention, either intensive outpatient or rehab, is applied; but then they are not followed up. So like any other chronic medical illness, if you apply some sort of intervention for a period of time, you're going to have good results. Like the diabetic, as long as he is taking his insulin, he will be well. But if he stops, then the blood sugar goes out of control." Baxter says the same is true with addiction: a lack of long-term follow-up too often means the problem returns. "As far as I'm concerned, that's incomplete treatment."

Just as the threat of losing their medical license is an effective lever to get doctors to comply with long-term monitoring and treatment, Baxter says some people have suggested that driver's licenses might be used as an incentive for people to stay well and stay out of trouble.

NIDA's Compton points out that there is another aspect to medicine's addiction problem: the lack of attention to addiction in medical education and training.

"Typically medical education has next to no explicit focus on addiction. Yet tobacco, alcohol, and other drugs will be problems seen in every medical practice. We are approaching this from a broader perspective," Compton says.

"There are elements of medicine that can be seen through a lens of learning about various addictions. During the educational process, physicians can become much better equipped to deal with the practices that they are going to have throughout their careers, which can be filled with either addiction behaviors themselves or the consequences. Heart disease, lung cancer, emphysema, complications of diabetes, liver problems, stroke, heart arrhythmias—all of those may be consequences of one form or another of drug use and drug addiction. So helping our colleagues address the underlying condition is a very important goal over the long haul."

There are too many cases where physicians treat cirrhosis of the liver, but don't help the patient break free from alcohol. Spending on treatment for lung cancer and heart disease and a multitude of other tobacco-related diseases dwarfs our investment in preventing and treating tobacco addiction. People addicted to drugs are far more likely than average to become infected with hepatitis or HIV, and then if they don't gain control over the addiction, they are far less likely than average to successfully manage their infections.

"We want to globally change the awareness, recognition, and the sense that it's not possible to do something for addicted patients. If you ask physicians, you'll find that many of them have a sense of nihilism about addicted patients. They think there's not much they can do about it and they tend to write them off. And that would be an incorrect assumption. So, we want to give them the tools to both identify, assess, and then intervene successfully with addicts."

One of the teaching tools being used to help physicians do a better job—certainly better than what is shown on *House*—is a Web-based course that includes videos of a physician and actors portraying patients as they demonstrate the steps for recognizing and dealing with potential abuse of painkillers. If Cuddy wanted to have her staff brush up on their skills, she could start by pointing them to the NIDA Centers of Excellence for Physician Information Web site (www.drugabuse.gov/coe), where they could browse the online courses and other resources.

One of the case presentations deals specifically with a physician who has begun injecting drugs.

This case is about an anesthesiologist who presents with fever, malaise, and several other somewhat nonspecific and vague findings, which turn out to be infective endocarditis caused by intravenous (IV) drug abuse . . . In this patient's (Dr. Johnson's) case, the students are given a little information at a time, which correlates with the evolution of the disease. In the early stage it would be difficult to make a specific diagnosis; but as time goes on, more and more of the clinical findings point toward endocarditis. In consideration of the patient's past history of trauma with chronic pain syndrome and treatment— and his job as an anesthesiologist—the suspicion of drug abuse arises early in the case as a diagnosis of endocarditis is being made.

From J. Allen, M. Cooley, R. C. Vari, D. Carlson, and C. E. Christianson, *Patient-Centered Learning: The Connor Johnson Case—Substance Abuse in a Physician,* University of North Dakota, November 8, 2009

The case presentation points out that "the key to recovery is early diagnosis and appropriate therapy." Of course, if House's colleagues had actually done an effective job of early intervention, it would have drained the drama out of many, many episodes of the series.

At the beginning of Season Six, House is in an inpatient psychiatric treatment facility. "Broken—part 1" (6-01) starts with graphic scenes of House going through drug withdrawal. Then he meets with the medical director to say he is ready to go home. "No painkillers. No hallucinations. Leg hurts, but it's manageable. Great job. Gonna miss you," House tells Dr. Darryl Nolan. But the doctor urges him to stay. "Your issues run deeper than Vicodin," he tells House.

House checked himself in voluntarily, so he is free to leave. But Nolan says he won't recommend that House's medical license be reinstated unless he stays for further treatment. NIDA's Dr. Compton says many people who become addicted to drugs have other issues as well.

"Absolutely. If anything, this is more the norm than the exception. Many times there are additional psychiatric symptoms, if not full disorders," he says.

"All the time," Luis Sanchez agrees. He points out that not only are physicians vulnerable to the same mental health challenges as anyone else, they often tend to minimize their own health problems. "I happen to have an M.D. behind my name . . . but that's because I went to medical school and graduated. I'm just like everybody else. Doctors forget that. The most common reason why a physician would develop depression, bipolar disorder, anxiety, stress, go down the whole long list, is not the medical school, not our training, it is our family history, it's our genetics. We forget that, because we focus on the patient, we don't focus on ourselves. We are trained to deny illnesses."

Anderson Spickard says that depression is the most common dual diagnosis, as it is called, that he sees among the physicians he has treated for addiction. "There is always an argument about whether the depression is primary or secondary. There is much more of a tendency now to treat the depression."

Work-Life Balance

In Season Three, Cuddy tries to get pregnant. But each pregnancy test she takes is negative. She is deeply frustrated, but she holds it all in and tries to keep her attempts to become a mother secret. Of course, House figures out what is going on. In "Finding Judas" (3-09), House exploits her sensitivity about the matter. When he thinks she mishandled the treatment of a child patient, he hits her where it hurts, yelling, "It's a good thing you didn't become a mom, 'cause you suck at it!" Wilson later finds her crying in her office. She seems to feel that her failure to conceive is a sign that indeed she would fail at motherhood.

Doctors are trained for years and years to succeed at medicine. But the young physicians who emerge from medical school in their mid-twenties often want to become husbands and wives and parents, too. Medical school doesn't include parenting skills classes.

Rebecca Harrison, M.D., is a hospitalist at Oregon Health & Science University in Portland, Oregon (like House, she treats patients in the hospital and does not have patients she regularly follows at an outside clinic or practice). She also helps manage clerkships for medical students. One day a student came in to talk with her. Harrison says the student was a "rising star," but the young woman was having doubts about pursuing a career in academic medicine.

Harrison wrote about the encounter in a journal article.

She worried about not having balance in her life if she entered academics. Her mother had recently become ill and suddenly her priorities were with her aging parents. She wanted a marriage, children and quality family time. She wanted to foster her passion for music. As I contemplated her dilemma, I realized, here lies the future of academic medicine.

From R. Harrison, "Evolving Trends in Balancing Work and Family for Future Academic Physicians: A Role for Personal Stories," *Medical Teacher* 30, no. 3 (2008): 316–318.

"She said, 'Oh, you're my role model,' because I have a family, and at the time my kids were very young," Harrison recalls. "This is not a unique scenario. Among the growing population of women in medicine this comes up a lot."

Even as young physicians make fresh starts on careers in medicine, they are enveloped by the history of their profession.

"Medicine, if you go back to [William] Osler and some of the great historical figures, they really took it all very seriously," Harrison says. "Their commitment to medicine was everything. They set the stage: altruism, you sacrifice yourself for the good of your patient. That was the culture."

In 1889, William Osler, M.D., became physician in chief of the then-new Johns Hopkins Hospital in Baltimore, Maryland. Even though more than a century has passed, the fundamental patterns of medical education and practice he helped establish then still echo through hospitals today. It's hard for doctors with families to try living up to the stereotypes of an earlier era . . . when physicians were almost all men who were backed up on the home front by wives who shouldered the burden of managing the household and children. Even some women who became doctors in earlier decades can have trouble connecting with younger doctors. Harrison remembers reading an article by a prominent senior physician who is a woman. The author seemed mystified that work-life balance was a topic worth talking about.

But it is being talked about. A lot. Harrison says she speaks at meetings around the world where sessions on work-life balance for physicians often go over their time limits because the discussions are so passionate and the personal stories so gripping.

"It's really hard to not feel pulled all the time, because medicine and motherhood, or parenthood, are very all-consuming. It's endless. It's not like a job that ends at five o'clock, in either case."

Nevertheless, Harrison says being a parent is a good thing for a doctor. And becoming a mom was a great thing for her.

"It was a really profound experience. It was a good experience. It's something that makes me more human and a better doctor and a better person. So overall, it's really, really positive. Was it hard? Oh, absolutely."

Though Cuddy did not become pregnant, she does eventually become a mother by adopting a child. It's not easy, though. A young woman who is pregnant agrees to give Cuddy her child in "Joy" (5-06), but then after the baby is born, the woman decides to keep it. Another traumatic disappointment for Cuddy. Maybe she is not fated to be a mother. Then in a Christmas-themed episode, "Joy to the World" (5-11), Cuddy discovers a newborn girl that has been abandoned because her teenage mother thought the baby had died right after she gave birth in an abandoned house. Cuddy successfully applies to become the foster mother of the newborn.

But as Cuddy is frantically trying to prepare for a home visit by a state worker in "Painless" (5-12), House makes her come in to the hospital to discuss a case. He wants approval for one of his extreme diagnostic tests . . . but he also wants to make her pay for not giving the hospital—and him—her undivided attention.

Cuddy: "And hearing me say no over the phone wasn't good enough?"

House: "I'm inconveniencing you because you inconvenienced me."

Cuddy: "You know that foster care official is coming in the morning."

House: "If they weren't, there would be no inconvenience."

Cuddy: "Do not force me to choose between my child and my—"

House interrupts her: "I'm forcing you to do your job! If you can't also . . ."

Cuddy surrenders: "Fine!"

In surrendering to House, Cuddy gives him a blank check to do whatever he thinks is right. Near the end of that episode, she admits to Wilson that she let House run loose because she was preoccupied by the stress of preparing for the foster care program home visit. (She passed the inspection.) Wilson tells her to go easier on herself. "Get help! Most men in your position have a deputy and two assistants at work and a wife and two nannies at home. You're not Superwoman. Don't be a martyr," he tells her.

Cuddy takes the advice and hires Cameron to be her assistant. But the charge House leveled at her—that maybe she couldn't handle her job and a baby—hangs in the air.

Rebecca Harrison has heard it, too. "I still hear people say that if I went part-time, I'd be a wuss," she says.

Well, if that's true, Harrison has a growing number of wusses keeping her company. According to a survey of physicians younger than fifty done by the Association of American Medical Colleges and the American Medical Association, four out of five would reduce their hours if they could afford to. When asked about the importance of various factors when thinking about what constitutes a desirable professional practice, the number one choice among the physicians responding to the survey was "Time for family/personal pursuits." It was ranked as very important by more than seven out of ten physicians. Flexible scheduling and "no or very limited on-call, night, or weekend responsibilities" also ranked in the top ten factors considered very important.

Percent who responded "Very Important" to the question: How important are the following factors when you think about a desirable professional practice?

	MEN	WOMEN
Time for family/personal pursuits	66%	82%
Flexible scheduling	26%	54%
No or very limited on-call, night, or weekend responsibilities	25%	44%
Minimal practice management obligations	10%	18%
Practice income	43%	33%
Long-term income potential	45%	33%
Opportunity to advance professionally	29%	27%

Michael J. Dill and Edward S. Salsberg. "The Complexities of Physician Supply and Demand: Projections Through 2025." Association of American Medical Colleges Center for Workforce Studies, November 2008. Available online at http://services.aamc.org/publications/showfile.cfm?file=version122 .pdf, accessed January 20, 2010.

The responses to this question elicited some notably different responses from male and female physicians.

Those different ratings are reflected in the survey finding that although almost all male physicians have full-time jobs, almost one in four female physicians is working part-time. But for doctors, part-time can have a different meaning than it does for most people, as the survey uncovered when it asked both whether doctors were working full-time or part-time and then also how many hours they worked each week.

"Well, lots of women checked part-time and then said they were working thirty to forty hours a week. There aren't many professions where forty hours a week would be considered part-time. But in medicine you could work three ten-hour shifts and you are only working three days a week and so it's viewed as part-time," says Edward Salsberg, the senior director of the Center for Workforce Studies at the Association of American Medical Colleges.

On average, male physicians said they worked fifty-five to fifty-seven hours a week, with doctors in their forties working slightly longer than those in their thirties. For women, the average workweek ranged between forty-five and forty-seven hours. Even when the researchers excluded the doctors who said they worked part-time, there was still a gender gap, with male physicians reporting a typical workweek as being fifty-five to fifty-eight hours, while women said they put in fifty-two to fifty-three hours a week . . . still a lot of hours.

Interestingly, a presentation Salsberg made on the survey results, to an annual meeting of the Association of American Medical Colleges, started off with a slide displaying images of TV doctors from Dr. Kildare and Marcus Welby, M.D., up to the cast of *Grey's Anatomy*.

"If you think about it, the TV shows are an important picture for the nation about what they think physicians are," Salsberg notes. The images from different decades reflected the changes not only in public perceptions, but also in the underlying reality of what it means to work as a physician.

"The funny part is, I sat with my staff when we first put this slide together, and they are all younger than I am, and they looked at it, and they didn't know who Marcus Welby was. And I looked at it, and I didn't know who McDreamy is. Just on our staff there was clearly a big generation split."

One thing people from every generation can agree on is that though the typical roles of men and women in society have shifted dramatically in recent decades, nonetheless it is still true that on average women handle a bigger share of the load of managing home and family. So when a woman says she's working as a physician only part-time, that doesn't mean she is just relaxing the rest of the time.

"In many cases, these women basically have two full-time jobs: taking care of their family as well as working as a physician," Salsberg notes.

The survey also documented an important difference between men and women in how much backup they can expect from spouses or partners. Less than a quarter of male physicians said their wife or partner works full-time. But more than two-thirds of female physicians said their husband or partner works full-time. So when a male physician calls his significant other and says he'll have to stay late because a patient or paperwork needs his attention, he's much more likely to be assured that the kids will still get picked up from school on time, the refrigerator will be stocked with food, and the dog will get walked.

Family responsibilities also account for much of a gap that the survey found in the percentage of physicians who have taken an extended leave from work. About 5 percent of male physicians under fifty said they had ever taken an extended leave from work that lasted three months or more. By contrast, almost 30 percent of women said they had taken at least three months off at some point in their careers.

In order to learn more about the situations of physicians who try to balance their duties to career and to family by working part-time, Rebecca Harrison and her colleague, Jessica Gregg, M.D., Ph.D., did in-depth interviews with physicians who were applying for a prestigious award for junior academic faculty members in internal medicine, the Mary O'Flaherty Horn Scholars in General Internal Medicine award. It allows recipients to work part-time for up to three years. They also interviewed the division chiefs of the applicants in order to get a sense of what bosses think about physicians who work part-time.

SAMPLE QUESTIONS

WORK, FAMILY, AND SOCIAL RESPONSIBILITIES

- Describe your current life roles, including how you have chosen to prioritize them. What are the challenges and rewards in these various roles?

- How would the Horn Scholars Program help you better fulfill your various roles?

CAREER GOALS / ASPIRATIONS

- Describe your professional interests, strengths, limitations, and aspirations.

- Which of these would you be willing to give up or accomplish over a longer time frame in order for you to fulfill ALL of your lifetime goals and commitments?

CURRENT EDUCATIONAL ROLE

- Describe current involvement in the education of medical students, residents, and fellows (include supervision of trainees in clinical settings), and indicate how this role would change for you if you were to spend 20 to 25 hours per week in career activities.

CURRENT CLINICAL RESPONSIBILITIES

- Describe the time devoted to patient care. Indicate the size and nature of the patient population for which primary direct care is assumed.

PERCEIVED BARRIERS AND SUPPORT FOR HALF OF A FULL-TIME POSITION

- Describe how you believe your colleagues, chief, and administrators will facilitate and/or hinder the success of your future career in half of a full-time position.

From R. A. Harrison J. L. Gregg, "A Time for Change: An Explora-
tion of Attitudes Toward Part-Time Work in Academia Among Women
Internists and Their Division Chiefs," *Academic Medicine* 84, no. 1
(January 2009): 80–86

The authors wrote that division chiefs did see some positive aspects to part-time work.

"Division chiefs describe several benefits to having part-time faculty in their divisions including recruitment and retention of high-quality faculty members and creation of more 'balanced' career paths. Some described these faculty having more time available for scholarship and presentations, which increases division visibility," they wrote.

But they also heard about the downside, including "the potential to be viewed as a less committed worker or one who is not fully integrated into the division."

The physicians themselves said the lighter work schedule would allow them to better manage family duties and other commitments outside of work, but some said they also foresaw risks, such as "slower promotion trajectory or even demotion, being overlooked for career opportunities, given less desirable work, or being marginalized within the division."

Harrison and Gregg suggest that leaders in academic medicine need to rethink how they measure productive and professional work, in order to focus less on hours or the number of patients seen. They admitted that changing old ways won't be easy, but if things don't change, then doctors who also want to do a good job as a husband or wife or parent will continue to hear echoes of the threat House blasted at Cuddy: "I'm forcing you to do your job! If you can't also . . ."

Although the American Academy of Medical Colleges survey of young physicians didn't ask specifically about whether doctors who work part-time are made to feel like slackers who aren't totally committed to their work, Salsberg says he does hear about that sort of attitude.

"I only know about it from anecdotes, but from the anecdotes I've heard, I think it's real. I do certainly think it's changing. If you think about the fact that roughly fifty percent of medical students are women . . . twenty years down the road, when fifty percent of the practicing doctors are women, it's going to be very different."

Underlying the skepticism about part-time physicians is an assumption that someone who isn't on the job or on call all the time is somehow less able to provide good care. But there are also arguments on the other side . . . that part-timers could be the better doctors, because they would probably be less harried and fresher when they are at work, and they would have more time to think and learn about developments in their specialties.

So far we've been talking mostly about how women in medicine juggle their professional responsibilities with traditional family obligations. But work-life balance is not an issue just for women.

"For men in the modern era who want to be more engaged parents and be more present with their children and in their family life, I think all of the same issues are in place, when I look around at colleagues, it tends to be women who elect to, for example, work part-time, rather than the men. And the women may feel that the pressure is more on them to be making these difficult choices about work versus family. But that's a case-by-case, family-by-family situation," says Joseph Carrese, M.D., M.P.H. He is an associate professor in the Division of General Internal Medicine at the Johns Hopkins School of Medicine in Baltimore, Maryland.

Carrese says he does see men trying to become more involved at home.

"There is an expectation that they will be more equal partners. That is something they want for themselves. I think that's something that their partners expect from them. I think that's definitely more likely to be the case than the model of a generation or two earlier, where the guy, particularly in an academic institution or even in clinical practice, was out there working eighty to a hundred hours a week and could pull that off because there was a full-time person at home managing the home front and all of the responsibilities that go with that."

Carrese is in his early fifties, in the middle of his medical career. A couple of years ago he coauthored a medical journal article about work-life balance with a fellow physician who is a generation older. Coauthor Michel Ibrahim, M.D., Ph.D., is a professor at the Johns Hopkins Bloomberg

School of Public Health and the editor in chief of *Epidemiologic Reviews*. He was also the dean of the University of North Carolina Gillings School of Public Health in Chapel Hill, North Carolina.

Actually, they are not merely fellow physicians; Carrese is Ibrahim's personal doctor. The article they wrote grew out of a discussion they had at the end of an office visit. In the article, Ibrahim recalls asking Carrese, "How are you doing?"

> *"Oh, I'm fine, but trying to balance career and family is not easy. I juggled my schedule a few weeks ago so I could teach a course to medical students in the evening—a time of the day that I usually reserve for my family. As it turned out, my daughter's high school soccer team made it to the regional finals, and the game was scheduled at the same time as the course. This created a major conflict for me: teach this special class (which is partly about balance in your life!) or attend my daughter's soccer game."*

From J. A. Carrese and M. A. Ibrahim, "Success, Regret, and the Struggle for Balance," *Annals of Family Medicine* 6, no. 2 (March-April 2008): 171–172

Ibrahim wrote that the comment triggered some painful memories of times he'd put his career ahead of his family. That's what physicians of his generation did. Ibrahim became a full professor by age forty, eventually rising to become a dean.

Carrese, by comparison, notes that as he enters his fifties, he is an associate professor. And he says he recognizes attitudes like those that House exhibited when he yelled at Cuddy that she had to choose whether to be a mom or a hospital leader.

"It gets to the point about the character on *House* whose professionalism and focus are being challenged because of her outside relationships and family responsibilities. In the institutional context that I work in, there are high expectations, both in terms of productivity and success. And in order to advance in this environment, the people who are more likely to be rewarded are the ones who are more likely to be single-minded about this. If you take a more balanced view towards work-life issues, you may not succeed at the same pace or to the same extent," Carrese says. "There are choices for a lot of us. Some people can do it all, but most of us need to make choices about this."

Ibrahim, now in his midseventies, suggests that medicine might benefit by adjusting career paths to better synchronize with the natural seasons of life.

"When I am working now, I am not really looking for a promotion or becoming a dean or a president. I am doing work that I like doing, so I have more time than I ever had in the past," he says. "So therefore, I began to spend time with my children. They love it and I love it. We've begun now to really bond, two or three decades later than usual."

Meanwhile, now that Carrese's children are growing up and heading out on their own, he is entering a season of life that can allow more focus on work without neglecting family needs. So he points out that most young families would benefit if more time were reserved for raising children early in a physician's career.

"They don't want to postpone the interactions with kids and family. They'd rather focus more on work later on," he says . . . and Ibrahim agrees.

They both say medicine, particularly academic institutions, should look at some of the adaptations that certain corporations have made.

"People can have flex careers, part-time careers, more flexibility about productivity standards and the time line under which those accomplishments are expected, and then I think there is more opportunity for people to strike different, and perhaps better, work-life balances and so stay as part of the institution," Carrese says. "To the extent that institutions keep the old rules in place and are rigid about it, it continues to be a problem."

Like the problems Cuddy experienced on *House*.

"In the *House* setting, this character is working in an environment that appears to be almost Neanderthal, certainly hostile to work-life balance and well-being. If we work for companies and institutions where the culture and the expectations make this more difficult, almost impossible for us to succeed while doing the right thing for our families and our children, then that's part of what needs to change here," he says.

The potential consequences of a "move up or move over" culture involve more than career disappointments or conflicts for individual doctors. There are effects on institutions and the broader field of medicine itself.

"If you are not successful at the pace that is expected, there is the chance that you won't be able to stay. If that disproportionately affects women, or think about diversity more broadly, people who are approaching their lives in different ways, then the institution and the field as a whole loses out on those voices and the contributions of those people," Carrese says. "I think that's a real problem for the field. Certainly different people bring different perspectives and different issues to the table. If you are cutting out an entire gender or certain segments of the population because they have a different way of approaching this, it's not just problematic for those individuals, I think it's a problem for the institution and then beyond that the whole field."

He points out that members of the generation of today's college students have strong attitudes about what sort of life they want. And these young adults are now making decisions about their future careers.

"I know my kids have pretty strong ideas about their quality of life and their work-life balance. If medicine doesn't make these adjustments, people will go to other fields. Not just other fields within medicine, that's already happening, but they'll become investment bankers or go to corporate America. Already we're seeing the numbers in general internal medicine dropping precipitously, in terms of who's coming to this field out of medical school. Part of it is economic, but a big chunk of it is work-life issues," he says. "Medicine as a field has to be responsive to this, because we may end up losing out on the top people as they elect to go into other fields entirely."

Ibrahim seconds that prediction.

"That's true," he says. "They will be driven away from medicine and medicine will be the loser."

Drs. Carrese and Ibrahim say the comments their article generated were mostly from people who appreciated their effort to raise these issues in the open . . . and particularly their noting that the traditional focus on career left casualties on the family side of the work-life balance.

"The comments fascinated me, because I didn't realize that it would be received with such acceptance. Most of the comments said, 'Right on target. We always felt that way and it's so good of you to say it candidly and honestly,'" Ibrahim says.

Some of the responses pointed out that it's almost impossible to achieve a perfect balance between career and family. As one doctor put it, "I will never be doctor of the year or mother of the year, and must acknowledge that I never really had the capability to be either. But with balance and some small success I'm an OK doctor and an OK mom. And most days that is good enough."

Another point made is that "balance" is not the same as saying each side gets equal time. The choice of how much effort and time to devote to work and how much to family and other duties is an individual one. Indeed, as some doctors noted, being a physician can be very rewarding, and very enjoyable, so spending the bulk of one's time at work doesn't necessarily mean there is an imbalance. It may just mean that a person really likes caring for patients and doing the other things that doctors get to do.

One doctor who responded to the journal article by Carrese and Ibrahim wrote this:

In the movie Patton *George C. Scott who played Patton was challenged about his love of fighting. He became quiet, thoughtful and in more of an admission than statement said something to the effect of "God forgive me, but I do love it so." When I struggle with balance I sometimes remember this movie, not because I want to be compared to Patton, but that I do love my work.*

By the way, Dr. Carrese says he did manage to resolve that scheduling conflict so he didn't have to choose between his class and his daughter's big soccer match. He says he works hard to minimize conflicts, but that when he is on call at the hospital they can be unavoidable.

"I try to schedule this so as to avoid my kids' soccer and baseball seasons, but invariably there is something I'll miss in a stretch like this, but my two kids are very understanding and forgiving about that, I think mainly because the vast majority of the time I am there to spend time with them, and when I'm not it is the exception rather than the rule. They also understand the nature of my job as a doctor and that when I'm not with them I am trying to help other people, either patients or students or trainees, and so that makes it more acceptable to them," he says.

Some of the letters pointed out examples of department leaders at medical institutions who seemed to dismiss concerns about work-life balance. One person told Carrese and Ibrahim of a supervisor who scoffed and said that there was really no such problem and that it was actually easy to do well on the job and still have plenty of time and attention for family. But that commenter added that this supervisor was actually just in denial about the toll that his devotion to his career had taken on his family. Other observers note how difficult it is for anyone to recognize and understand the perspectives of people who grew up in a different generation, and as a result one person's attempts to properly balance career and family may be seen by another person as merely slacking.

One journal article about the effects of generational change included this basic list of distinctions between common attitudes of Baby Boomers and Generation Xers:

BOOMERS (BORN 1945 TO 1962)	GENERATION X (BORN 1963 TO 1981)
Work hard out of loyalty	Work hard if balance allowed
Expect long-term job	Expect many job searches
Pay dues	Paying dues not relevant
Self-sacrifice is virtue	Self-sacrifice may have to be endured, occasionally
Respect authority	Question authority

From J. Bickel and A. J. Brown, "Generation X: Implications for Faculty Recruitment and Development in Academic Health Centers," Academic Medicine 80 no. 3 (March 2005): 205–210

Another look at generational differences comes from a company that advises clients on workforce management issues. They summarized distinctions between Generation X and the next generation in this table:

GENERATION X	MILLENNIALS
Born 1965–1976 **51 million**	**Born 1977–1998** **75 million**
Accept diversity	Celebrate diversity
Pragmatic/practical	Optimistic/realistic
Self-reliant/individualistic	Self-inventive/individualistic
Reject rules	Rewrite the rules
Killer life	Killer lifestyle
Mistrust institutions	Irrevelance of institutions
PC	Internet
Use technology	Assume technology
Multitask	Multitask fast
Latch-key kids	Nurtured
Friend—not family	Friends = family
Mentoring Do's	**Mentoring Do's**
• Casual, friendly work environment	• Structured, supportive work environment
• Involvement	• Personalized work
• Flexibility and freedom	• Interactive relationship
• A place to learn	• Be prepared for demands, high expectations

From D. Scheef and D. Thielfoldt, "What You Need to Know About Mentoring the New Generations," Café Conversations

The GenX-Millennials generational shift as it specifically plays out in medical school was investigated by researchers who gave personality tests to medical students who entered during the years 1989–1994 and 2001–2004. Then they compared results of those born between 1965 and 1980 (Generation Xers) with results of those born in 1981 or later (Millennials).

Millennial students scored significantly higher than Generation X students on factors including Rule-Consciousness, Emotional Stability, and Perfectionism; Generation X students scored higher than Millennials on Self-Reliance. Millennials also were significantly different from Generation Xers on several other factors.

From N. J. Borges, R. S. Manuel, C. L. Elam, and B. J. Jones, "Comparing Millennial and Generation X Medical Students at One Medical School," *Academic Medicine* 81, no. 6 (June 2006): 571–576

Generational conflict is not new. How it plays out at medical schools and for medicine in general may depend in part on whether young physicians who stick to a focus on career rise to the top and try to perpetuate the attitudes of many of their predecessors . . . or the growing number of physicians who are trying to achieve a different balance eventually occupy enough of the dean's offices and CEO positions to change the culture of medical institutions.

Dr. Carrese says he sees signs of change. He says he recently attended a meeting at his institution where several of the presenters were women talking about work-life issues.

"Part of the discussion that was taking place in front of the whole division, including the male leadership, was the importance of this issue and the importance of having these voices at the table and making space for women to have part-time careers," he says. "I think that's a conversation that might not have taken place a generation ago."

Of course, before you can worry about balancing work and family, you have to have a family. Just finding time to date, marry, and have children can be tough for busy physicians. The typical doctor is in her or his midtwenties when graduating from the intense years of medical school. Then there is residency training, which may take three to five years— even as much as seven years for some programs that include research training years. Then there may be a year or two of fellowship training.

Even when young physicians are done with their formal training, they may feel that they need to devote their full attention to establishing themselves in their careers. So when do they take time to have children, for example? During residency? Soon after finishing? Or only after they feel secure in their jobs? By that time they may be forty years old!

Recently, medical training underwent a major change with the imposition of limits on the number of hours residents are allowed to work in a hospital. In 2003 the accrediting body for medical residency programs in the United States declared: "Starting today, all 7,800 residency programs in the United States must comply with the Accreditation Council for Graduate Medical Education's duty hours standards, which limit resident duty hours to a maximum of 80 hours a week and set other restrictions on duty hours." Residents are also now limited to working no more than 30 hours without going home. Eighty hours a week and 30-hour shifts would be a massive increase in the workload of most people, but before the new limits took effect, it was common for residents in some specialties to work as much as 120 hours in a single week and 36 hours or more in a single shift at the hospital.

Naturally, working those hours is exhausting. Concerns about fatigue clouding the medical judgment of residents prompted the limits. The issue got national attention with a widely publicized case of a young woman in New York who died while in the care of residents who had been working long hours. But changes did not come quickly. The death of Libby Zion occurred in 1984. The state of New York eventually imposed work hour limits on residents in 1998. And it was almost two decades after the death of the eighteen-year-old woman before the national standards took effect.

The counterarguments to reducing work hours included the potential effects on training, patient care, and hospital finances. If residents, who are paid salaries, work fewer hours a week, then teaching hospitals may need to add staff to get the same amount of work done; but insurance companies generally pay for the services provided, not how many people were needed to provide those services. Beyond that financial matter, there are legitimate questions about how residents will learn everything they need to know if they are in the hospital fewer hours and thus are involved in fewer cases. Some observers say it is becoming more common for residents in certain specialties to do fellowship programs after basic residency. So while each workweek may be a bit shorter, the years of training may grow longer.

While it would seem obvious that residents who are less exhausted will provide better care, the studies that have been done since the eighty-hour workweek took effect have not found clear evidence of an improvement in patient outcomes or a consistent reduction in medical errors. The leading explanation for this paradox is that when residents work shorter shifts, they end up handing off their patients to another team more often. Miscommunication and other slipups in those handoffs may be wiping out any benefits of the shorter shifts.

Meanwhile, the intensity of health care has increased dramatically. These days patients are sent home from the hospital with IVs and wound care needs and rehabilitation schedules that in previous decades would have kept them in the hospital. The patients that remain in the hospital are acutely sick. Indeed, many of today's general hospital ward patients would have been in intensive care units in earlier times. Similarly, the patients who populate ICUs today are so sick that in an earlier era many, if not most, probably would not have survived. It all adds up to more and more complex care having to be provided as rapidly as possible . . . often by residents who now have a hard deadline for clocking out.

"You hand off at noon or one o'clock. It doesn't matter what you have left. But the work volume and complexity has gone up. So when they are there they are working incredibly intensely. And they have all these cross-cover patients," Rebecca Harrison notes.

Cross-cover patients are those a physician who is on call manages for another care team that doesn't have anyone in the hospital during those hours, partly because of the restrictions on duty hours. Cross-coverage is stressful, especially for residents, because they have to make medical decisions without having been involved in that patient's care until that moment. In previous generations, physicians tended to spend more hours in the hospital, but the hours were generally less intense and they usually handled patients they were familiar with.

Back to the matter of balancing work and family . . . Residents say reducing their commitment to a maximum of eighty hours per week, while still double what most people consider to be full-time, has freed up as much as forty hours each week that they used to spend in the hospital. Much of that time may be consumed by getting some much-needed rest, and there is still plenty of studying and other work that isn't covered by the duty-hour limits. That said, while having a baby during residency was once almost unheard of among residents in surgery and other intense programs, now it is becoming more common. So today's physicians often feel it is possible to think about starting a family while they are still in their thirties, even if both people are working full-time.

The benefits and problems of reduced work hours for residents are discussed more extensively in my book about residents who are learning to become surgeons, *The Real Grey's Anatomy.*

The increased percentage of physicians who are women, more two-career couples, men trying to pick up a fairer share of the duties outside of the workplace, broader social shifts in the attitudes and desires of the generation of younger physicians, and specific changes such as the eighty-hour workweek for residents—all seem to point in the same direction: toward a different definition of the lifestyle of a physician. On the other hand, while the world is changing, today's young physicians have been trained by older doctors, some of whom still hold to older standards of what is considered professionalism in medicine.

Salsberg says this: "A professional is someone who carries out their work seriously and does their homework and is well prepared. Just because you are juggling a family and your job, to me, doesn't mean you are unprofessional."

"There is this professionalism question. What does it mean to be a professional? Does it mean you stay until your patient is cared for? Or do you hand off [to the next shift] because your program is going to get cited if they don't comply with the duty-hour regulations?" Harrison asks. "Sometimes students and residents get a double message."

Paying attention to work-family balance, the growing number of physicians who are working part-time, and other changes in medical workplaces isn't just about being nicer to young physicians. As noted earlier, there are real consequences for the profession and to the nation. If medicine is seen as too stressful, and other good-paying and rewarding careers offer better lifestyles, then fewer people may choose to go into medicine, and those already on the job may be more likely to burn out and switch careers or retire.

Harrison says it is vital that the medical profession show young people that the challenges are worthwhile. "If we can't convince them, we're going to lose them. And if we lose them, we're going to have problems," she says. "It's clear that lifestyle is very important in career choice for students. And medicine is lower on the list; it's deemed as uncontrollable."

Salsberg says their survey of physicians younger than fifty found about half feel they are able to balance their work and personal life to their satisfaction. However, less than half said they were able to control their work hours or schedule. Not surprisingly, those who work part-time said they were more satisfied with their work-life balance. The contrast was larger among women. About 46 percent of full-time female physicians said they were satisfied with their balance compared to 74 percent of those working part-time. Salsberg says concerns about filling the growing demands for health care are the reason his organization and others are trying to study the desire for work-life balance and its effects, such as the increase in part-time work by physicians.

"If younger physicians, say, were to work ten percent fewer hours, you'd need ten percent more doctors to get the same total number of hours," he says. "We pretty much confirmed that women do tend to work fewer hours than men, so based on the changing gender mix, you would need more physicians in order to stay even."

One question he and his colleagues are still trying to answer is how much of the shift away from full-time work is driven by the changing gender mix of physicians and how much is related to generational factors; that is, do younger physicians, whether male or female, place a greater value on time with family and other interests outside of work than did their predecessors? He says they are analyzing census data and other information to get a better fix on historical trends in medical work patterns.

"Yes, there has been a decrease in the hours worked by physicians in their thirties and forties compared to twenty and thirty years ago. What I don't know is whether that is driven solely by the changing gender mix or are males and females both working fewer hours," Salsberg says.

So how can medicine change so that more people are attracted to it as a career . . . and so those already on the job are likely to stay longer? Salsberg says one part of the answer is health care reform. No, not the kind of reform of health care insurance that usually grabs headlines, but rather reform of the way health care professionals do their daily jobs. Right now, doctors complain they spend far too much of their time hassling with paperwork. Just think of the piles of paper you get every time you go to the doctor. Especially when there is a hospital stay involved, the piles of statements and bills and explanations of insurance benefits and other dross can start drowning the kitchen table when you sit there to go through your mail. But at least once you get better, the medical paper blizzard dwindles. For physicians, however, the paper tide never, ever ebbs.

"If you are juggling your professional life and your family, when you come into the office you want to practice medicine. If you're going to put in thirty hours and you have to worry about picking the kids up, you don't want to spend twenty percent of your time, or whatever it is, on paperwork and administrative hassles," Salsberg says.

Indeed, no one ever decided to become a doctor so that he or she could spend one day a week just dealing with insurance forms and other medical paperwork.

One of the shocks that often hits physicians fresh out of medical school is how their days in residency training are consumed by administrative tedium. Of course, much of it is vital to tracking patient care, and as the low men or women on the hospital totem pole, interns are naturally stuck with the scut work. But even as physicians climb higher on the totem pole, paperwork still dogs them.

On *House* the team members may threaten to quit—or do quit—because they can't put up with House, but in the real world, the administrative drudgery may be a leading factor in decisions to cut back or get out of medicine.

Actually, "paperwork" isn't really the right term anymore. As hospitals and doctor's offices slowly drag themselves into the computer age, doctors and others in health care are spending more and more of their days tapping away at keyboards, staring into monitor screens, and wondering why all they get is a string of error beeps when they try to change a patient's medication. The promise of electronic health records may someday help reduce the amount of busywork in health care, but the transition period isn't easy. Many doctors report that they are spending more time or hiring more staff to deal with the computerized record systems than they did with old-fashioned paper records.

Health care is well behind other industries in taking advantage of computers. There are a variety of reasons, including patient privacy. Although research on the effects of the shift to electronic records is really just getting under way, some of the studies performed so far indicate that computers have yet to produce important gains in productivity. Indeed, there is some evidence that, at least at first, computers tend to slow physicians down.

In one study, the productivity of doctors did go up after they started using computers. But rather than actually getting more done, they may have just done a better job of documenting what they did. One thing about computers, they can be programmed to keep you from "turning the page" or "filing a note" until every box and field is properly filled out. Indeed, although the statistics from that study indicated that the doctors were more productive, the physicians said they felt like the electronic system was taking up more of their time. In their article on another study, researchers wrote that they were surprised to see that doctors shifted time away from interacting with nurses and patients, and instead spent it retrieving information from the computer.

One study of how nurses in an intensive care unit did their work before and after a computer system was installed concluded that managers should not expect the electronic system to reduce workloads. Another study of nurses in an ER found that they spent more time working at computers and less time talking to one another.

But then a program at Massachusetts General Hospital suggests that part of the problem is how people use computers, not the concept of using computers itself. The hospital managers decided to create an incentive system to encourage doctors to do their computer note taking faster. Within a year after the incentives were put into place, the average time it took to complete a patient note was cut in half.

As I explained in *The Medical Science of House, M.D.*, one of the truly odd things about Princeton-Plainsboro Teaching Hospital is the near absence of nurses or other health care professionals. In a real hospital, the attending physician would never roll a patient to an imaging lab, run the MRI or CT, collect a biopsy, run the pathology tests, etc., etc. You wouldn't want your physician doing those things because he or she probably wouldn't be as well trained or experienced as someone who specializes in nursing or radiology or pathology and so on. It would even be a violation of regulations and some laws for a physician to run certain lab tests without going through regular certification to demonstrate proficiency at those tasks.

Those other health care professionals, the ones practically invisible on *House*, offer another important hope for the future of medicine. As indispensable as they are today, it seems likely the role of professionals other than M.D.s will only grow in coming years.

"Nurse practitioners, physician assistants, but also social workers, nutritionists, physical therapists" are some of the professionals Salsberg expects we will increasingly rely on. "That's the thinking these days about how we're going to deliver more services to more people with greater needs, given the desire for cost containment. The thought is, 'How do we make better use of our physicians?' And the answer is, you build teams and you use physicians to do what a physician has to do."

The move toward more integrated care teams raises a question on which House might have some very strong opinions.

"Perhaps the more challenging part of this is the question 'Is the doctor always the team leader?' Most doctors will say they work well with nonphysicians, but they still like being the manager. It's a little trickier if you say that in some cases, for example people with chronic illness, it may well be that the nurse practitioner or the physician assistant can really do the ongoing management as well as the physician," Salsberg says. "In some of the directions we want to move in, physicians actually are not the best qualified. Think about something like diet or smoking or exercise. The physician's role is mostly to give a very brief message motivating the patient. 'If you don't stop smoking, you're gonna die.' But to actually spend a half hour with the patient and to talk to them, to give them the tools to change their diet or to stop smoking is not what physicians are necessarily best qualified to do."

Salsberg says that making better use of other team members can help physicians control their workload, if doctors can loosen up a bit. "It also means a change in personality; to accept the fact that it is the team performance, not necessarily your individual performance, that is most important.

"Thinking about House, on the one hand House does a good job teaching others, challenging his coworkers. On the other hand, it's pretty clear that he's the top guy," Salsberg notes.

Yes, indeed, House is the top guy . . . even though Cuddy is supposed to be his boss. Rebecca Harrison hopes that after facing some of the doubts and criticism Cuddy had to deal with when she decided to become a mom as well as a physician and hospital administrator, an administrator in real life would try to find ways to improve the workplace culture and the work-life balance.

"Probably this administrator character, who has gone through this experience herself, who gets now what it's like to be a mother, and still has ambition for her career, might rethink how she could run a group of doctors and attend to these issues and at the same time get warm bodies to take care of patients. It's a struggle, but there's room for growth there," Harrison says.

The stories on *House* also point out that friction between the personal and professional sides of life is not restricted to the pull of becoming a parent or other forces that are often identified with the growing number of women becoming physicians. Foreman also gets involved in clashes between who he is (and was) as a person and how he wants to be seen as a physician.

"House Training" (3-20) shows just one example of Foreman confronting the gap between the world he grew up in and the world he now works in. Early in the episode, Foreman's parents make a surprise visit. It seems they have to come see him because he won't go visit his childhood home. "You haven't been home in eight years," Foreman's father says in a sharp-toned manner.

The featured patient in this episode is African-American, and she berates Foreman, accusing him of abandoning the community he grew up in and acting like he is better than those he left behind. Foreman disputes her conclusions, but the accusations still have an effect. This patient's treatment does not go well. Foreman makes a lethal error when he thinks the patient has cancer and doses her with radiation that ends up destroying her ability to survive a simple staph infection. As the patient declines, Foreman opens up to her. He tells her about the mistakes he made growing up, including stealing cars and breaking into houses. He goes on to tell her that even though he did things in his youth that you wouldn't want to put on your medical school applications, he turned his life around. And yet, after pulling himself up into a prestigious career and gaining the respect of his colleagues, he sometimes feels like an imposter and that at any time the fact that he doesn't really belong there will be discovered.

"Imposter syndrome" is one of the stresses that diversity experts see as more people from historically underrepresented groups become doctors and scientists.

> *Underrepresented minorities face additional difficulties. Being the only minority in a lab, research group, or department is an isolating experience. Minority individuals may feel that they are under a microscope or that they are carrying the burden of an entire race of people. Because so few minority mentors and role models exist at the faculty level, some minority trainees report that they endure the "imposter syndrome," that is, a lingering feeling that they do not deserve their professional status or achievements. Such manifestations of lowered self-esteem have the potential to subvert minority trainees' desires to "aim high" professionally.*
>
> From NRC (National Research Council) Report, *Assessment of NIH Minority Research and Training Programs, Phase 3, 2005*

Foreman tells his dying patient that he felt like he had left his old life so far behind that he felt suffocated when he did visit the neighborhood he grew up in. He says he no longer felt at home there.

"We certainly don't view an African-American going into medicine as 'leaving the neighborhood,'" Salsberg says of the attitude at the Association of American Medical Colleges. Actually, he points out that physicians often go back to practice in neighborhoods like the ones in which they grew up, adding that neighborhoods with high proportions of minority residents are often medically underserved and need more physicians. But he also points out that "we don't want to suggest that only minority physicians can treat minority patients, of course. The same is true for rural areas. A medical student who comes from a rural community is more likely to go back to a rural community than others."

And certainly many physicians who grew up in the kind of neighborhood Foreman describes end up practicing or doing research in communities that are very different. Either way, there are benefits to overcoming historical patterns, including by encouraging greater diversity among physicians.

"The question might be, is there pressure on him or her to go practice back in their home communities that have great needs? Our attitude is that it is important to have diversity, but there is no greater responsibility to go work in an underserved area, and they don't have any greater responsibility to go into primary care. We need minority surgeons and therapists and the full range," Salsberg says.

Foreman receives a bit of wisdom about balancing work and personal relationships from an unexpected source in "Teamwork" (6-08). As he is doing a lumbar puncture on a patient who is a porn star . . . and whose wife also is a porn star . . . Foreman asks him if he ever gets jealous when his wife is shooting a sex scene. The porn actor replies, "It's a job. Once you start letting your work life rule your home life, especially if you are in the same line of work, your relationship's gonna be short."

Suicide

One day near the end of Season Five, Lawrence Kutner doesn't show up to work. In "Simple Explanation" (5-20), House sends Foreman and Thirteen to find out why, telling them he needs to know how to fill in the blank on the form for "reason for termination." When they go to Kutner's apartment, they find him dead of a gunshot wound. His death is ruled a suicide.

For most causes of death, including heart disease, cancer, and other diseases, the rates among physicians are lower than those among the general population. It makes sense. After all, physicians are not only better educated and tend to make more money than the average person, they specifically know more about the causes of illness and death. By contrast, most reports on suicide estimate the rates among physicians are as high as or even higher than those among the general populace. And the contrast is even greater when you look at female physicians. In the general population, men tend to commit suicide more often than women; but among physicians, the rate among women appears to be at least as high as that among men.

*Each year, approximately 30,000 Americans die by suicide—
outnumbering homicides and deaths from HIV/AIDS. Suicide is the
leading cause of violent death in the world, claiming almost a million
lives each year, more than homicide and armed conflict combined.
In the United States, suicide is the third-leading cause of death for
individuals between the ages of 10 and 24. It claims more than 4,000
young lives annually.*

From *Suicide Prevention: A Briefing for Physicians,*
Pennsylvania Medical Society

Dan Fox, Ph.D., president emeritus of the Milbank Memorial Fund,
says that when compared to the lower-than-average rates of deaths
caused by physical diseases among physicians, the suicide death rate
stands out. "They *appear* to have a high rate of suicide because in
general they are healthier than the rest of the population. At any age
cohort, except the oldest old, they are less likely to die of the chronic
diseases that we help along by the way we live. Therefore untreated
clinical depression leading to suicide leaps out at you."

*The risk of all-cause mortality was 56% lower than expected in men,
and 26% lower in women, compared to the general population. Standardized mortality ratios (SMRs) were markedly lower for diseases
strongly linked to smoking, e.g., cardiovascular diseases, respiratory
diseases, and lung cancer. Suicide was the only cause of death where
risk was greater than the general population. Overall, we found that
physicians are at substantially lower risk of dying compared to the
general population for all causes of death except suicide.*

From D. M. Torre, N. Y. Wang, L. A. Meoni, J. H. Young,
M. J. Klag, and D. E. Ford, "Suicide Compared to Other Causes of
Mortality in Physicians," *Suicide & Life-Threatening Behavior* 35,
no. 2 (April 2005): 146–153

Charles F. Reynolds III, M.D., at the University of Pittsburgh says
underlying rates of mental health issues do not seem to be higher among

physicians, and yet there is something different about doctors and their lives that appears to magnify the risk of suicide.

"There do seem to be some differences. Rates of depression and mental illness seem to be the same in physicians as in the general population: about one in ten men and one in five women will experience clinical depression during the course of a lifetime. What's different in physicians is that the rate of completed suicide is several-fold higher as compared with the general population, including the well-educated, well-compensated segments of the population. So it seems to be a work hazard specific to physicians," he says. "It's most noteworthy among women physicians. The rate of completed suicide among women physicians is three- to four-fold greater than in the general population. In the general population you see a gender gap, with rates of completion higher among men. You don't see that gap in physicians, where rates of completion are pretty much comparable between men and women physicians. Our best guesstimate is that somewhere around three hundred or four hundred physicians a year end their lives by suicide. That's the equivalent of about two medical school classes. That's a tremendous loss for society and obviously a loss for the doctors' patients and their families."

Reynolds says the methods of suicides are somewhat different, too. In general, men tend to use firearms and women are more likely to overdose, but among physicians overdoses are the most common method among both men and women. As for the risk factors for suicide among physicians, Reynolds points to untreated or poorly treated mood disorders like depression or bipolar disorders, often complicated by substance use.

There is another complication, too: the competitive drive common among physicians. Doctors were academic successes in school. They usually did very well in high school, went to good colleges where they also performed well enough to get into medical school. Then in medical school and residency they competed against other smart and accomplished classmates.

In "Games" (4-09), House tries to figure out why one of the new doctors on the show dislikes her patient. The patient is addicted to drugs and seems to be the opposite of the striving, successful personality type typical of physicians. House suspects that the patient represents a sort of failure that the doctor fears.

"Why are you afraid to lose?" House asks Dr. Amber Volakis. She says winners are happier. When House points out that the patient appears to be happy with his life, despite his failures, she calls the patient an idiot. But as House continues to press, Amber concedes that she may indeed feel compelled to win. Still, she says, it helps her to be a better doctor.

"Let's assume that's true. I get how that can make me a screwed-up person. But how is my willingness to do anything to get the right answer bad for my patients?" Amber says.

Reynolds says examinations of cases of suicide by physicians often reveal personal or professional setbacks. It may be that a history of success at school and then at work means some physicians have little experience coping with failure, so that they are unprepared when they do stumble. In addition, the undertone of competition with classmates and colleagues may create barriers to reaching out for help.

In "Painless" (5-12), Kutner wonders why Taub is taking the attempted suicide of a patient so personally. Eventually he gets Taub to admit he almost lost someone close, though he resists revealing the details.

Kutner probes. "So it's not your parents. Then it's your wife . . . someone you're close to . . ."

"A colleague. We were residents together. I should have done more to stop it. He had the mother of all God-complexes: so busy treating everyone's problems he was blind to his own. Helped himself to a vial of insulin. It's a miracle he survived. His friends and family almost didn't. He was a selfish ass," Taub says.

Later in the episode, Kutner guesses that Taub was still holding back, that the resident who attempted suicide was not a friend, but actually Taub.

"That selfish ass with the God complex who almost made the stupidest decision of his life—wasn't your colleague, was it? It was you," Kutner says.

"No." Taub's apparent discomfort makes his denial less than convincing.

No one saw warning signs before Kutner's character committed suicide several episodes later in Season Five. In that episode, House, Taub, Foreman, and Thirteen visit Kutner's adoptive parents, who say they also don't have any idea why Kutner ended his life. This sort of anguished bewilderment is common after a suicide. Reynolds says that in order to try to understand what happened, investigators will sometimes do psychological autopsies.

"We try to pull together medical records, including psychiatric records, of any treatment received. We also interview loved ones and professional colleagues to try to get a handle on whether or not the person in fact had a mental illness, like depression, whether they were receiving treatment, how well or otherwise the treatment was going. It's basically a pulling together of diverse sources of information that allow us to reconstruct a retrospective about what might have been going on," Reynolds says.

House can't leave mysteries unsolved, so he searches for any such clues as to what pushed Kutner toward suicide. He knows that when Kutner was a child, he witnessed the murder of his biological parents. House speculates that lurking pain of that trauma may have overwhelmed him. As House combs Kutner's apartment for clues, he develops a new theory. Maybe Kutner didn't commit suicide, maybe it was a murder that was made to look like a suicide. Cameron says House wants it to be murder, because then he wouldn't feel guilty about missing any warning signs of suicide risk. Wilson also senses that House may be more upset about his failure to predict Kutner's suicide than about his colleague's death itself.

"You worked with him every day for two years and you never saw this coming," Wilson says.

"No one saw it coming," House replies.

"But you see everything coming. This has never been about what you missed. This is about why you missed it. You're terrified that you're losing your gift, losing who you are."

Earlier in that episode, House pesters the fellows for clues.

"He didn't say anything? To any of you? Family problems? Bad relationship? Financial pressures?" House asks. Then he mocks their denial that they had missed seeing any warning signs.

"He didn't slit his wrists and . . . peacefully drift away. He shot himself. He didn't leave a note. That means panic. Which could have been preempted if the idiots who worked alongside him for eighty hours a week had seen this coming," House says.

"This isn't our fault! Something like twenty-five percent of suicidal people show no outward signs of depression," Thirteen insists.

"No. Twenty-five percent of suicidal people have friends who didn't notice anything and don't want to feel guilty," House says.

That exchange—the mix of surprise, denial, and guilt—sounds familiar to Reynolds. "That's a common problem, actually. When it happens, it's a real shocker."

Another physician who has studied and fought against suicide says that just because people deny there were warning signs doesn't mean no one knew of any difficulties.

"When somebody commits suicide and you really do an evaluation, it wasn't that they just got up and killed themselves; somebody knew that they were having problems," says retired U.S. Air Force surgeon general Lieutenant General Charles H. Roadman II, M.D.

Roadman helped lead a study of suicide by air force personnel.

"What we found was that eighty percent of the suicides had predisposing issues of either a broken relationship, trouble with money, or trouble with the law," he says.

What they didn't find was an excess level of schizophrenia or clinical depression among those who had committed suicide. After the air force studied suicide, it acted. Roadman says they trained over 80 percent of USAF personnel in how to recognize and prevent suicide. Suicide prevention was added to the curriculum at the U.S. Air Force Academy. The barriers they had to overcome included the stigma of mental health problems and also dealing with a mind-set that reporting suspected problems was "ratting" on a colleague.

"And then changing identification of their buddy from snitching to 'buddy care.' Buddy care is where you see someone in trouble, and you do something to identify them and get them help, rather than just let them languish on their own and then run out of options," Roadman says.

Of course, they also needed somewhere to go for help. The U.S. Air Force established multidisciplinary teams to respond.

Before the suicide intervention program went into effect in the mid-1990s, about fifty to seventy air force personnel committed suicide each year (a rate of about ten to sixteen per one hundred thousand people). Afterward, the number of suicides dropped to less than thirty a year. However, after the initial success, the suicide rate began to climb again; so leaders ramped up training again, and the rate went back down. On average, researchers say the training and treatment program reduced the rate of suicide by a third.

Even as program leaders saw the encouraging data on air force suicide rates, they noted that the rates in the other branches of the military stayed about the same or rose. Since then, the other services have started to implement some of the suicide prevention approaches pioneered by the air force.

Roadman says it is important to note not only that the program worked . . . but how it worked. Rather than just deploying health care personnel to increase the amount of psychiatric treatment, they used a community public health approach to understanding and addressing the social aspects of suicide risk.

"What it really says is that whatever was going on that we were doing, it was in fact effective. The difference between this and the psychiatric treatment approach is this takes a public health prevention, upstream approach," he says.

He offers a comparison to strategies for reducing heart attack deaths. The medical approach is to train people to do CPR, improve ambulance response and hospital capacity. While those things can prevent deaths of people having heart attacks, in order to prevent heart attacks from happening in the first place, society has to address the upstream issues, including the reasons people put on too much weight and have too little physical activity in their daily lives.

Researchers who tracked the effects of the U.S. Air Force suicide prevention program also recorded declining rates of accidental deaths and moderate-to-severe family violence, indicating that the public health approach had benefits beyond the issue of suicide itself.

"Oh, absolutely," Roadman says, noting that people commit suicide when they feel unable to cope with whatever problems they face. "Coping skills, or lack of them, will manifest themselves in marital problems, child abuse, traffic accidents, all these collateral issues."

While there is no single "commander" who can order health care personnel to learn about suicide and take effective action, there are national standards for medical education, as well as state medical licensing requirements that some experts say could be used to address the specific threat of suicide among physicians and other health care workers. Some efforts are under way. Charles Reynolds points to programs that teach medical students to recognize depression in themselves and their colleagues and then to seek help. In *The Real Grey's Anatomy*, I wrote about the Resident Wellness Program at Oregon Health & Science University. It is one example of an effort to counteract the professional competitiveness in medicine and the reluctance of doctors to seek care, which combine to push too many doctors to hide their problems for too long. Such a program might have helped Taub deal with the crisis that led him to attempt suicide during his residency.

Thirteen displays the reluctance of doctors to get care when she tries to cover up possible symptoms of Huntington's disease. Real doctors also sometimes try to mask the fact that they get sick just like anyone else. And they sometimes remark that patients can seem momentarily confused when they see a doctor with the sniffles from an allergy or other common illness.

Dan Fox says the aversion to acknowledging normal human frailty extends beyond individual doctors to medical institutions. He says that he and colleagues were rebuffed in their attempts to survey physicians in order to better understand the extent of depression and other mental health issues. One institution after another turned down their requests to have doctors fill out a form with the very same questions that new patients typically answer about their health histories.

Fox refers to parallels between physicians and pilots as he highlights the lessons medicine should learn from the air force experience with combating suicide.

"Unless something like that happens in medicine, you're going to keep having unnecessary suicides. The air force analogy is relevant, because before the policy change and the culture change, the first thing that happened to you if you sought help for mental distress was that you got grounded. And the worst thing that can happen to you in the air force is that you're not allowed to fly. That's where the prestige is. Ditto in medicine; if a medical board sanctions you, you can't touch a patient. And that's the nightmare," Fox says.

Changes in medical licensing may offer some levers to encourage action. Rather than being licensed for life, almost all physicians now have to be recertified during their careers. Recertification and other quality improvement measures may turn up signs of trouble.

"If your mental illness, or your physical illness for that matter, is so severe that it is impairing you, there are going to be quality changes. If you are depressed, you're going to forget things. Forgetfulness, distraction—it's all part of being depressed. You are going to forget and your quality is going to waver. So then the question becomes, why is your clinical quality wavering?"

Charles Reynolds also sees hope for physicians in the progress demonstrated by the air force.

"Medicine, like the military, is pretty hierarchical. So I think a top-down approach to try to bring about cultural changes could be helpful," he says.

But he wants to be sure that increased scrutiny during license renewal is geared toward treatment of mental health issues, rather than discouraging doctors from seeking help for fear that it could derail recertification.

"What we are trying to do is to get the boards' questions on renewal applications not to ask things like 'Have you been in treatment for a mental illness?' but rather 'Do you have any kind of medical condition that would make it difficult for you to function normally as a physician?' We are trying to move away from specific diagnoses and the stigma that is attached to them," he says.

Reynolds would use the same approach to substance abuse, asking only about current impairment, not about attendance in rehabilitation programs or other treatment.

However, Roadman says he thinks the U.S. Air Force experience applies mostly to other military branches and similar organizations, such as police and fire departments. He cautions against trying to draw too many parallels between military and medical hierarchies. And beyond that comparison, Roadman doubts that the successful techniques he helped put into use could be applied to address suicide and broader mental health issues in the general population. He points out that, by definition, everyone in the military is employed and insured. No one is homeless. Members of the armed forces are also generally healthy. People with organic brain disease or other serious problems are not enlisted.

"If you have an open population, a lot of unemployed, a lot of organic brain disease, a lot of languages, a lot of homelessness, it doesn't have as much applicability, because you don't have the chain-of-command ability to find all of these predisposing factors. And you have disease that actually requires medication and psychiatric treatment," Roadman says.

Roadman also points out that the upstream, community prevention approach he championed was designed and put into action before the wars in Afghanistan and Iraq. He says the military is learning that problems, including suicide risk, that result from traumatic brain injuries, post-traumatic stress disorder, and other effects of war require different solutions. Nonetheless, he says society would benefit by rejecting the stigma often attached to mental illness.

"If you can frame this not as mental illness, but you frame this as the environment producing stresses beyond your ability to cope, then it becomes a different problem. 'You are stressed' versus 'You are mentally ill,'" Roadman says.

And then there have to be caregivers and systems ready to respond to those who seek help. Unfortunately, mental health services are often hard to find or afford. Despite recent attempts to equalize the treatment of mental and physical ailments, even those who have good health care insurance may find, for example, that they don't have the same access to and coverage of treatment of depression as they would for heart disease treatment.

Any discussion of suicide in the media raises questions about the potential impact on viewers who may be vulnerable. At the end of the episode in which Kutner committed suicide, the show provided contact information for organizations that offer advice and aid to anyone who may be contemplating suicide or dealing with other mental health issues. A full screen graphic displayed the toll-free telephone number of the National Suicide Prevention Lifeline at 1-800-273-TALK (1-800-273-8255) and the Web site of the National Alliance on Mental Illness: www.nami.org.

WARNING SIGNS OF SUICIDE FROM THE AMERICAN ASSOCIATION OF SUICIDOLOGY

Get help immediately by contacting a mental health professional or calling 1-800-273-8255 for a referral should you witness, hear, or see anyone exhibiting any one or more of the following:

- Someone threatening to hurt or kill him/herself, or talking of wanting to hurt or kill him/herself

- Someone looking for ways to kill him/herself by seeking access to firearms, available pills, or other means

- Someone talking or writing about death, dying, or suicide, when these actions are out of the ordinary for the person

Seek help as soon as possible by contacting a mental health professional or calling 1-800-273-8255 for a referral should you witness, hear, or see anyone exhibiting any one or more of the following:

- Hopelessness

- Rage, uncontrolled anger, seeking revenge

- Acting reckless or engaging in risky activities, seemingly without thinking

- Feeling trapped—like there's no way out

- Increased alcohol or drug use

- Withdrawing from friends, family, and society

- Anxiety, agitation, unable to sleep or sleeping all the time

- Dramatic mood changes

- No reason for living; no sense of purpose in life

From the American Association of Suicidology, *Understanding and Helping the Suicidal Individual,* www.suicidology.org

Nine

Miracle Stuff

"It's still miracle stuff after all these years."

"It is pretty, all pink."

Those are the words of one of the world's most experienced transplant surgeons and one of his veteran assistants as they put the finishing touches on a procedure to implant a donated kidney into a patient. Technically there was really nothing remarkable about the operation. It was methodical, almost routine.

But even for a senior surgeon who has implanted countless organs into patients, organ transplants are, as he says, "miracle stuff." It's not just the fact that an organ taken from one person can survive and function inside someone else. It's the immediate and profound impact on the life of the recipient. Most treatments for chronic diseases minimize the damage or delay the progression of the underlying disease, but medical therapy often can't restore full health and vitality.

By contrast, for organ transplant recipients, the week before and the week after the transplant are different worlds. Indeed, a transplanted kidney starts producing urine before the patient leaves the operating room.

Kidney failure means spending several hours several times a week tethered to a dialysis machine that filters blood. A pancreas that doesn't produce sufficient insulin may require finger pricks for blood checks and insulin therapy every few hours. When the liver, lungs, or heart are too sick to be aided by medicines or surgery, death closes in on the patient. But replace the sick organ with a healthy one, and life and strength surge. A young man, for example, with both kidney failure and a diseased pancreas gets both organs replaced and the next day no longer has either kidney failure or diabetes. Tedious and draining kidney dialysis sessions . . . no longer needed. Frequent blood sugar tests, insulin injections, and concern about a sudden diabetic coma are relegated to history. "Miracle stuff."

Of course, organ transplants cannot magically restore perfect health. Patients typically have to take drugs to reduce the risk of organ rejection. They have to watch for infections and perhaps progression of the underlying disease that damaged their organs in the first place. The big catch, though, is that so many people who would benefit from an organ transplant never get one because there just are not enough organs donated.

According to recent statistics from the United Network for Organ Sharing (UNOS) and the Organ Procurement and Transplantation Network (OPTN), there are more than one hundred thousand Americans waiting for an organ transplant. Here's a breakdown of the waiting lists by organ type:

All organs	105,254
Kidney	82,949
Kidney/Pancreas combo	2,202
Pancreas	1,495
Liver	5,747
Heart	3,030
Lung	1,857
Intestine	229
Heart/Lung	75

Note: Some people are waiting for more than one organ.

Source: www.unos.org/data, accessed on January 16, 2010

Almost half a million transplants have been performed in the United States since the Organ Procurement and Transplantation Network (OPTN) began collecting national waiting list data more than twenty years ago. But even at the current rate of almost thirty thousand transplants a year, many people die before a suitable organ becomes available. According to a report from the Mayo Clinic, almost eighty people receive a transplanted organ in the United States each day, but another twenty people die with their names still on transplant waiting lists.

Except for many kidney and partial liver transplants, organs are usually retrieved from the bodies of people who died suddenly, often after a car crash or other injury. If more people registered as donors and told family members they wanted their organs offered to others if possible, the waiting list death toll could be reduced.

So why don't more people agree to donate their organs at death? Experts say that myths and misunderstandings about organ donation are a huge problem.

As researchers and professionals in the area of organ donation, we often wonder where members of the public get "crazy ideas" about organ donation like the existence of a black market, the corruption of the organ allocation system, and the untrustworthiness of doctors. The answer may have been quite literally in front of us for years.

> S. E. Morgan, T. R. Harrison, L. Chewning, L. Davis, and
> M. DiCorcia, "Entertainment (Mis)Education: The Framing of
> Organ Donation in Entertainment Television,"
> *Health Communication* 22, no. 2 (2007): 143–151

By "in front of us," these researchers mean in front of TV viewers. "Shows like *House* are contributing to that misinformation," says Susan E. Morgan, Ph.D. She is a professor in the Department of Communication at Purdue University in West Lafayette, Indiana.

In recent years, Morgan and other communications researchers have done surveys and experiments to learn more about where people get their "crazy ideas" about organ donation. The results document that even though viewers know TV shows are fiction, entertainment programs exert a powerful influence.

In one study of popular shows, including *House*, titled "Entertainment (Mis)Education," Morgan and her colleagues categorized the common myths seen on TV. Many of them involve corruption in the medical system: that there's an extensive black market for organs, that doctors manipulate the system and decide who lives and who dies, that donors may be declared dead prematurely in order to get their organs, that doctors are vultures who are eager for patients to die so that their organs can be procured. There are also stories about undeserving or ungrateful recipients, including alcoholics, prisoners, abusers, and other "bad" people. Over and over again, rich people are shown buying anything they want, even organs, regardless of official rules. Donors are frequently depicted as merely sources of spare parts.

"Doctors, especially the main character in the television drama *House*, are seen 'gaming the system,' that is, evaluating a patient as being sicker and in greater need of a transplant than they really are or otherwise manipulating the organ allocation system to favor patients of their choosing," the researchers wrote. They also noted that "characters in both *Law & Order* and *House* make comments about how easy it was for (the late baseball superstar) Mickey Mantle to get an organ transplant, with the implication that Mantle was an undeserving recipient whose transplant was made possible by his wealth and position."

In another study, researchers surveyed viewers who saw episodes of top shows that included organ transplant story lines. They asked about whether they agreed with a list of statements about the organ donation process. The authors wrote, "Two were accurate, truthful statements about organ donation ('Doctors work just as hard to save a patient who is an organ donor as one who is not,' and 'An organ is matched to a recipient through a national computerized system') and five were false statements about organ donation ('There is a black market for selling organs in the United States,' 'People can recover after being declared brain dead,' 'Doctors have personal pull in deciding which patient gets the organ,' 'A hospital's transplant committee determines priority of patients on the waiting list at that hospital,' and 'The rich and/or famous can pay their way for higher priority on a transplant waiting list or "pull strings" to get a transplant faster').''

Ratings of Belief Statements
About Organ Donation, by TV Program

	NUMB3RS	CSI: NY	HOUSE	GREY'S ANATOMY
True statements:				
Doctors work hard	4.11 (.988)	4.42 (.933)	4.24 (.987)	4.28 (.978)
Matched through computer	4.09 (.697)	3.97 (.813)	3.89 (.913)	4.02 (.809)
False statements:				
Hospital committee	3.74 (.899)	3.69 (.967)	3.85 (.897)	3.59 (.951)
Black market	4.27 (.776)	3.93 (.933)	3.87 (1.038)	3.65 (.994)
Recover from brain dead	2.77 (1.207)	2.52 (1.149)	2.48 (1.229)	2.70 (1.133)
Doctors' personal pull	2.71 (1.053)	2.40 (1.131)	2.77 (1.112)	2.56 (1.081)
Rich and/or famous	3.31 (1.321)	3.10 (1.384)	3.11 (1.352)	2.91 (1.187)

Note: Numbers in parentheses are standard deviations. Ratings of the belief statements were made on a 5-point scale where 1 = Strongly Disagree, 5 = Strongly Agree.

From S.E. Morgan, L. Movius, and M. J. Cody, "The Power of Narratives: The Effect of Entertainment Television Organ Donation Storylines on the Attitudes, Knowledge, and Behaviors of Donors and Nondonors," Journal of Communication 59 (2009): 135–151(Table 3)

Among other things, the results of this study indicate that the effects of TV shows are very specific; that is, rather than just adding some common background to popular ideas about organ donation, viewers absorbed the specific lessons of the episodes they watched. Morgan says that when they surveyed viewers of *House, CSI: NY, Numb3rs,* and *Grey's Anatomy,* they thought they would see some general attitudes and beliefs about organ donation. Instead, they found that the viewers' answers depended on the story lines of the specific episodes the viewers had seen.

"If [the episodes] featured a black market, it increased a belief in black markets. If they showed doctors killing patients for their organs, it increased a belief that doctors might kill patients for their organs. So there was a correspondence between the myth that was portrayed and increased belief in that particular myth," Morgan says. "And that wasn't what we had necessarily expected."

In addition to watching House try to trick those in charge of evaluating transplant candidates in "Sex Kills" (2-14), viewers have watched as he helped a man commit suicide in order to donate his heart to his son in "Son of Coma Guy" (3-07) and as he encouraged a patient to agree to an operation in which he would donate part of his liver to his wife in "Simple Explanation" (5-20) even though they both knew the man would probably die from the trauma of the surgery and so his entire liver would go to his wife. They have seen the team chase after recipients of organs that apparently were infected in "Not Cancer" (5-02). They have seen an emergency department doctor almost send a patient to the OR for removal of his organs even though he was actually paralyzed, not brain dead, in "Locked In" (5-19).

While the findings about the effect of specific episodes, along with other experiments involving health knowledge and entertainment TV, point to the potential educational effect of prime-time TV, researchers say the cumulative effect of the various myths in these shows tends to reinforce mistrust of the organ transplant system.

"There is massive mistrust of the entire system, from the paramedics who pick you up at an accident site who might let you die if they see that you are an organ donor, to the emergency room doctors who would do the same thing, to physicians that would perhaps hasten your death to procure your organs for some of their other patients. The organ procurement system is seen as corrupt and as favoring some people on the waiting list over others," Morgan says.

In all the TV shows that Morgan has reviewed, she says all but one of the messages about organ donation have been negative.

"There is only one good message. There is a general portrayal of people who decide to register to be organ donors as good people. That's taken as evidence that you must be a good person to be willing to do that," she says. But even that positive message tends to be complicated by a sense that those who do register to be organ donors are doing something that a hardheaded, rational person wouldn't necessarily agree to. In other words, organ donors are soft touches, too trusting.

Researchers say the more that TV medical shows appear to be trying to be accurate, the more that viewers believe the parts of the stories that are, in fact, inaccurate. So when House and his colleagues use the names of tests and drugs and symptoms properly, they are laying out a trail of credibility that is then more likely to lead viewers astray when the story takes an entirely fictional turn.

Although participants acknowledged that they knew that entertainment television represented fictional accounts, this concession was followed by the assertion that "there's always a kernel of truth." Indeed, the "kernel of truth" perception is exacerbated by the format of medical and legal shows. The scripts of these shows use technically accurate terminology, creating a sense of greater credibility. In addition, many storylines are based on real-life stories that audience members can easily recognize from news coverage.

From S. E. Morgan, T. R. Harrison, L. Chewning, L. Davis, and M. DiCorcia, "Entertainment (Mis)Education: The Framing of Organ Donation in Entertainment Television," *Health Communication* 22, no. 2 (2007): 143–151

When it comes to organ donation and transplants, there are plenty of kernels that can lead viewers on. For example, not only are there indeed black markets for organs in some other countries, there are just enough allegations and questionable cases reported in the United States to justify suspicions about broader conspiracies.

In a recent program for HDNet, former CBS News anchor Dan Rather told of a global black market in kidneys that has some U.S. connections. He interviewed people who said they had been involved with buying or selling kidneys in Moldova in Eastern Europe and in China. He showed pictures of a clinic in Turkey that had been raided by police. His story referred to an FBI roundup in 2009 of forty-four people, including public officials, religious leaders, and others in New Jersey. The suspects were charged with money laundering and corruption, but the federal complaint also referred to boasts by one of the suspects that he had been buying organs for years.

Rather also interviewed a woman who said she knew of living kidney transplants in California and New York in which donors were paid in violation of laws and regulations. The woman and unnamed sources for the report alleged that surgeons failed to make sure that the organ donations were entirely voluntary.

In 2007, a transplant surgeon in California was charged with prescribing overdoses of drugs to speed the death of a man in order to harvest his organs for transplant. The following year, though, a jury found the doctor not guilty. Medical ethics charges were also dropped eventually. The surgeon said that all he had done was give painkillers to a dying man. As it turned out, the man's organs were not suitable for transplantation.

In 2009, Apple CEO Steve Jobs received a liver transplant. Some people then said that it seemed he had perhaps jumped ahead of others who had been on the transplant waiting list. While Jobs did wait less time than some other patients, the waiting list formula also includes measures of severity of disease and life expectancy. Jobs's surgeon said he rose to the top of the list simply because he was the sickest patient on the list when a suitable organ became available. Jobs also apparently took advantage of the fact that organ waiting lists are shorter in some parts of the country than in others. Although he lives in California most of the time, Jobs got his transplant in Tennessee, which at the time had a relatively short forty-eight-day wait for liver transplants . . . much shorter than the average wait in California.

Although Dan Rather was unable to independently confirm any specific cases of black market kidney transplants in the United States . . . and the transplant doctor in California was acquitted of all charges of hastening the death of a potential donor (and it was pointed out that the family had already agreed to remove him from machine support before any transplant preparations were considered) . . . and Steve Jobs's doctors said he played by the rules when he needed a new liver . . . each of these stories provides those kernels of truth that TV writers can build on to draw viewers into gripping and persuasive dramas. Then while viewers say (and truly believe) they aren't accepting fiction as fact, the distinction between the kernels of truth and the bulk of the dramatic stories on TV grows fuzzy.

Sometimes the confusion comes from the language used. For instance, entertainment shows or news stories may refer to a "black market" in human organs existing in the United States, meaning cases in which a person agreed to donate one of his or her kidneys for cash or other payment and not for purely altruistic reasons, as required by the official rules in this country.

"When the term 'black market' gets mixed up with the urban legend of the guy waking up in a bathtub of ice [and realizing one of his kidneys has been stolen]. That's a black market: people killing you for your organs, taking them without your consent. That's a black market. What's happening here in the United States is that people are lying [about the reasons they are agreeing to donate a kidney]," says Tenaya Wallace, an organ donation advocate.

A national survey in 2009 done by Donate Life America, an organ donation advocacy group, and paid for by a pharmaceutical company that makes anti-rejection medicine found that:

- Fewer than two out of five licensed drivers in the United States is registered as an organ donor

- Only half of the survey respondents said they believed doctors fight just as hard to save their lives if they know they are organ donors

- Less than half said they understood that it is impossible for a brain dead person to recover from his or her injuries

From Donate Life America, "While the Majority of Americans Express Interest in Organ and Tissue Donation, Too Few Take Steps to Register as Donors," April 13, 2009 (available online at www.donatelife. net/pdfs/DLA_Survey_Press_Release_and_Survey_Responses.pdf, accessed on January 19, 2010)

Another media researcher, Brian L. Quick, Ph.D., assistant professor of communication at the University of Illinois at Urbana-Champaign, suspects the confusion is abetted by a sleeper effect. So that even if people know that the *House* episode about the patient with locked-in syndrome who is almost sent for organ harvesting by a busy emergency department doctor—"Locked In" (5-19)—is just a scary story . . . and that the surgeon in California charged with attempting to hasten a potential donor's death was found not guilty . . . over time the wall between the memories of what's real and what's made up begins to break down.

"I think initially someone might watch a show and go, 'There's no way a doctor would let someone die just because they are an organ donor.' But then over time, I'm willing to bet that that person would forget who the source was. They may just remember seeing something about a doctor letting a person die because they were an organ donor, but they forget it was on [a dramatic TV show]. They just remember that belief. It's problematic," Quick says.

So what's the big deal if viewers aren't exactly sure whether they heard something on the news or on *House*?

"With *House*, I would say, there are facts that a show can get wrong that don't matter. If they get stuff wrong about acute intermittent porphyria, it has absolutely no consequence that I can think of, as somebody who does media effects research. It's not going to have an impact. [But] there are facts that *House* can get wrong that do have a social impact, like willingness to donate. Because we have an organ shortage in this country and a lot of people are being buried with organs that could save other people's lives," Morgan says.

Despite those tragic consequences of misinformation, Morgan says sometimes even strong advocates of organ donation haven't really understood how make-believe stories on TV can have very real effects. She says her concerns were initially dismissed by many in the organ transplant advocacy community.

"It took them about a year after the completion of the first study to start to come around. There is a Listserv for that community. A lot of people made some really fairly insulting accusations about how I thought so little of the American public that I thought that Americans couldn't distinguish between Hollywood and reality. But I was thinking, 'Where else are they going to get their information about organ procurement and organ donation?'" Morgan says.

And then even when advocates decided to fight back against misinformation, Morgan says their tactics were sometimes clumsy and ineffective. For example, Morgan recalls how some transplant advocates reacted to shows portraying a black market in human organs.

"Their response to that is 'Well, that's illegal, so that doesn't happen in the United States.' Good Lord, there's a black market for everything. Drugs are illegal and we have an epidemic of drug abuse in this country. People aren't stupid; they see that there is a black market in other things and that if you have the money and have the influence you can get pretty much anything you want," she says.

One day in the mid-2000s a new effort to shift the media conversation about organ donation was born.

"I was on a panel at a Donate Life America conference about the portrayal of organ and tissue donation. Susan Morgan was also on the panel. I'd read her research. And basically at the end of her presentation she said that the organ and tissue donation community needs to get more organized and have a stronger voice when it comes to Hollywood. So I said. 'Yeah, we should do that!' And the Donate Life community said, 'Good. Go do that. You are in L. A. Get that done!' " Tenaya Wallace chuckles as she recalls how she suddenly found herself in charge of fighting Hollywood myths about organ donation.

Donate Life America, formerly the Coalition on Donation, is a national organization funded by regional organ procurement organizations to lead efforts in encouraging more people to register to donate their organs after death. Wallace was working at the affiliate in Los Angeles. She became the campaign director of Donate Life Hollywood . . . the campaign being to battle against the media myths that Morgan and other researchers showed scared people away from registering as donors or consenting to donate the organs of loved ones who have just died.

At first, Donate Life Hollywood intended to collaborate with the Hollywood, Health & Society program (see Chapter 1) because of their shared interest in the accuracy of health information on prime-time television shows. But Donate Life Hollywood wanted to take a more aggressive tack and advocate for more organ donation, rather than just provide information and resources to TV writers and producers.

Wallace says they've had an impact. The producers of the series *Samantha Who?* agreed to re-edit a scene that made eye donations seem "yucky" before the episode was repeated or issued on DVD. They convinced the creators of an ad campaign promoting college loans to delete tongue-in-cheek advice to "sell a kidney" to raise money for school. But they also try to hand out positive feedback with awards and other recognition.

Indeed, Wallace says the first letter written to *House* creator David Shore was an "atta boy" for "Not Cancer" (5-02):

Dear Mr. Shore,

House M.D. *was the first show in the 2008 fall season to contain an organ donation/transplant storyline. We in the donation and transplant community are very happy to see that the common myths and misconceptions that keep people from signing up to be a donor were not included in your "Not Cancer" storyline.*

That's how the letter from Donate Life Hollywood began. It went on to recap the most common negative portrayals of the organ donation and transplant system, and what's at stake: the people who die every day because not enough people agree to be organ donors.

Wallace says she tries to show Hollywood writers that they don't really need to exaggerate or sensationalize organ transplantation, because the real stories are full of all the human drama that any writer could hope for.

"These are incredible stories," she says. "These are the things that Hollywood loves. This is life and death. This is hope. This is triumph, transformation, second chances, all of this kind of stuff. Unfortunately most of the television shows take us into the underground, the world of darkness where something shady is going on; when really the everyday stories of organ and tissue donation are so much more interesting and so much more inspiring and so much more dramatic than that."

In 2009, Donate Life Hollywood staged its first film festival featuring some of these stories, along with transplant experts and writers.

Wallace points to the short-lived TV series *Three Rivers*, which was based on stories about an organ transplant team, as an example of how fiction can have a real impact. The series lasted only eight episodes.

"But it also saved twelve lives in eight episodes," she says. She's not talking about the lives of TV characters. Wallace says the *Three Rivers* series directly led to organ donations that went to a dozen people who had been waiting on transplant lists.

"There were four families that said yes to donation and referred to the television show as the reason why they were giving consent. It's not uncommon that a really good show that models behaviors to sign up as an organ donor would increase the number of people registered as donors . . . but there has never, ever been a television show where people actually referred to the show at the point at which someone has died and they are saying yes to donation. There were four families across the country, from four different states, that said, 'I saw that show and I want my loved one to save lives like they do on the show,'" she says.

Although *House* writers were praised for "Not Cancer" (5-02), a year later another episode featuring an organ transplant raised questions. In "Wilson" (6-10), Wilson donates part of his liver to a friend who is also his patient. Wilson feels guilty after giving the man a high dose of chemotherapy that destroyed his liver. However, a transplant expert says not only was the chemotherapy dose outrageously high, but the portrayal of the patient didn't ring true, most importantly in that the patient would not have been a candidate for an organ transplant. (The transplant expert asked that we not print her name because she doesn't really want her colleagues to know how big a fan of *House* she is.)

"They know [the patient] will be dead before the day is over, even though he's sitting up and eating and drinking and having a conversation. He tells Wilson, 'You're my friend, you have to give me half of your liver.' Wilson, of course, does it. You can see the ridiculousness of it. First of all, cancer patients are not candidates for transplant, unless it is liver cancer. There is no way that somebody with leukemia or other hematologic cancer would have gotten a liver transplant."

Not every patient who might benefit from an organ transplant gets one, because there aren't enough donors. But in this episode, the patient had a donor, Wilson. The transplant expert says sometimes people who could benefit from a living donor transplant (kidney or partial liver) do come in believing that the usual rules governing transplants don't apply to their cases.

"They might come in with a family member who is willing to donate. It's a rare event, but when it happens they wonder why they can't [get a transplant]. Those situations can arise. If you come in with your own donor, you may feel like the rules can be bent for you, because you are not taking a resource out of the general pool; you are bringing your own. So there's the idea that the situation should be looked at a little differently. That can be a little hard to deal with. Something like this is exactly what you're afraid of: somebody coming to you and saying, 'Well, I have my own donor. What do you care if I'm taking a risk?'"

One problem is that the procedure could hurt the donor.

"The live donor is taking a risk. You still have a responsibility to the donor; you don't want to harm the donor. You can't take it for granted that every single donor that comes in is going to walk out without a problem. There have been donor deaths. There are donors that then needed to have transplants. And there have been donors that had complications."

Harm to donors is one reason that many programs sharply reduced the number of living partial-liver transplants in recent years.

"It was rising, rising, rising. Then there was a death in New York. And all of a sudden it went down, down, down. Live donation really went down all over the country and the same thing happened in our program."

A report of one case described how a fifty-seven-year-old man donated a lobe of his liver to his brother. In this case, the recipient was a physician. The donor died three days after the operation, apparently of aspiration pneumonia. After two donor deaths in the early 2000s, the rate of living liver transplants in the United States dropped by half, from a peak of about 500 a year to about 250 a year. Part of the decline in living donor transplants may also be due to changes in criteria that allowed more livers from deceased donors to be approved for transplant, thus easing the demand for livers. Donor deaths have been rare, about one in seven hundred. But many more, about one in a dozen, suffer complications serious enough to send them back to the hospital.

Those very real risks are the reason transplant programs try to make sure that living donors fully understand what they are doing and haven't been pressured to agree. The scenario in "Wilson" would have triggered questions.

"The fact that it happened so quickly would have set off alarm bells. The donor has to have time to think about it."

Donors are supposed to be checked by multiple experts.

"Every person has a surgeon that goes over everything, a hepatologist [liver expert] that goes over everything, and an independent donor advocate that goes over everything, a financial person, a social worker, a nurse coordinator. It's a very lengthy process."

Nothing like the rush job shown on *House*. And the transplant team would have been on the lookout for signs of coercion. They would probably have wondered if the guilt trip being dumped on Wilson by his patient interfered with Wilson's ability to think clearly about the risks of the procedure. In the episode, House does try to talk Wilson out of donating part of his liver, saying, "If you die, I'm alone."

The transplant expert says sometimes it seems that donors may not have a clear understanding of what it means to donate a kidney or part of a liver.

"Some people are concerned about how the scar will look. I understand that people don't want to have a scar, but that's not the worst thing that can happen to you. It makes you kind of wonder if the person really understands what they are about to go through, if the worst thing in their mind is the scar."

She says she has encountered donors who don't have health care insurance and don't appear to understand that if they go through with the donation, they might not be able to get insurance, because they will be considered at higher risk.

The scenario in "Wilson" also seemed so unnecessary. Although there is a severe shortage of organs, livers from deceased donors usually become available in time for the sickest patients. If Wilson's patient really might die within a day, he would probably jump to the top of the waiting list and get a liver soon.

The expert points out another common misunderstanding about living liver donations: whether the organ comes from a living or deceased donor actually makes no difference in the rules.

"We apply the same rules to live donation as to cadaveric donation.

You have to be able to be a candidate for a cadaveric donor to be a candidate for a live donor. You have to meet the same criteria. Because there are things that can happen. If the liver you put in doesn't work, you'll have to change it for another liver."

So even if it seems that the recipient isn't taking an organ that could be given to someone else, sometimes things go wrong and that's exactly what happens. A recipient at risk of imminent death because a transplant organ is failing jumps up to the top of the waiting list, bumping other patients down.

The expert excuses the cavalier portrayal of a live donor scenario because everything on *House* is portrayed in a cavalier fashion. That's just the tone of the show. But she worries about some viewers having their hopes raised.

"You can't take medical shows too seriously. The problem comes when somebody is watching it and actually thinks that this is how something happens. That's when it's a problem . . . Somebody watching this could actually walk away thinking that cancer was not a contraindication," the transplant expert says. "It was as inaccurate as you can get about the process. And the message [the show] gave was wrong, because you can imagine all these people now saying, 'Well, why can't I get a liver?' such as people with metastatic colon cancer or other diseases that are not candidates for transplant."

The transplant expert ends up torn between annoyance at the inaccuracies she saw and forgiveness because the show is so fun to watch.

"I didn't like the concept that somebody with cancer, somebody who had a clear contraindication, was able to be transplanted, and that [Wilson] put himself at risk. It just wasn't realistic and it was the wrong message. But I liked the episode. I did, I loved the episode."

Tenaya Wallace says although the "Wilson" episode appears to misrepresent the rules governing live liver donation in the United States, in general she doesn't have a problem with *House*.

"Any of the transgressions are really because House transgressed. House always transgresses," Wallace says with a laugh. "That's his thing, right?"

So even when House does something wrong, as he did in the "Wilson" episode when he tried to pressure a family member of a crash victim to approve the donation of the victim's organs, she believes that viewers usually understand that just because House does something doesn't mean it's right.

"It was pretty manipulative, but honestly I kind of just shrugged my shoulders, because that's what House would do."

Ten

When Miracles Run Dry

Even with seemingly miraculous treatments such as organ transplants, and even with House in charge of the case, not every patient can be cured. In "Known Unknowns" (6-07), Wilson was preparing a speech to a medical conference. House took a look at his draft text.

"Euthanasia: let's tell the truth. We all do it," House read aloud and then turned to Wilson. "That's a great opening line. Are you insane?"

House feared that if Wilson gave the speech, he would sabotage his career. So in typically outlandish style, House drugs Wilson and gives the speech in his place. He includes Wilson's account of how he refused a dying cancer patient's request for a lethal drug overdose, instead telling the patient how to overdose himself and then leaving the man alone in his hospital room.

"When he first came to my office, I told him I would be with him every step of the way. But I left him alone at the end. I broke that promise. To cover my ass, I failed," House reads from Wilson's speech. "This is a burden no one should have to carry alone. And this is a decision no one should make alone."

The audience members listen intently. At the end there is a roar of questions, but as House heads to the door, only one audience member reaches him, thanking him for his courage in speaking out about the ethical challenges of treating a person who is suffering and has no hope of a cure.

In "Informed Consent" (3-03), a patient asks to die rather than continue with tests and treatments that he is sure are futile. Chase tells the team what he has seen other doctors do. "We give him a syringe full of morphine. Every doctor I've ever practiced with has done it. They don't want to, they don't like to, but that's the way it is," Chase says.

Are lethal overdoses really a common, though veiled, practice in medicine?

A number of years ago, researchers in Oregon did a survey study that included 70 percent of licensed physicians in the state. According to the responses, such requests are common. One in five physicians said that during the preceding year a patient had asked for a lethal prescription. About 7 percent of the physicians (187 out of 2,671 who responded to the survey) said they had written a lethal prescription sometime in their careers. In most, but not all, of those cases, the physicians said their patients took the lethal medication. Other surveys have produced somewhat different results, but they confirm that some physicians in some circumstances do give their patients prescriptions intended to end their lives.

Under the laws that would govern Princeton-Plainsboro Teaching Hospital in New Jersey, like those in almost every other state, physicians are not authorized to write prescriptions with the intent of accelerating death. (However, prescribing a dose of a drug that could be lethal would usually be considered appropriate if the primary intent was to relieve pain or other symptoms.) But that's not the case in Oregon and Washington. Voters in Oregon were the first in the nation to approve a system allowing physicians to prescribe lethal medications for certain patients. Twice, actually. In 1994, 51 percent of voters approved the Oregon Death with Dignity Act (DWDA). Three years of legal action, including court injunctions, followed. Just days after a federal appeal lifted an injunction against the act, voters again expressed their support; this time more strongly. In November 1997, a ballot measure seeking to repeal the Death with Dignity Act was voted down 60 percent to 40 percent. An attempt by the George W. Bush administration to declare that physicians who wrote lethal prescriptions would be subject to federal sanctions was ultimately turned away by the Supreme Court of the United States.

Voters in Washington State approved a similar law in 2008.

Although the term "physician-assisted suicide" is commonly used to describe what happens under the Oregon system, the law actually says that ending one's life in accordance with the law is not suicide. It is also not euthanasia, since the law requires that patients take the lethal dose of medicine themselves. Doctors may not give an injection or even put pills in a patient's mouth.

During the first twelve years of legalized physician-assisted suicide, Oregon officials reported that 460 people died from taking medications prescribed under the act. A total of 724 prescriptions were issued. Many patients never use the prescriptions. During the first nine months that lethal prescriptions were legal in Washington, sixty-three were written and thirty-six people died from ingesting the medications. There are specific rules governing the lethal prescriptions:

To request a prescription for lethal medications, Oregon's Death with Dignity Act requires that a patient must be:

- An adult (eighteen years of age or older)

- A resident of Oregon

- Capable (defined as able to make and communicate health care decisions)

- Diagnosed with a terminal illness that will lead to death within six months

Patients meeting these requirements are eligible to request a prescription for lethal medication from a licensed Oregon physician. To receive a prescription for lethal medication, the following steps must be fulfilled:

- The patient must make two oral requests to his or her physician, separated by at least fifteen days.

- The patient must provide a written request to his or her physician, signed in the presence of two witnesses.

- The prescribing physician and a consulting physician must confirm the diagnosis and prognosis.

- The prescribing physician and a consulting physician must determine whether the patient is capable.

- If either physician believes the patient's judgment is impaired by a psychiatric or psychological disorder, the patient must be referred for a psychological examination.

- The prescribing physician must inform the patient of feasible alternatives to DWDA, including comfort care, hospice care, and pain control.

- The prescribing physician must request, but may not require, the patient to notify his or her next of kin of the prescription request.

From *Death with Dignity Act Requirements*, Oregon Department of Human Services, March 2006 (available online at www.oregon.gov/ DHS/ph/pas/docs/Requirements.pdf, accessed on March 20, 2010)

Here's how House read Wilson's description of the case he presented to the medical conference in "Known Unknowns" (6-07).

"Patient S, a fifty-five-year-old man. End-stage lung cancer. His pain was beyond the point where we could even pretend to treat it. I showed him how to use the morphine pump. I told him too much morphine would kill him, but not to worry. The machine only gives out so much. To override it you need to enter a special code. I went to the door and told the nurse, 'The code is 328.' I said it loudly," House told the audience.

That brief description rankles Susan Tolle, M.D. Tolle is the director of the Center for Ethics in Health Care at Oregon Health & Science University in Portland. She was one of the researchers who surveyed Oregon physicians about requests for lethal prescriptions before they were legal, and she's been tracking how the system established by the Death with Dignity Act works. She says that a few years ago she met with a group of television writers (not from *House*) and that, just as in the scene from *House*, they wanted to know about the use of morphine to hasten the deaths of terminal patients. She told them morphine is the wrong drug.

"No," she says she told them emphatically. "It's not a good way to kill yourself. We know that everyone thinks about it and talks about it, but actually as a single drug what is usually mixed up is too dilute." She says a patient who attempted to overdose by repeatedly pushing the button on a morphine pump would likely fail. "What would happen is, you would push it a bunch and you would make yourself sleepy. You'd fall asleep and you'd stop pushing the button," she says.

Almost all of the people who have taken lethal prescriptions in Oregon have swallowed large doses of secobarbital or pentobarbital, two types of barbiturates that are commonly prescribed to treat short-term insomnia.

But what really angers Tolle is the claim that Wilson's patient was suffering untreatable pain. "That is a factual error," she says. "There is actually no pain we cannot treat, if we are willing to be aggressive enough, which would include a rarely used category called terminal sedation." She says she is offended by *House* and other shows that perpetuate the myth that end-stage cancer and other terminal conditions often inflict uncontrollable pain.

"The show sometimes plays to people's deepest fears. One fear many people have is that their pain will be untreatable, unrelenting, and overwhelming as they are dying. That should not be the case, if someone is well trained and willing to consult with someone else who is even better trained if they are having trouble managing someone's symptoms," Tolle says.

Indeed, while some patients in Oregon said they wanted lethal prescriptions because they were concerned about pain, Tolle and other experts say they don't know of a single case in which pain was the main reason a patient wanted to use the Death with Dignity law.

End-of-life Concerns of People Who Requested Lethal Prescriptions in Oregon

CONCERN	NUMBER	%
Losing autonomy	414	90.8%
Less able to engage in activities making life enjoyable	398	87.3%
Loss of dignity	282	85.2%
Losing control of bodily functions	264	57.9%
Burden on family, friends/caregivers	167	36.6%
Inadequate pain control *or* concern about it	101	22.1%
Financial implications of treatment	12	2.6%

Note: patients could choose multiple concerns.

UNDERLYING ILLNESS	NUMBER	%
Malignant neoplasms (cancer)	373	81.1%
Amyotrophic lateral sclerosis (ALS/Lou Gehrig's)	35	7.6%
Chronic lower respiratory disease (emphysema, etc.)	18	3.9%

UNDERLYING ILLNESS	NUMBER	%
HIV/AIDS	8	1.7%
Other Illnesses	26	5.7%

From data reported by the Oregon Department of Human Services, March 2010 (available online at www.oregon.gov/DHS/ph/pas/docs/yr12-tbl-1.pdf, accessed on March 20, 2010)

Cancer is the most common disease among patients who request a lethal prescription, but in contrast to the case that Wilson referred to in "Known Unknowns" (6-07), people who use the law more closely resemble the patient in "Informed Consent" (3-03), who wanted to call a halt to all the tests and treatments he believed were futile.

"He says no more tests. He wants to die, and he wants us to help him do it," Cameron says. House mocks the request. "He's thought this through; it's not an impulsive decision," Cameron insists. But House brushes aside the man's desire to die, saying he must be depressed. The Oregon and Washington laws do say physicians should look for signs of psychiatric problems, including depression.

Kenneth Stevens, M.D., would likely side with House. The former chair of the Department of Radiation Oncology at Oregon Health & Science University worries that some of his colleagues don't try hard enough to provide patients with alternatives to lethal prescriptions. He is a vocal opponent of Oregon's Death with Dignity law. "Assisted suicide and euthanasia are really a reversal of the doctor's role of taking care of the patient," he says.

"I have never prescribed a lethal prescription, and as far as I know I haven't directly killed anybody." But Stevens says patients do ask about lethal prescriptions. "I have had situations. I do a lot of prescribing of morphine and morphine-like drugs. I have had patients say, 'How many of these do I need to take to kill myself?' when I give them a prescription. And my response has always been that the purpose of the pain medication and the purpose of my care for you is to help take care of your symptoms. I'll be here for you to do that."

Stevens says he wouldn't withhold pain medication, even if he knew that a patient was contemplating taking an overdose, but his emphasis is on trying to show patients that they have alternatives. He recalls a woman who was stunned when she learned she had a dangerous cancer.

"Upon learning that she had cancer, she developed a very hopeless feeling. She told me she was going to wait until she was eligible for Oregon's assisted suicide law and die that way," Stevens says. He says he asked her to come back and talk more about her options. After a few weeks, she agreed to undergo treatment. Although this woman did not match the requirements of the Death with Dignity law, because she still had treatment options and wasn't likely to die within six months, Stevens says the point is that patients can change their minds.

It is true that the overwhelming majority of patients who consider physician-assisted suicide do not actually use it. Susan Tolle and her colleague Paul Bascom, M.D., explored a number of cases of people who were considering physician-assisted suicide in an article published in the *Journal of the American Medical Association*. They noted that while about half of dying patients want the option of physician-assisted suicide to be available, only about one in ten seriously considers it. In Oregon, only one in one hundred dying patients specifically requests a lethal prescription. Ultimately, just one in one thousand receives and uses a lethal prescription. The authors wrote that "when physicians commit themselves to remain present with patients and to respond to their suffering, in almost all cases, the patient's wishes can be met without PAS [physician-assisted suicide]."

Stevens's description of the personalities of those who request lethal prescriptions echoes the determined and insistent character of the patient who asked House and his colleagues to help him die in "Informed Consent" (3-03).

"These people that were requesting assisted suicide were very determined, very sort of authoritarian. They had had extreme autonomy in their lives, very controlling personalities. One doctor said talking to the patient was like talking to Superman when he's going after a train; he just couldn't stop this person from their desire to die at their own hands with an overdose," Stevens says.

An Oregon physician who campaigned in support of the Death with Dignity laws in Oregon and Washington puts a different spin on why people request lethal prescriptions.

"You have control of the timing and the manner of your inevitable death," says Nancy Crumpacker, M.D., a retired cancer doctor. "They are independent, and they've always made their health care decisions very thoughtfully and carefully and not just done what the physician said to do," she says. "They don't let other people make decisions for them."

In 2007, the *Oregonian* newspaper ran a series of reports (available online at http://next.oregonianextra.com/lovelle/) documenting the final months of life and then the death by lethal prescription of retired newspaper employee Lovelle Svart. Both Crumpacker and Stevens agree that her case typifies many of those who use the Oregon law.

"She fits. She fits to a T," Crumpacker says of Svart.

Stevens puts a darker interpretation on the trajectory of Svart's case, especially the final gathering of friends and family that included a newspaper reporter and photographer. "She had invited all these people to her exit party. How could she back out on it?" Stevens asks.

Tolle says that a dozen years of experience have provided enough data to be confident about painting a picture of the type of person most likely to ask for and use a lethal prescription. It is not the sort of weak and vulnerable person that critics of the law had feared it would be.

"It's not the poor, the downtrodden, the vulnerable, the minority," Tolle says. According to data gathered from case reports required by the law, the typical patient who used the Oregon Death with Dignity Act was a well-educated white person with cancer. Almost 99 percent had insurance (almost 70 percent had private insurance, the rest were in the Medicare or Medicaid programs). If you want to try to predict who might use the law, one of the leading "risk factors" is higher education.

Almost half of those who had taken a lethal prescription in Oregon had a college degree, nearly double the rate among Oregon adults in general.

To help pump up the drama, *House* and other shows often simplify complex situations into stark either/or choices. So it is with the depiction of dying patients. The doctors argue whether to give the patient a lethal overdose or leave him to suffer horribly. By contrast, the Oregon experience shows that while death may be inevitable, it needn't be painful.

Even critics of physician-assisted suicide criticize the way *House* portrays end-of-life care. "People deserve a life that's not TV. That's too bad. They could have helped educate the public about the benefits of hospice," Kenneth Stevens says.

Hospice, that is, care for people who are dying, is not part of what House does. He is interested only in conquering the disease. A review of all of the episodes of *House* from the beginning through most of the sixth season reveals the word "hospice" used only once. In "The Honeymoon" (1-22), House mocks Cameron's reluctance to cut open a patient. When she says it is premature to do exploratory surgery, House shoots back that it is premature to put the patient on a list for hospice care. In other words, he sees hospice as just another word for surrender.

That's a common, but quite wrong, attitude according to physicians on all sides of the physician-assisted suicide issue. Nancy Crumpacker says they all agree that people deserve to have the best possible management of their symptoms, whether or not the goal is cure. And though she says people often think that hospice care means giving in to death, it is not. The goal of hospice is to live better during the time that remains. She sees no important difference between hospice and other medical care.

"Well, it is medical care. But instead of a person having to leave their home and go see a physician, they've got access [to care] in their home. A nurse is part of that. There's pastoral care. There's physical therapy. There might be a medical social worker. There's a whole system that can come together, where this person doesn't have to leave their home to get people who are experts in managing the problems that come up at the end of life," Crumpacker says.

Actually, hospice care is provided not only at home, but in all settings, including hospitals and long-term care facilities. Almost 90 percent of people who have used the Oregon Death with Dignity law were enrolled in hospice, indicating that they were being seen by specialists in end-of-life care. According to Medicare data analyzed by researchers at Dartmouth University (www.dartmouthatlas.org), Oregonians are more likely than average to take advantage of hospice services, while patients in House's home state of New Jersey are somewhat less likely than average to use hospice. Oregonians are also far more likely to die at home, according to the Dartmouth reports. Only about 26 percent of Oregonians die in a hospital, compared to the national average of about 32 percent. Almost 40 percent of people in New Jersey die in a hospital. It seems House isn't the only New Jersey physician who wants to keep doing tests and treatments until the patient's last breath.

Tolle says it is no coincidence that the state that was first to legalize physician-assisted suicide is also ahead of the pack when it comes to providing comprehensive care to people at the end of life. After voters approved the Death with Dignity Act, but before it took effect, she and colleague Melinda Lee, M.D., wrote an editorial comment that appeared in the *Annals of Internal Medicine* (January 15, 1996), titled "Oregon's Assisted Suicide Vote: The Silver Lining." While she says she took some heat for the "silver lining" phrase, she says that all the public attention to end-of-life care prompted physicians to do a better job of addressing the reasons some people ask for lethal prescriptions.

"We have really moved a lot of physicians along and developed a lot more palliative care programs in a lot more hospitals. They provide the expertise, the consultations, and they raise the bar. And there has been a lot more public expectation that you actually can and should be more aggressive in treating pain, particularly in people with advanced illness," Tolle says. She notes that in addition to helping more patients die at home among family and friends, Oregon doctors have also increased their use of pain medications. One survey found that just before physician-assisted suicide became legal in the state, 85 percent of Oregon physicians said they had taken a class to learn more about controlling pain and dealing with other end-of-life issues.

Some commentators have argued that legalizing physician-assisted suicide would undermine the provision of comprehensive end-of-life care by providing an easier alternative. The initial response to voter approval of assisted suicide in Oregon suggests the opposite. The public has been telling the health care community for a long time that, when it comes to care of the dying, we are not meeting their needs and those of their loved ones. It took a wake-up call like this, however, to motivate the health care system to make necessary changes.

From M. A. Lee and S. W. Tolle, "Oregon's Assisted Suicide Vote: The Silver Lining," *Annals of Internal Medicine* 124, no. 2 (January 15, 1996): 267–269

Although House regularly demonstrates that he knows more than other doctors about almost everything, it seems he must have skipped end-of-life care training.

"There are just a number of things that are misleading, misrepresented, outdated, problematic, and not particularly helpful in promoting the best end-of-life care," Tolle says of the story lines on *House*. She says House should get help from someone who knows the right way to care for a dying patient. "Step up to the plate, Doctor. Get the help you need. There are people who are trained in palliative medicine. If you can't manage this, get them in there."

Tolle says the way House treats dying patients "suggests a lack of both skill and moral courage."

Eleven

Mistakes and Punishment

Doctors are human. Even House is not perfect. But when physicians make mistakes, people may die . . . and the doctors must cope with regret, second-guessing, and sometimes discipline.

Oh, No

Foreman misdiagnoses a patient in "House Training" (3-20). The mistake proves fatal. He thinks the woman has a rare blood cancer known as lymphomatoid granulomatosis. He prescribes treatment with high doses of radiation. But then after the treatment, he discovers that she did not have cancer. The patient turns out to have an infection, and because of the radiation treatment, her bone marrow and the basis of her immune system have been destroyed.

Foreman turns to Wilson for advice on how to break the bad news to his patient. Wilson's advice: Don't minimize the hurt. Don't pussyfoot around it. Give her time to process the news and then try reaching out to her.

"Wait until she's done thinking, until you think it's appropriate, then maybe you can touch her," Wilson says. "Put your hand on her arm like this. Let her know that she's still connected to another human being."

The hallway lesson in delivering bad news doesn't do the trick. When Foreman tells the woman that she will probably die within hours because of his mistake, she is shocked and then her disbelief at the news quickly turns to anger at Foreman. She yells at him. "Get the hell away from me!"

Later, Foreman returns to the patient's room. He asks for her forgiveness. He doesn't get it. "This isn't like you ran your cart into mine at the supermarket," the patient says.

There is no clearly effective treatment for lymphomatoid granulomatosis, the disease Foreman believed his patient had. However, total body irradiation is not even one of the common choices. Radiation may be used if the disease is localized in certain areas of the body, but if it is widespread, then steroids; antiviral drugs in combination with immunosuppressive therapy; chemotherapy; and other treatments are sometimes used. So, putting aside the error in diagnosis, Foreman's management of the case doesn't seem to match the disease he thought his patient had.

Then after he realized the real problem was an infection, he told the patient there would be no point in even attempting antibiotic therapy . . . despite the fact that people with weakened immune systems (including those with AIDS) are often treated successfully with antibiotics. So perhaps he compounded his error.

But the real point of the episode is to see Foreman dealing with the deadly consequences of an error, not the error itself or whether he could have somehow rescued the patient. The real test before him is breaking bad news and admitting error. He doesn't perform very well.

Doctors do make mistakes. And sometimes the mistakes cause permanent injury or death. When it happens, what's the best way to tell the patient or family? First though, while it seems obvious that doctors should tell patients when something has gone wrong, it is generally not required by law in the United States. Disclosure is required by law in

Canada. But, of course, physicians regularly hold themselves to higher standards than the legal minimums. According to surveys, most doctors say that patients should be told about significant errors, but they don't always practice what they preach. One review of the issue pointed to a survey of physicians that asked about their experiences when they or their family members were patients. They said that errors were disclosed in less than a third of cases. Another survey asked doctors how they would respond in various scenarios involving serious errors such as operating on the wrong body part or giving a patient an overdose of insulin.

> They found that only 42% would use the word "error," while the rest would use the term "adverse event." Only 50% of respondents would provide specific details of what happened; some would provide details only if patients asked specific questions that required the answers. Only one-third would offer an apology and very few physicians would discuss the prevention of future errors.
>
> From W. Levinson, "Disclosing Medical Errors to Patients: A Challenge for Health Care Professionals and Institutions," *Patient Education and Counseling* 76, no. 3 (September 2009): 296–299.

Oncologist Richard Penson confronted the professional and personal consequences of medical mistakes during a workshop he helped organize. He says the session began with one of the leaders telling how she missed the diagnosis of a disease that eventually led to the patient's death.

"The experience was generally really good, because there was a sense of solidarity, that we're professionals, trying to do our best, but everybody has a horrible experience with making a mistake," Penson says.

He points to studies that indicate that each time someone is admitted for hospital treatment, there is about a one in twenty-five chance of a significant medical error occurring at some point during the stay. And while physicians, nurses, and administrators constantly try to reduce the number of errors, people will always make mistakes; so health care providers also need to learn the best way to help their patients after something goes wrong. Penson says he finds it helpful to follow a protocol called SPIKES that is used for delivering bad news, whether or not an error occurred.

SPIKES involves:

Setting up the conversation with a patient by finding a private place, involving family, sitting down, connecting (with eye contact or touching the patient, as Wilson advised Foreman)

Assessing the patient's **Perception** by asking what he or she knows about the situation

Obtaining the patient's **Invitation**, in other words finding out how much detail the patient wants to hear

Giving **Knowledge** and information to the patient by warning that bad news is coming and always using common words, not medical jargon

Addressing the patient's **Emotions** by watching carefully for signs of sadness, shock, and other reactions and by asking questions

Strategy and **Summary**: offer a plan for what's next or set up a time to meet again to make plans

Adapted from W. F. Baile, R. Buckman, R. Lenzi,
G. Glober, E. A. Beale, and A. P. Kudelka, "SPIKES—A Six-Step
Protocol for Delivering Bad News: Application to the Patient
with Cancer," *The Oncologist* 5, no. 4 (2000): 302–311

While there is a big difference between telling a patient unpleasant news about his or her illness and revealing a medical error, Penson says the communication techniques are basically the same.

"Those same strategies are really important. Say to the patient, 'This is what happened. It was my fault. I am really sorry.' Say it clearly," he says. He adds that doctors shouldn't hold back negative information, because it is better that patients hear the information from the doctor, rather than from someone else. He also advises steps that Foreman didn't take: explaining to the patient what will be done at the hospital to prevent a similar mistake in the future and connecting the patient with the hospital's attorney in order to begin discussions about a legal settlement.

Penson says being open with a patient may not be easy, but it is better than trying to hide.

"A major goal, which is an important goal if you are just breaking bad news about cancer or treatment failure or something, but an even more important goal when you are a clinician responsible for a patient and you've done something wrong, is to try and keep the trust there. You can't always keep the trust there, but actually it's amazing how often you can," he says.

Penson says doctors aren't born knowing how to deliver bad news; they have to learn. He says he does things differently now than he did before he took classes on delivering bad news. For instance, while Foreman's attempt to reach out and touch the patient he harmed just makes her angrier, Penson says he's become a hugger.

"Even as a caring cancer doctor, I had never hugged a patient. Now I hug almost every patient. Every time I meet a patient I ask, 'Are you a hand shaker or a hugger?' I would say ninety percent of my patients say, 'I'm a hugger.' and so I give them a hug at the end of the conversation," he says.

He has also learned that doctors who try to downplay or sugarcoat bad news are setting up themselves and their patients for problems.

"They will say, 'You've got a shadow on the scan, but I think it's fine. Don't worry about it.' Then a month or two later, there's a big mass. And the patients says, 'You said not to worry about it.' Whereas the right strategy is to say, 'You've got something on your CT scan. We hope that it's fine, but we will be repeating the scan in two months' time.'" Penson says that method sets the scene without giving the patient unrealistic expectations. He says that if the doctor knows the specific odds of various outcomes, patients should be told. Rather than saying, "It's probably nothing," it is better to point out that "Four out of five times it's not a problem," making clear that in one out of five cases things do not go well.

While Penson says physicians should get formal instruction on communicating with patients, the scene in "House Training" (3-20) showing Foreman getting some quick pointers from Wilson in the hallway is realistic.

"I think that's a relatively valid portrayal of medicine. It really is an apprenticeship in large part," he admits. "I would say most clinicians in practice now have little formal training [on this topic] and have picked up, by experience and 'curbside' advice, how to do things. That's the norm and that's not a good thing."

Penson says his institution, Massachusetts General Hospital in Boston, prods doctors to improve by using part of their pay as a carrot.

"They take two thousand dollars off our pay each year. We can earn it back by doing things like washing our hands when we go in and out of patient rooms. This year there are three things we have to do, and one of them is to take a course on exactly this sort of thing: we all have to do an hour-and-a-half-long course on empathy or breaking bad news. I think people do take it seriously. How you break bad news makes a difference, a measurable difference in clinical outcomes for patients."

Whether it's delivering bad news or simply trying to explain a diagnosis or treatment during the routine course of a case, doctors, like most people, speak differently to "outsiders," including patients, than they do among themselves. Some of the difference is meant to help patients understand, since they come to the conversation with very different backgrounds. It's not only that few patients have extensive training in medicine. When we are patients, the words of a doctor carry not just sterile information; they can have life-changing consequences. Good doctors are aware of the emotional punch their words may carry.

In one case I observed, when a group of doctors was briefing the next shift about the patients on their hospital service, they bluntly described a woman who was not expected to survive. They all felt that further treatment was futile. Since there was nothing they could do to help the woman, a key topic was how to present the situation to the family, so that they would agree that the right thing to do was to turn off the machines that were pumping air in and out of the woman's lungs . . . and to give instructions that there should not be any attempt to do CPR when the woman's heart stopped beating. Several of the doctors said firmly that they would refuse to do CPR. Indeed, they said that useless pounding on the patient's chest would be an assault. Some of the doctors became visibly angry when told that a specialist on another service hadn't officially agreed that further intervention was hopeless.

But then when two of the doctors went to meet with the patient's family, their attitude was markedly changed. In place of the firm and matter-of-fact demeanor they showed when they were in their workroom surrounded only by their peers, the doctors conveyed their sympathy in soft tones. They weren't faking. When talking to fellow physicians, they were focused on the medical facts. When meeting with family members, they were trying to help ease the emotional storm of loss and grief. They confirmed that there was nothing they could do, and they answered questions about what would likely happen when the machines were disconnected, without going into unnecessary detail.

They were still providing care, though the focus of their attention had shifted from the patient to the family.

In "House Training," Foreman says he heard that if you do a good job of delivering bad news, patients will thank you, despite the fact that the information itself is devastating. Wilson warns him against expecting thanks. However, when the two doctors I was observing finished confirming to family members that their loved one would not recover, it was clear that the family members were thankful for the attention and care the doctors had demonstrated, even as they also felt profound loss.

A similar contrast may be seen when physicians realize that one of their peers may have provided less-than-ideal care. In one such case, a patient was transferred from a small-town hospital to a large medical center because the original surgeon realized that the problem was too complicated. When doctors got the first details about the case, some reacted with harsh annoyance that the surgeon took on a case that was too difficult and then left them to fix things. But when family members arrived the doctors were diplomatic. Here again, it's not just a show for outsiders. The doctors didn't have all the details and they didn't want to be seen as prejudging the actions of the surgeon; so they don't let the family members see that their hunch is that the original surgeon may have mishandled the case.

Foreman should have learned the basics of how to deliver bad news as a medical student, and then he should have studied the topic further and put the lessons into practice as a resident. The fact that Foreman grabbed Wilson in the hallway for a quick lesson in delivering bad news indicates that his medical education was seriously deficient.

The national organization that oversees medical residency programs insists that they teach residents how to communicate with patients.

Residents must demonstrate interpersonal and communication skills that result in the effective exchange of information and collaboration with patients, their families, and health professionals. Residents are expected to: communicate effectively with patients, families, and the public, as appropriate, across a broad range of socioeconomic and cultural backgrounds.

From the Common Program Requirements:
General Competencies established by the Accreditation
Council for Graduate Medical Education

Not only do medical students and residents read about delivering bad news to patients and attend lectures on the topic, they may practice on "standardized" patients (people who are trained to act like real patients). Some of these training classes even involve people who have actually been through cancer or other serious diseases . . . and know firsthand how it feels to get terrible news. Then, during the years of training that follow medical school, residents watch senior physicians deliver bad news to real patients. There is really no excuse for a physician supposedly as skilled and experienced as Foreman to be so ignorant of how to communicate with his patients at moments when they depend on him to get it right.

The consequences of an error affect not only patients, but also the doctor and others involved. As Foreman leaves his patient's room after telling her the bad news in "House Training," he punches a wall in anger and frustration, possibly breaking his hand. Cameron treats his hand and tries to make him feel better. Foreman brushes her away. "I killed a woman. Don't you think it's appropriate I feel like crap for at least a little while?"

Doctors may feel branded by the guilt and shame of a serious error.

"That's a lifelong experience. They will never lose that. And that's a good thing. It's a torturous scar, but it is part of how we endeavor to do the best," Penson says.

The aftereffects may include what doctors call "treating the last patient"; that is, being biased by the fear of repeating a mistake. The season after Foreman made a fatal error by mistaking an infection for cancer, he faces another case where he must choose between the two diagnoses. In "97 Seconds" (4-03), Foreman is working at another hospital after having left Princeton-Plainsboro Teaching Hospital. This time he again believes that cancer is the cause, but his new boss is not like House and urges Foreman to play it safe.

"Large cell lymphoma's incredibly aggressive. She'll be dead in a week if we follow the textbooks," Foreman says. His new boss, unlike House, tends to favor textbook treatment. "Unless it's infection, in which case you radiate her and she'll be dead in a day. And I know you've had some experience with that," she says, referring to the patient Foreman misdiagnosed the previous season. "I've seen doctors do this before," she continues. "Go back to the scene of the crime—if you're right this time, you purge yourself of past ghosts."

Foreman ignores her advice. He treats the patient for lymphoma, not an infection. This time he is right. But while House would have congratulated him, his new boss fires him for following his gut, instead of following the less risky course.

In a perfect world, physicians would not have to learn how to deal with the aftereffects of errors, they just wouldn't make them. But in the real world people will always make mistakes. There is increasing attention and effort being devoted to reducing errors in health care, both through research into the causes as well as creating payment and regulatory systems that encourage better care. The prestigious Institute of Medicine confronted errors in health care in two major reports. The first, *To Err Is Human*, released in 1999, outlined the extent of the harm caused by interventions that are meant to help people, extrapolating from studies to estimate that between 44,000 and 98,000 Americans die each year as a result of medical errors. The report went on to recommend actions and policies intended to help us better understand and then reduce errors. Then in 2001, the Institute of Medicine released *Crossing the Quality Chasm*, which took a broader look at how often medical care falls short of the best practices and issued "a call for action to improve the American health care delivery system as a whole, in all its quality dimensions, for all Americans."

Those who toil to improve the quality and safety of health care spend relatively little time looking into how to improve the accuracy of diagnosis and effectiveness of treatments for the bizarrely rare kinds of cases featured on *House*, simply because they are so rare. The real threat to most patients comes from all the little, common errors in routine cases. The numbers add up.

The massively obese patient featured in "Que Sera Sera" (3-06) has read even scarier numbers about the toll of medical errors. He tells the team he wants to be discharged even though the doctors have not yet figured out what caused the "coma" that brought him to the hospital.

"There are over three hundred thousand deaths caused each year by medical mistakes and hospital associated infections," the patient says as he asks to be sent home. Later in the episode, his fears about the hazards of hospitalization appear to be realized when he loses his sight during a brain biopsy. "You stuck a needle in my brain and ten seconds later I was blind! How's that difficult to diagnose? Who the hell knows what else you guys have done to me? I should have never come here!"

Ten years after the release of *To Err Is Human*, medical errors remain a very real problem. But some observers say there has been more progress toward changing the culture and practice of medical care than they dared to expect.

"I think it's actually breathtaking. I think it's really fairly impressive how far we've come. Now, we've also learned how hard this is, so despite a huge amount of activity and a lot of transformation, I'm convinced we're safer, but I'm not convinced we're that much safer, so there's still a long ways to go," says Robert Wachter, M.D. He is the chief of the Division of Hospital Medicine at the University of California, San Francisco and the chief of the Medical Service at the UCSF Medical Center.

A decade after the release of *To Err Is Human*, Wachter wrote an article for the journal *Health Affairs* reviewing the progress toward better, safer care. He says he sees evidence of progress every day.

"When I and the other members of my team came into the [patient's] room, the first thing we did was make sure we cleaned our hands, something we didn't think about ten years ago. Before the patients were taken off for a procedure or given a medicine, a nurse double-checked to be sure that this was the correct patient by asking the patient his or her name and date of birth, confirming that it was the right patient. I've had patients say to me, 'Why do people ask me that all the time?' It almost gets annoying," he says, while pointing out that constantly rechecking a patient's identity is an important way to reduce the chances that a busy doctor or nurse will give someone the wrong test or treatment. Wachter also notes that today's residents, while still incredibly busy, get more time off than earlier classes, because of limits on duty hours that are intended to reduce errors committed by tired doctors. "I had residents who were reasonably well rested, still busy, still a little harried, but by and large working no more than eighty hours a week, as opposed to the hundred hours a week that I worked [as a resident]."

Wachter says those residents also seem more aware of the kinds of tricks our minds can play on us, especially in stressful situations, that may lead doctors away from the correct diagnosis, including the sort of "treating the last patient" trap that Foreman was warned about. He also gives an example of how procedures have changed in order to recognize and reduce complications of potentially hazardous procedures. For example, he says that when a patient needed a procedure called thoracentesis, which involves sticking a needle into the chest to draw out fluid collecting around the lungs, it used to be common practice to have a resident perform the procedure.

"It's an inherently dangerous procedure, with a chance of puncturing the lung and causing the lung to deflate of about five to ten percent," he says. Now the protocol at the UCSF Medical Center is to call on a team specifically trained to perform thoracentesis using a small ultrasound machine to guide the needle. "Out of about two hundred of these that we've done, we've had one complication, instead of the normal amount that you'd expect of about ten or fifteen complications. All of that, people don't even notice anymore. It just becomes standard operating procedure. But all of it represents staggering amounts of change."

Wachter sees changes at the management level, too, including ongoing comparisons of error rates at different hospitals.

"I went to our Root Cause Analysis meeting, where we took a bad error that happened in the hospital and analyzed it in great detail, with twenty people sitting around the table, all of whom have significant expertise now in doing this, expertise that we didn't have five years ago. From that, a working group was formed to go out and fix all the systems. They'll come back a month later, reporting to us what they fixed or where they hit speed bumps," he says. "Again it's like, no big deal. We do this all the time now. But none of that existed ten years ago. People didn't think about it this way. We didn't have the expertise. We didn't have the structures. We didn't have the people. We didn't have the technology."

Medical care is incredibly complex and each patient is different. Wachter admits it is difficult to know for sure exactly how much safer an individual patient is today.

"Could I prove to you that we harmed fewer patients this week because of all those things? That's actually a hard thing to do, because it's so hard to measure errors; but I'm quite convinced that it was much safer than it was ten years ago."

And while his journal article recapping the last decade of quality improvement efforts pointed to "unmistakable progress," it also highlighted "troubling gaps."

"Communication is still really glitchy. When a patient comes into the hospital and I am admitting them on my service, in order to really make sure we do the right thing, we might need to communicate effectively with thirty different people. My team [communicating] with the outpatient doctor, with the family, with four or five different specialists calling in to figure out what's going on with their heart or kidney or brain, with the overnight shift, with the radiologists," he says. "I care a lot about this and we work pretty hard, so we try, but it's still very haphazard. It's still very dependent on paging people and finding them. It's almost impossible logistically for all of us to sit down together."

He can only dream about the luxury of having the sort of face-to-face conferences that are a staple of House's days.

Then there are the electronic medical records that were supposed to eliminate prescription errors and other problems related to bad handwriting, misplaced papers, and incomplete information. While many large hospitals have moved to electronic systems, much medical care still depends on a real paper trail. Wachter says it's not that doctors don't want to embrace the computer age (though changing old habits is always a challenge); the real hurdles include figuring out how to pay for the costly electronic systems and devising software that can adequately deal with systems far more complex than those used to manage retail inventories, air fares, or checking accounts. But he dreams of catching up to the user-friendly electronic systems that have become part of everyday life.

"I just watch my kids on Facebook and they are communicating in real time with twenty different people who are spread around the world. And if the right way of communicating something, rather than using text, is a picture or a video or music, it's all just seamless and it flows in ways that are much more nuanced and much more robust than what we have [in hospitals]," he says. "I don't think that would fix [health care communication problems] exactly, but I think the complexity of what we are trying to do means that we are left with still glitchy communication being a prime reason that care is still not as safe as it should be."

Wachter and others say that most electronic medical record systems are barely growing out of the "1.0" stage, so they resemble the clunky word processing or spreadsheet software of the early 1990s.

"Very few of them have gone through the versions 2.0, 3.0, 4.0 that you need to make these better, to get feedback from doctors and nurses who say, 'This just sucks. It does not allow me to do my work. It must've seemed really good to an IT geek, but in real life you can't take care of a patient when you have to click through thirty-seven screens to get to what you need to do,'" he says.

The UCSF Medical Center is feeling the growing pains. Wachter points out that even at this major academic medical center, just up the road from Silicon Valley, where there is no shortage of computer smarts, the electronic system that was adopted eight years ago was recently scrapped. The hospital staff will now have to learn a new system and the budget will take a multimillion-dollar hit.

"Ultimately we felt like it was in our interests and in the interest of our organization to sever that relationship at a cost to us of many tens of millions of dollars. And we're not that unusual. A lot of places have gone through the same thing," Wachter says. And that sort of experience is one reason that many health care institutions are moving slowly. "It's not shocking that organizations are a little bit wary about jumping into the pool until the systems really mature."

Still, he says that there has been progress and that recent increases in federal funding to support electronic health record systems should help accelerate the transition.

And what would Wachter do if he had dictatorial power to order changes to improve the quality of health care? He says he would continue to boost spending on electronic systems and then, when they have matured, mandate their use. He would also like to mandate practices that have proven benefits and yet have not been universally adopted.

"To me it is immoral that most American hospitals have hand hygiene rates of fifty to seventy percent, which means thirty to forty percent of the time your doctor or nurse will not have cleaned their hands before they touch you in the hospital. I think that sort of thing needs to be a standard."

Wachter would also boost public spending on research into quality improvement. After all, unlike the incentives that support research into a new drug or device, there's really no profit motive that would prompt private industry to focus on the quality of health care. However, there are changes already happening in how hospitals and providers get paid that may change some of those incentives. For example, Medicare will no longer pay health care facilities for treatment needed to deal with the results of certain errors that are never supposed to happen, such as operating on the wrong body part. So now administrators know that their hospital will take a financial hit if these glaring errors occur.

Wachter says he would also like to see medical education evolve to put more emphasis on the kinds of things that young doctors and nurses need to know but that aren't included in standard textbooks.

"Every medical student learns biochemistry. Every medical student needs to learn the science of safety and quality. It is just as complicated; and I suspect they'll use it more in their careers than the Krebs cycle," he says.

FYI, the Krebs cycle describes how cells take oxygen and glucose and turn it into carbon dioxide, water, and energy.

While the changes Wachter would like to see won't be easy to achieve, he thinks neither are they impossible.

"None of that is entirely unrealistic," he predicts.

But what would House think? He rails against mandates and standards and guidelines, always preferring to follow a hunch and trusting in his own brilliance. Certainly, House is not the only physician who resists what is derided as "cookbook medicine." Wachter, though, sees signs of a cultural shift; that more physicians are willing to accept that if the recipe is good, they should use it.

"I think so. It's a slow process. It's a heavy lift. We were trained in this culture of entrepreneurialism and that everybody does it their own way and we like to be innovative and try new things," he says. But increasingly he thinks his colleagues are moving away from holding up strongly independent physicians like House as their role models. "House in some ways is the embodiment at some level of the old model of the incredibly innovative, entrepreneurial, free-spirited, uncontrollable, brilliant diagnostician. That's all cool, and every now and then this person comes up with something just so out of the box that you don't want to tie that person's hands behind his back. But on the other hand, those people generally stink at doing some other things that are really very important when it comes to delivering high-quality and safe care, such as being an effective team member, standardizing the way we do certain things which should be standardized, and when we know the right thing to do, coming up with a checklist or a cookbook that ensures that we do it that way every single time."

He spells out the sharp contrast between House and another kind of leader: Chesley "Sully" Sullenberger, the U.S. Airways pilot who ditched his jet in New York's Hudson River without losing a single life.

"They both do really cool things. But the tradition of medicine was to [have doctors] like House being defined as the great doctor, but I think we're moving more towards someone like Sullenberger, who is clearly an amazing team player, who understands the role of checklists and systems. That will increasingly be what the model is for a great doctor. That's a big, big shift and the trepidation about that is understandable," Wachter says. But he adds that practicing medicine will never be just reading from a cookbook. "There are pieces of medicine that are so individualistic and so nuanced that you don't want it to be all cookbook and you don't want our hands to be tied so we can't try new things and new techniques, because then we'll never move the ball down the field. It's an incredibly interesting tension. It's partly why my job is a lot of fun, because I've got to try to figure out what's the sweet spot between all of these different forces."

While Wachter is encouraged by the progress he is seeing, the ultimate goal of an error-free health care system remains distant.

"There are still plenty of glitches. Those of us who care about, and write about, and do research in the area of patient safety are not going to be unemployed anytime soon."

Discipline

When physicians violate the rights of patients, they may face discipline. When they abuse their staff, they may face discipline. When they willfully abuse their privileged access to medicines, they may face discipline.

House evades sanctions. He has to . . . or his career and our viewing pleasure would whimper to a halt.

The licensing body that would regulate the physicians at Princeton-Plainsboro Teaching Hospital is the New Jersey State Board of Medical Examiners. The board's Web site lists summaries of actions against physicians who were not able to evade the consequences of their actions. There is no listing of any actions, much less any complaints, against Gregory House, M.D. After all, he is just a fictional character.

And yet an article on the Web site of another licensing board, the Medical Board of California, carries the headline "Medical Board of California vs. Gregory House, M.D.," and this notice:

> *The Accusation against Dr. Gregory House was issued on July 10, 2007 as a result of a patient complaint. It alleges that Respondent committed violations of the Business and Professions Code sections 2234(b) (gross negligence) and 2234(c) (repeated negligent acts) in connection with the care and treatment of two patients. Additionally, Respondent was accused of violating Business and Professions Code section 2239 (excessive use of drugs and alcohol), 2238 (violation of statute regulating drugs), and 2234 (unprofessional conduct).*
>
> From C. A. Aristeiguieta, "Medical Board of California vs.
> Gregory House, M.D.," *Medical Board of California*
> *Newsletter* 104 (November 2007): 4

The charges pertain to House's conduct in the episode "Son of Coma Guy" (3-07). But it was just a story. How could a real medical licensing board post this notice of alleged violations? Well, this case is just part of a story, too. It is part of a Medical Board of California newsletter article about staff members watching the episode, then discussing their concerns and how they might handle a doctor who acted like House.

The author went on to point out that he has encountered physicians who "fit the pattern of Dr. House." Of particular concern in those real-world examples, just as on *House*, was that not only did the doctors' actions violate ethics, regulations, and even laws, but that their colleagues knew of the transgressions and yet did not intervene.

Even when physicians are disciplined, it may be difficult for members of the public to find the records of the findings and sanctions. There is a national data bank, but medical license regulation is the responsibility of the states. Errors or omissions in reporting disciplinary actions can mean the records are not available as intended. That's what journalists Tracy Weber and Charles Ornstein found in their reporting for www.ProPublica.org and the *Los Angeles Times*. Their story, "Dangerous Caregivers Missing from Federal Database," published February 15, 2010, reported that the national data bank was missing records of disciplinary actions against probably thousands of health care workers.

"States either didn't know they needed to report or simply didn't report and the federal government asked no questions. So you had a confluence of bad things," Ornstein says. "Some states said they assumed it was being reported by a national organization or they assumed a parent agency was doing it or maybe a predecessor did it. But nobody from the feds asked questions."

Ornstein and Weber investigated the national data bank as it expanded to include more categories of health care professionals, including nurses, pharmacists, psychologists, and other licensed health professionals. Ornstein says it seemed obvious that some records were missing. For example, when they looked at records from Ohio that were supposed to cover every disciplinary action against any pharmacist in the entire state over a ten-year period, there was one case listed.

When notified by the news organization of the gaps, the federal administrator in charge of the database told the investigative reporters, "We take this very seriously."

The national repository for disciplinary actions is called the National Practitioner Data Bank, www.npdb-hipdb.hrsa.gov. It is administered by the Health Resources and Services Administration, part of the U.S. Department of Health and Human Services. As its Web site notes, one purpose of this national repository is to try to prevent physicians and other licensed health care practitioners from simply moving from state to state to hide past disciplinary actions.

The ProPublica journalists are not the only ones to point to holes in the data bank. The advocacy group Public Citizen released a report in May 2009 that said that as of 2007, almost half the hospitals in the United States had never reported a disciplinary action to the National Practitioner Data Bank. Either they were not filing reports or their doctors must be as angelic as House is brilliant. Public Citizen also noted odd variations in reporting. While the report authors said it was reasonable to assume that doctors around the country were similar, including experiencing similar rates of disciplinary action, the actual rates of reported actions varied widely from state to state.

In any case, members of the public generally can't read the reports in the National Practitioner Data Bank. Access is restricted to state licensing boards, hospitals and other health care institutions, certain professional societies, and certain public agencies.

But members of the general public often can find out about serious disciplinary actions taken by individual states. Each state has its own method of reporting. In New Jersey, a good place to start is the Web site of the New Jersey State Board of Medical Examiners, www.state .nj.us/lps/ca/bme. Each month a listing of public disciplinary notices is posted at www.state.nj.us/lps/ca/bme/disnotice/bmepdn.htm. The notices include the name and license number of the physician and a summary of the violation and the action taken. Of course, few people would check these notices every month.

You don't have to check the notice each month to learn about public actions taken against a physician in New Jersey. The state has a related

Web site, the New Jersey Health Care Profile, http://12.150.185.184/dca, that displays a link to "Search for a Health Care Professional." The information on this site is more comprehensive, listing not only public disciplinary actions, but also the education, board certifications, practice information, and professional activities of the physicians. The Web site includes information provided by other states, including some disciplinary actions, but as the New Jersey Web site cautions (and the experience of investigative journalists and others demonstrates), the interstate information "may not be comprehensive."

Members of the public may also be able to get information about physicians, including education, certifications, and known disciplinary actions, through a national service called DocInfo, www.docinfo.org. It is managed by the Federation of State Medical Boards (FSMB). For about $10, anyone can get a report on a physician. The Web site promises, "We not only search the state where the physician is currently practicing, we also search all known practice locations throughout the United States."

Happy hunting. Here's hoping your doctor is as brilliant as House . . . without his flaws.

ADDITIONAL READING

CHAPTER 1: IT'S JUST A SHOW

Davin, S., ed. *Medical Dramas: From Production to Consumption*. Cardiff: University of Wales Press, 2006. Information available online at www.uwp.co.uk/book_desc/1952.html, accessed on March 28, 2010.

Entertainment Education and Health in the United States. Menlo Park, Calif.: Kaiser Family Foundation, spring 2004. Available online at www.kff.org/entmedia/loader.cfm?url=/commonspot/security/getfile.cfm&PageID=34381, accessed on March 28, 2010.

Hollywood, Health & Society Program, Los Angeles, California, www.learcenter.org/html/projects/?cm=hhs, accessed on March 28, 2010.

Impact of TV's Health Content: A Case Study of ER *Viewers*. Menlo Park, Califs.: Kaiser Family Foundation, 2002. Available online at www.kff.org/entmedia/upload/Survey-Snapshot-ER.pdf, accessed on March 28, 2010.

Television as a Health Educator: A Case Study of Grey's Anatomy. Menlo Park, Calif.: Kaiser Family Foundation, 2008. Available online at www.kff.org/entmedia/mh091608pkg.cfm, accessed on March 28, 2010.

CHAPTER 2: A FEW ZEBRAS FROM THE HERD

Locked In

"Belgian Coma 'Writer' Rom Houben Can't Communicate." BBC News. Available online at http://news.bbc.co.uk/2/hi/europe/8526017.stm, accessed on March 12, 2010.

Caserta, R. "Comatose for 23 Years, Belgian Feels Reborn." The Associated Press, November 25, 2009. Available online at http://abcnews.go.com/International/wireStory?id=9171552, accessed on March 12, 2010.

"Living with 'Locked-In' Syndrome." BBC World Service. Available online at www.bbc.co.uk/worldservice/news/2009/11/091127_lockedin.shtml, accessed on March 12, 2010.

Monti, M. M., A. Vanhaudenhuyse, M. R. Coleman, M. Boly, J. D. Pickard, L. Tshibanda, A. M. Owen, and S. Laureys. "Willful Modulation of Brain Activity in Disorders of Consciousness." *New England Journal of Medicine* 362, no. 7

(February 18, 2010): 579–589. Epub February 3, 2010. Abstract available online at www.ncbi.nlm.nih.gov/pubmed/20130250, accessed on March 12, 2010.

Smith, N. *I Think There's Something Wrong with Me*. London: Bantam Press, 2007.

Smith, N. "My Wife Gave Me Life After Death." *Sunday Times of London*, August 19, 2007. Available online at http://entertainment.timesonline.co.uk/tol/arts_and_enter tainment/books/book_extracts/article2283235.ece, accessed on March 12, 2010.

A Can of Worms

Elliott, D. E., J. V. Weinstock. "Helminthic Therapy: Using Worms to Treat Immune-Mediated Disease." *Advances in Experimental Medicine and Biology* 666 (2009): 157–166. Abstract available online at www.ncbi.nlm.nih.gov/pubmed/20054982, accessed on February 13, 2010.

Hong Kong Health Department. Caution against improper weight control. February 8, 2010. Available online at www.dh.gov.hk/english/press/2010/100208.html, accessed on February 13, 2010.

Image of an antique tapeworm diet ad available online at www.diet-blog.com/archives/2007/05/24/vintage_weight_loss_sanitized_tapeworms.php, accessed on February 13, 2010.

To browse clinical trials that are testing the effects of parasitic worms on human health, go to www.clinicaltrials.gov and enter "helminth" in the search window. Note: some of the trials listed will be those that give people worm eggs, while others will be experimental treatments meant to kill parasitic worms.

Weinstock, J. V., and D. E. Elliott. "Helminths and the IBD Hygiene Hypothesis." *Inflammatory Bowel Diseases* 15, no. 1 (2009): 128–133. Available online at www3.interscience.wiley.com/cgi-bin/fulltext/121370235/HTMLSTART, accessed on February 13, 2010.

That's Gotta Hurt

Bhaskar, P. A. "Scrotal Pain with Testicular Jerking: An Unusual Manifestation of Epilepsy." *Journal of Neurology, Neurosurgery & Psychiatry* 50 (1987): 1233–1234. Available online with free registration at http://jnnp.bmj.com/content/50/9/1233.full.pdf, accessed on March 10, 2010.

Potts, J. M. *Genitourinary Pain and Inflammation: Diagnosis and Management*. Totowa, N.J.: Humana Press, 2008.

Death Cats

Dosa, D. M. "A Day in the Life of Oscar the Cat." *New England Journal of Medicine* 357, no. 4 (July 26, 2007): 328–329. Available online at http://content.nejm.org/cgi/content/full/357/4/328, accessed on June 7, 2010.

Dosa, D. M. *Making Rounds with Oscar: The Extraordinary Gift of an Ordinary Cat*. New York: Hyperion, 2010. Information available online at www.daviddosa.com, accessed on June 7, 2010.

Biological Liar

Benson, D. F., A. Djenderedjian, B. L. Miller, N. A. Pachana, L. Chang, L. Itti, and

I. Mena. "Neural Basis of Confabulation." *Neurology* 46, no. 5 (May 1996): 1239–1243. Abstract available online at www.neurology.org/cgi/content/abstract/46/5/1239, accessed on June 3, 2010.

Kapur, N., and A. K. Coughlan. "Confabulation and Frontal Lobe Dysfunction." *Journal of Neurology, Neurosurgery & Psychiatry* 43, no. 5 (May 1980): 461–463. Available online at www.ncbi.nlm.nih.gov/pmc/articles/PMC490577/, accessed on June 7, 2010.

Kopelman, M. D. "Two Types of Confabulation." *Journal of Neurology, Neurosurgery & Psychiatry* 50, no. 11 (November 1987): 1482–1487. Available online at www.ncbi.nlm.nih.gov/pmc/articles/PMC1032561/, accessed on June 7, 2010.

Miller, B. L., and J. L. Cummings, eds. *The Human Frontal Lobes: Functions and Disorders (The Science and Practice of Neuropsychology)*, second edition. New York: The Guilford Press, 2006.

Weems, Mason. *A History of the Life and Death, Virtues and Exploits of General George Washington*. Philadelphia: J.B. Lippincott Co., 1918. The story of the cherry tree is in Chapter 2, "Birth and Education." Available online at http://xroads.virginia.edu/~cap/gw/weems.html, accessed on June 8, 2010.

Premature Autopsy

Poe, E. A. "The Premature Burial." 1850. Available online at http://classiclit.about.com/library/bl-etexts/eapoe/bl-eapoe-premature.htm, accessed on June 7, 2010.

Selected news reports of premature declarations of death:

" 'Dead' Man Wakes Up Under Autopsy Knife." Reuters, September 17, 2007. Available online at www.reuters.com/article/idUSN149975820070917, accessed on June 7, 2010.

Haydon, Harry. "Bee Sting Man Wakes in Coffin." *Sun (London)*, January 26, 2010. Available online at www.thesun.co.uk/sol/homepage/news/2825012/Bee-sting-man-wakes-in-coffin.html, accessed on June 7, 2010.

"Man Wakes Up in Coffin at His Own Wake." AFP, January 21, 2008. Available online at www.smh.com.au/news/world/man-wakes-up-in-coffin-at-his-own-wake/2008/01/21/1200764121109.html, accessed on June 7, 2010.

Mauser, Daniel. "Dead Baby Wakes Up Before Funeral." August 8, 2009. Available online at http://guanabee.com/2009/08/dead-baby-wakes-up-before-funeral, accessed on June 7, 2010.

"Morgue Opens Body Bag, Finds Woman Is Alive." *Albany (NY) Times Union*, November 18, 1994. Available online at http://articles.baltimoresun.com/1994-11-18/news/1994322010_1_clarke-morgue-albany-medical, accessed on June 7, 2010.

"Medical Examiner Not Liable for False Declaration of Death." News 14 Carolina, April 7, 2010. Available online at http://charlotte.news14.com/content/top_stories/624225/medical-examiner-not-liable-for-false-declaration-of-death, accessed on June 7, 2010.

CHAPTER 3: PROFESSIONAL OPINIONS

What Do Doctors Think?

Koch, T. "The Doctor in This House: Lessons from TV's Gregory House, M.D." *Canadian Medical Association Journal* 178 (January 2008): 67–68. Available online at http://canadianmedicaljournal.ca/cgi/content/full/178/1/67, accessed on March 25, 2010.

Neely, K. "Is There a Doctor in Greg House?" *Atrium: The Report of the Northwestern Medical Humanities & Bioethics Program.* Northwestern University Feinberg School of Medicine, fall 2006, issue 3, pp. 19–20. Available online at http://bioethics.northwestern.edu/atrium/pdf/atriumissue3.pdf, accessed on March 25, 2010.

House 101

Czarny, M. J., R. R. Faden, M. T. Nolan, E. Bodensiek, and J. Sugarman. "Medical and Nursing Students' Television Viewing Habits: Potential Implications for Bioethics." *American Journal of Bioethics* 8, no. 12 (December 2008): 1–8. Abstract available at www.bioethics.net/journal/j_articles.php?aid=1709&display=abstract, accessed on February 8, 2010.

Czarny, M. J., R. R. Faden, and J. Sugarman. "Bioethics and Professionalism in Popular Television Medical Dramas." *Journal of Medical Ethics* 36, no. 4 (April 2010): 203–206. Abstract available online at http://jme.bmj.com/content/36/4/203.abstract, accessed on April 1, 2010.

Trachtman, H. "The Medium Is Not the Message." *American Journal of Bioethics* 8, no. 12 (December 2008): 9–11.

Wicclair, M. R. "The Pedagogical Value of *House, M.D.*—Can a Fictional Unethical Physician Be Used to Teach Ethics?" *American Journal of Bioethics* 8, no. 12 (December 2008): 16–17.

Wicclair, M. R. "Medical Paternalism in *House M.D.*" *Medical Humanities* 34 (2008): 93–99.

Rights and Wrongs

Czarny, M. J., R. R. Faden, and J. Sugarman. "Bioethics and Professionalism in Popular Television Medical Dramas." *Journal of Medical Ethics* 36 (2010): 203–206. Abstract available online at http://jme.bmj.com/content/36/4/203.abstract, accessed on April 1, 2010.

White, N. J. "*Grey's Anatomy, House* Present Skewed Ethics." *Toronto Star,* March 31, 2010. Available online at www.healthzone.ca/health/newsfeatures/article/787835--grey-s-anatomy-house-present-skewed-ethics, accessed on March 31, 2010.

Wicclair, M. R. "Medical Paternalism in House M.D." *Medical Humanities* 34 (2008): 93–99.

The Hospital Is a Mean World

Baran S. J., and D. K. Davis. *Mass Communication Theory: Foundations, Ferment, and Future.* Boston: Wadsworth Cengage Learning, 2009.

Federal Bureau of Investigation. Uniform Crime Reports. Available online at www
.fbi.gov/ucr/ucr.htm, accessed on March 28, 2010.

Gallup Poll. "Americans Perceive Increased Crime in U.S." October 14, 2009. Available
online at www.gallup.com/poll/123644/Americans-Perceive-Increased-Crime.aspx,
accessed on March 28, 2010.

Gerbner, G., and L. Gross. "Living with Television: The Violence Profile." *Journal of
Communication* 26 (1976): 173–199. Available online at www.unf.edu/~pharwood/
courses/fall05/3075fall05/crimegerbner.pdf, accessed on March 28, 2010.

Greenberg, B. S., N. Edison, F. Korzenny, C. Fenandez-Collado, and C. K. Atkin.
"Antisocial and Prosocial Behaviors on Television." In B. S. Greenberg, ed., *Life
on Television: Content Analyses of U.S. TV Drama*. Norwood, N.J.: Ablex Publishing Corporation, 1980, pp. 99–128.

Hetsroni, A. "Four Decades of Violent Content on Prime-Time Network Programming: A Longitudinal Meta-Analytic Review." *Journal of Communication* 57,
no. 4 (December 2007): 759–784. Abstract available online at www3.interscience
.wiley.com/journal/118502309/abstract, accessed on March 28, 2010.

Hetsroni, A. "If You Must Be Hospitalized, Television Is Not the Place: Diagnoses, Survival Rates and Demographic Characteristics of Patients in TV Hospital Dramas."
Communication Researcher Reports 26, no. 4 (October 2009): 311–322. Abstract
available online at www.informaworld.com/smpp/content~content=a916620082,
accessed on March 28, 2010.

Van den Bulck, J. "The Relationship Between Television Fiction and Fear of Crime."
European Journal of Communication 19, no. 2 (June 2004): 239–248. Abstract
available online at http://ejc.sagepub.com/cgi/content/abstract/19/2/239, accessed
on March 28, 2010.

Lighten Up

"I Want My Med TV." "ScriptDoctor" column quoting Dr. Mazzarelli. Available online
at http://holtzreport.com/thescriptdoctor/columns/I_Want_My_Med_TV.11.pdf,
accessed on June 6, 2010.

WPHT-AM 1210 Philadelphia. *The Anthony Mazzarelli Show*. Program information
and podcasts available online at http://philadelphia.cbslocal.com/personality/dr
-anthony-mazzarelli/, accessed on November 15, 2010.

CHAPTER 4: SHOW WITHIN A SHOW

An overview of HIPAA prepared by the American Medical Association is available
online at www.ama-assn.org/ama/pub/physician-resources/solutions-managing
-your-practice/coding-billing-insurance/hipaahealth-insurance-portability-ac
countability-act/hipaa-privacy-standards.shtml, accessed on February 15, 2010.

Encephaloceles information from the National Institute of Neurological Disorders
and Stroke. Available online at www.ninds.nih.gov/disorders/encephaloceles/enceph
aloceles.htm, accessed on February 15, 2010.

The Statement of Principles of the Association of Health Care Journalists outlines standards for journalists who cover health and medicine, including consider-ations of the rights of patients. Available online at www.healthjournalism.org/secondarypage-details.php?id=56, accessed on February 15, 2010.

Tsai, E. C., S. Santoreneos, and J. T. Rutka. "Tumors of the Skull Base in Children: Review of Tumor Types and Management Strategies." *Neurosurgical Focus* 12, no. 5 (2002): Article 1. Available online at http://thejns.org/doi/pdf/10.3171/foc.2002.12.5.2, accessed on February 15, 2010.

U.S. Department of Health and Human Services. Health Information Privacy. This Web site has information about the privacy rule that is part of the Health Insur-ance Portability and Accountability Act of 1996 (HIPAA). Available online at www.hhs.gov/ocr/privacy, accessed on February 15, 2010.

U.S. Department of Health and Human Services. HIPAA Administrative Simplification. Regulation Text. 45 CFR Parts 160, 162, and 164 (Unofficial Version, as amended through February 16, 2006). Available online at www.hhs.gov/ocr/privacy/hipaa/administrative/privacyrule/adminsimpregtext.pdf, accessed on February 15, 2010.

Video of surgery to remove a frontal encephalocele. Available online at www.orlive.com/childrenshospitalboston/videos/craniofacial-procedure-to-treat-encephalocele, accessed on February 15, 2010.

CHAPTER 5: HOUSE AND HEALTH CARE REFORM

Dramatic Reform

"Academics: Media Added to Reform Confusion." Covering Health blog. Association of Health Care Journalists. Available online at www.healthjournalism.org/blog/2010/02/academics-media-added-to-reform-confusion/, accessed on February 10, 2010.

Adelson, J. W., and J. K. Weinberg. "The California Stem Cell Initiative: Persua-sion, Politics, and Public Science." *American Journal of Public Health* 100, no. 3 (March 2010): 446–451. Abstract available online at www.ncbi.nlm.nih.gov/pubmed/20075315, accessed on February 10, 2010.

Butler, A. C., F. M. Zaromb, K. B. Lyle, and H. L. Roediger 3rd. "Using Popular Films to Enhance Classroom Learning: The Good, the Bad, and the Interesting." *Psychological Science* 20, no. 9 (September 2009): 1161–1168. Epub July 23, 2009, www.ncbi.nlm.nih.gov/pubmed/19645691, accessed on December 30, 2009.

How Healthy Is Prime Time? An Analysis of Health Content in Popular Prime Time Television Programs. Kaiser Family Foundation and the USC Annenberg Nor-man Lear Center's Hollywood, Health & Society, September 2008. Available online at www.learcenter.org/pdf/Howhealthyisprimetime.pdf, accessed on March 28, 2010.

Neumann, P. J., J. A. Palmer, E. Nadler, C. Fang, and P. Ubel. "Cancer Therapy Costs Influence Treatment: A National Survey of Oncologists." *Health Affairs* 29, no. 1 (January/February 2010): 196–202. Abstract available online at http://content.healthaffairs.org/cgi/content/abstract/29/1/196, accessed on March 28, 2010.

The Public and the Health Care Delivery System. NPR/Kaiser Family Foundation/ Harvard School of Public Health, April 2009. Available online at www.kff.org/ kaiserpolls/posr042209pkg.cfm, accessed on March 28, 2010.

Turow, J., and R. Gans. *As Seen on TV: Health Policy Issues in TV's Medical Dramas.* A Report to the Kaiser Family Foundation, July 2002. Available online at www .kff.org/entmedia/20020716a-index.cfm, accessed on March 28, 2010.

Wallack, L. "Health Care Reform: Asking the Right Questions." *Portland Oregonian,* January 29, 2010. Available online at www.oregonlive.com/opinion/index.ssf/ 2010/01/health_care_reform_asking_the.html, accessed on February 10, 2010.

Showdown

"Insurer Blames Health Costs for California Rate Hikes." The Associated Press, February 24, 2010. Available online at www.latimes.com/business/la-fiw-anthem25 -2010feb25,0,3310051.story, accessed on March 4, 2010.

Common Surgeries and Price Comparison in California: www.oshpd.ca.gov/com monsurgery. Instructions: www.oshpd.ca.gov/commonsurgery/Documents/Instruc tions.pdf. Common Surgeries and Price Comparison is a new Web tool allowing health care consumers to view and compare the price of twenty-eight common elective inpatient procedures at hospitals across California. Other states may also report hospital costs and other health care cost and quality information.

Compare hospital costs in Oregon: www.oregon.gov/OHPPR/RSCH/comparehospi talcosts.shtml. The data presented on this Web site represents the average payments for commercial inpatient claims for Oregon patients in acute-care hospitals who were discharged during calendar year viewed. The Web site contains data on the average payments for common conditions or procedures.

Facts on health care costs and insurance compiled by the Kaiser Family Foundation (not affiliated with Kaiser Permanente). Available online at http://facts.kff.org/ results.aspx?view=slides&topic=3, accessed on March 4, 2010.

Information collected from states and other sources is also available online from the Agency for Healthcare Research and Quality at www.ahrq.gov.

Massachusetts Attorney General Report: Investigation of Health Care Cost Trends and Cost Drivers. Available online at www.mass.gov/Cago/docs/healthcare/ Investigation_HCCT&CD.pdf, accessed on March 4, 2010.

Statement by Brian A. Sassi, president and chief executive officer, Consumer Business Unit, on rate adjustments in California. February 13, 2010. Available online at www.anthem.com/ca/shared/f0/s0/t0/pw_b142527.pdf, accessed on March 4, 2010.

The U.S. House of Representatives Committee on Energy and Commerce, Subcommittee on Oversight and Investigations held a hearing on "Premium Increases by Anthem Blue Cross in the Individual Health Insurance Market," on Wednesday, February 24, 2010. Transcripts and other information available online at http:// energycommerce.house.gov/index.php?option=com_content&view=article&id= 1905:premium-increases-by-anthem-blue-cross-in-the-individual-health-insurance-market&catid=133:subcommittee-on-oversight-and-investigations&Itemid=73, accessed on March 4, 2010.

What's All This Gonna Cost?

About CPT (Current Procedural Terminology). American Medical Association. Available online at www.ama-assn.org/ama/pub/physician-resources/solutions -managing-your-practice/coding-billing-insurance/cpt/about-cpt.shtml, accessed on June 6, 2010.

I discussed the cost of being treated by House in a conversation with Roger Siegel on NPR's *All Things Considered* on June 9, 2010. Available online at www.npr .org/templates/story/story.php?storyId=127593663, accessed on September 11, 2010.

New Jersey Hospital Price Compare. Available online at www.njhospitalpricecompare .com, accessed on June 6, 2010.

CHAPTER 6: TO TEST OR NOT TO TEST

Asscher, E., and B. J. Koops. "The Right Not to Know and Preimplantation Genetic Diagnosis for Huntington's Disease." *Journal of Medical Ethics* 36, no. 1 (January 2010): 30–33. Abstract available online at www.ncbi.nlm.nih.gov/ pubmed/20026690, accessed on February 3, 2010.

Bernhardt, C., A. M. Schwan, P. Kraus, J. T. Epplen, and E. Kunstmann. "Decreasing Uptake of Predictive Testing for Huntington's Disease in a German Centre: 12 Years' Experience (1993–2004)." *European Journal of Human Genetics* 17, no. 3 (March 2009): 295–300. Epub September 10, 2008. Abstract available online at www.ncbi.nlm.nih.gov/pubmed/18781186, accessed on February 3, 2010.

Etchegary, H. "Genetic Testing for Huntington's Disease: How Is the Decision Taken?" *Genetic Testing* 10, no. 1 (spring 2006): 60–67. Abstract available online at www .ncbi.nlm.nih.gov/pubmed/16545005, accessed on February 3, 2010.

GINA: Genetic Information Nondiscrimination Act of 2008. National Human Genome Research Institute, National Institutes of Health. Available online at www.genome .gov/10002328, accessed on January 26, 2010.

Huntington Study Group Web site: www.huntington-study-group.org.

Huntington's Disease Society of America Web site: www.hdsa.org.

Information on coenzyme 10 is available at www.nlm.nih.gov/medlineplus/druginfo/ natural/patient-coenzymeq10.html, accessed on February 2, 2010.

Information on creatine is available at www.nlm.nih.gov/medlineplus/druginfo/natural/ patient-creatine.html, accessed on February 2, 2010.

Meiser, B., and S. Dunn. "Psychological Effect of Genetic Testing for Huntington's Disease, An Update of the Literature." *Western Journal of Medicine* 174, no. 5 (May 2001): 336–340. Available online at www.ncbi.nlm.nih.gov/pmc/articles/ PMC1071392/, accessed on February 1, 2010.

Nagaraja, S. M., S. Jain, and U. B. Muthane. "Perspectives Towards Predictive Testing in Huntington Disease." *Neurology India* 54, no. 4 (December 2006): 359–362. Abstract available online at www.ncbi.nlm.nih.gov/pubmed/17114842, accessed on February 3, 2010.

National Institutes of Health National Human Genome Research Institute. *Learning About Huntington's Disease.* Available online at www.genome.gov/10001215, accessed on January 30, 2010.

National Library of Medicine Web site: www.nlm.nih.gov.

National Society of Genetic Counselors Web site: www.nsgc.org.

Robins Wahlin, T. B. "To Know or Not to Know: A Review of Behaviour and Suicidal Ideation in Preclinical Huntington's Disease." *Patient Education and Counseling* 65, no. 3 (March 2007): 279–287. Epub September 26, 2006. Abstract available online at www.ncbi.nlm.nih.gov/pubmed/17000074, accessed on February 3, 2010.

Scully, J. L., R. Porz, and C. Rehmann-Sutter. " 'You Don't Make Genetic Test Decisions from One Day to the Next'—Using Time to Preserve Moral Space." *Bioethics* 21, no. 4 (May 2007): 208–217. Abstract available online at www.ncbi.nlm .nih.gov/pubmed/17845479, accessed on February 3, 2010.

Wexler, Alice. *Mapping Fate: A Memoir of Family, Risk, and Genetic Research.* Berkeley: University of California Press, 1996. The story of a family at risk for Huntington's disease and the scientific research that led to the identification of its genetic source.

CHAPTER 7: WHO'S THE BOSS?

Help Wanted

Davies, H. T. O., and S. Harrison. "Trends in Doctor-Manager Relationships." *British Medical Journal* 326 (March 22, 2003): 646–649. Available online with free registration at www.bmj.com/cgi/content/full/326/7390/646, accessed on April 1, 2010.

Hariri, S., A. L. Prestipino, and H. E. Rubash. "The Hospital-Physician Relationship: Past, Present, and Future." *Clinical Orthopaedics and Related Research* 457 (April 2007): 78–86. Abstract available online at www.ncbi.nlm.nih.gov/pubmed/17259902, accessed on April 1, 2010.

Rundall, T. G., H. T. Davies, and C. L. Hodges. "Doctor-Manager Relationships in the United States and the United Kingdom." *Journal of Healthcare Management* 49, no. 4 (July-August 2004): 251–268; discussion 268–270. Abstract available online at www.ncbi.nlm.nih.gov/pubmed/15328659, accessed on April 1, 2010.

Firing Line

Cejka Search, Inc.: Physician, Allied Health and Health Care Executive Search Firm Web site: www.cejkasearch.com, accessed on March 29, 2010.

Physician compensation data: www.cejkasearch.com/compensation/amga_physician_compensation_survey.htm, accessed on March 29, 2010.

I Want My Toys

Angrisano, C., D. Farrell, B. Kocher, M. Laboissier, and S. Parker. *Accounting for the Cost of Health Care in the United States.* McKinsey Global Institute, January 2007, p. 16. Available online at www.mckinsey.com/mgi/publications/US_healthcare, accessed on February 17, 2010.

ECRI Institute. *Wasting Millions by Making Purchases Based Solely on Physician Preference?* Plymouth Meeting, Pennsylvania, 2009. Available online at www .ecri.org/press/pages/Physician_Preference_Items.aspx, accessed on February 17, 2010.

Fauber, John. "Faculty Disclose Outside Payments: Some UW Doctors Get 6-Figure Sums from Drug, Medical Firms." *Journal Sentinel.* Posted online: June 20, 2009, www.jsonline.com/features/health/48692952.html, accessed on November 28, 2010.

Fauber, John. "Journal Editor Gets Royalties as Articles Favor Devices." *Journal Sentinel.* Posted online: December 24, 2009, www.jsonline.com/watchdog/watch dogreports/80036277.html, accessed on November 28, 2010.

Lerner, J. C., D. M. Fox, T. Nelson, and J. B. Reiss. "The Consequence of Secret Prices: The Politics of Physician Preference Items." *Health Affairs* 27, no. 6 (November-December 2008): 1560–1565. Available online at http://content.healthaffairs.org/ cgi/content/abstract/27/6/1560, accessed on November 17, 2010.

CHAPTER 8: DOC, YOU DON'T LOOK SO GOOD

Kicking the Habit

"Experts Call for Balance in Addressing Under Treated Pain and Drug Abuse." News release from the American Pain Foundation. Available online at www .painfoundation.org/newsroom/press-releases/2006/experts-call-for-balance .pdf, accessed on February 20, 2010.

Greenup, R. A. "The Other Side of the Stethoscope." *Academic Psychiatry* 32, no. 1 (January-February 2008): 1–2. Available online at http://ap.psychiatryonline .org/cgi/content/full/32/1/1, accessed on February 6, 2010.

Allen, J., M. Cooley, R. C. Vari, D. Carlson, and C. E. Christianson. *Patient-Centered Learning: The Connor Johnson Case—Substance Abuse in a Physician.* University of North Dakota, November 8, 2009. Available online at www.drugabuse.gov/coe/ pdf/Connor-Johnson.pdf, accessed on February 23, 2010.

Cases Against Doctors. U.S. Department of Justice, Drug Enforcement Administration. Available online at www.deadiversion.usdoj.gov/crim_admin_actions/, accessed on February 20, 2010.

Center for Professional Health at Vanderbilt Medical Center Web site: www.mc .vanderbilt.edu/cph, accessed on February 6, 2010.

Miller, N. S., L. M. Sheppard, C. C. Colenda, and J. Magen. "Why Physicians Are Unprepared to Treat Patients Who Have Alcohol- and Drug-Related Disorders." *Academic Medicine* 76, no. 5 (May 2001): 410–418. Available online at http:// journals.lww.com/academicmedicine/Fulltext/2001/05000/Why_Physicians_ Are_Unprepared_to_Treat_Patients.7.aspx, accessed on February 24, 2010.

Schindler, B. A., T. Parran, Jr., and C. J. Daetwyler. "The Clinical Assessment of Substance Use Disorders." Online teaching module available at http://webcampus .drexelmed.edu/nida/module_1/default.htm, accessed on February 23, 2010.

Spickard, A., and F. T. Billings, Jr. "Alcoholism in a Medical School Faculty." *New England Journal of Medicine* 305, no. 27 (December 31, 1981): 1646–1648.

Spickard, A., and B. R. Thompson. *Dying for a Drink: What You and Your Family Should Know About Alcoholism.* Nashville: Thomas Nelson, 2005.

Work-Life Balance

Accreditation Council for Graduate Medical Education. "ACGME Duty Hours Standards Now in Effect for All Residency Programs." Chicago: ACGM, 2003. Available online at www.acgme.org/acWebsite/newsReleases/newsRel_07_01_03.pdf, accessed on November 28, 2010.

Asaro, P. V., and S. B. Boxerman. "Effects of Computerized Provider Order Entry and Nursing Documentation on Workflow." *Academic Emergency Medicine* 15, no. 10 (October 2008): 908–915. Epub September 10, 2008, www.ncbi.nlm.nih.gov/pubmed/18785946, accessed on November 28, 2010.

Bickel, J., and A. J. Brown. "Generation X: Implications for Faculty Recruitment and Development in Academic Health Centers." *Academic Medicine* 80, no. 3 (March 2005): 205–210.

Borges, N. J., R. S. Manuel, C. L. Elam, and B. J. Jones. "Comparing Millennial and Generation X Medical Students at One Medical School." *Academic Medicine* 81, no. 6 (June 2006): 571–576.

Boulis, A. K., and J. A. Jacobs. "Gender and the Career Interests of Graduating Medical Students." Paper presented August 14, 2004, at the annual meeting of the American Sociological Association, Hilton San Francisco & Renaissance Parc 55 Hotel, San Francisco, California. Available online at www.allacademic.com/meta/p109543_index.html, accessed on January 20, 2010.

Brotzman, G. L., C. E. Guse, D. L. Fay, K. G. Schellhase, and A. M. Marbella. "Implementing an Electronic Medical Record at a Residency Site: Physicians' Perceived Effects on Quality of Care, Documentation, and Productivity." *Wisconsin Medical Journal* 108, no. 2 (April 2009): 99–103. Available online at www.ncbi.nlm.nih.gov/pubmed/19437936, accessed on November 28, 2010.

Carrese, J. A. and M. A. Ibrahim. "Success, Regret, and the Struggle for Balance." *Annals of Family Medicine* 6, no. 2 (March-April 2008): 171–172. Available online at www.annfammed.org/cgi/reprint/6/2/171. Comments available online at www.annfammed.org/cgi/eletters/6/2/171. Both accessed on January 20, 2010.

Dill, M. J., and E. S. Salsberg. *The Complexities of Physician Supply and Demand: Projections Through 2025.* Association of American Medical Colleges Center for Workforce Studies, November 2008. Available online at http://services.aamc.org/publications/showfile.cfm?file=version122.pdf, accessed on January 20, 2010.

Goitein, L., T. D. Shanafelt, J. E. Wipf, C. G. Slatore, and A. L. Back. "The Effects of Work Hour Limitations on Resident Well-Being, Patient Care, and Education in an Internal Medicine Residency Program." *Archives of Internal Medicine* 165 (2005): 2601–2606. Available online at: http://archinte.ama-assn.org/cgi/reprint/165/22/2601.pdf, accessed on November 28, 2010.

Greim, J., D. Housman, S. Lenz, E. Mort, T. G. Ferris, G. S. Meyer, and J. S. Einbinder. "Improving Physician Note Entry Rates Through an Incentive Program." *AMIA Annual Symposium* Proceedings, November 6, 2008: 939. Available online at www.ncbi.nlm.nih.gov/pubmed/18999141, accessed on November 28, 2010.

Harrison, R. A. and J. L. Gregg. "A Time for Change: An Exploration of Attitudes Toward Part-Time Work in Academia Among Women Internists and Their Division Chiefs." *Academic Medicine* 84, no. 1 (January 2009): 80–86. Available online at http://journals.lww.com/academicmedicine/Fulltext/2009/01000/A_Time_for_Change__An_Exploration_of_Attitudes.25.aspx, accessed on January 21, 2010.

Harrison, R. "Evolving Trends in Balancing Work and Family for Future Academic Physicians: A Role for Personal Stories." *Medical Teacher* 30, no. 3 (2008): 316–318. Abstract available online at www.informaworld.com/smpp/content~content=a793158768, accessed on January 20, 2010.

Holtz, Andrew. *The Real Grey's Anatomy*. New York: Berkley, 2010.

Iglehart, J. K. "Revisiting Duty-Hour Limits: IOM Recommendations for Patient Safety and Resident Education." *New England Journal of Medicine* 359 (2008): 2633–2635. Available online at: http://content.nejm.org/cgi/content/full/359/25/2633, accessed on November 28, 2010.

Lerner, Barron H. "A Case That Shook Medicine: How One Man's Rage Over His Daughter's Death Sped Reform of Doctor Training." *Washington Post*, November 28, 2006. Available online at www.washingtonpost.com/wp-dyn/content/article/2006/11/24/AR2006112400985.html, accessed on November 28, 2010.

"Libby Zion" (obituary). *New York Times*, March 6, 1984. Available online at: www.nytimes.com/1984/03/06/obituaries/libby-zion.html?scp-2&5q-libby+zion+obituary&st-nyt, accessed on November 28, 2010.

National Institutes of Health. *Women in Biomedical Careers*. http://womeninscience.nih.gov, accessed on January 21, 2010.

National Research Council. *Assessment of NIH Minority Research and Training Programs: Phase 3*. Washington, D.C.: National Academies Press, 2005. Available online at www.nap.edu/catalog.php?record_id=11329, accessed on September 12, 2010.

Saarinen K., and M. Aho. "Does the Implementation of a Clinical Information System Decrease the Time Intensive Care Nurses Spend on Documentation of Care?" *Acta Anaesthesiologica Scandinavica* 49, no. 1 (January 2005): 62–65. Available online at www.ncbi.nlm.nih.gov/pubmed/15675984, accessed on November 28, 2010.

Scheef, D., and D. Thielfoldt. "What You Need to Know About Mentoring the New Generations." *Café Conversations*. Available online at www.thelearningcafe.net/downloads/Articles-Generations0904.pdf. accessed January 30, 2010.

Suicide

Andrew, L. B. "Physician Suicide." eMedicine.com, July 10, 2008. Available online at http://emedicine.medscape.com/article/806779-overview, accessed on February 6, 2010.

Center, C., M. Davis, T. Detre, D. E. Ford, W. Hansbrough, H. Hendin, J. Laszlo, D. A. Litts, J. Mann, P. A. Mansky, R. Michels, S. H. Miles, R. Proujansky,

C. F. Reynolds III, and M. M. Silverman. "Confronting Depression and Suicide in Physicians: A Consensus Statement." *Journal of the American Medical Association* 289 (June 2003): 3161–3166.

Centers for Disease Control and Prevention. "Understanding Suicide Fact Sheet." Available online at www.cdc.gov/violenceprevention/pdf/Suicide-FactSheet-a.pdf, accessed on February 27, 2010.

Hampton, T. "Experts Address Risk of Physician Suicide." *Journal of the American Medical Association* 294 (2005): 1189–1191.

Knox, K. L., D. A. Litts, G. W. Talcott, J. C. Feig, E. D. Caine, and J. Romano. "Risk of Suicide and Related Adverse Outcomes After Exposure to a Suicide Prevention Programme in the US Air Force: Cohort Study." *British Medical Journal* 327 (December 13, 2003): 1376. Available online at www.bmj.com/cgi/content/full/327/7428/1376, accessed on March 9, 2010.

Pennsylvania Medical Society. *Suicide Prevention: A Briefing for Physicians.* Available online at www.pamedsoc.org/MainMenuCategories/PatientCare/Disease Management/Suicide.aspx, accessed on February 27, 2010.

Reynolds, C. F. III, and P. J. Clayton. "Commentary: Out of the Silence: Confronting Depression in Medical Students and Residents." *Academic Medicine* 8, no. 42 (February 2009): 159–160.

Sansone, R. A., and L. A. Sansone. "Physician Suicide: A Fleeting Moment of Despair." *Psychiatry* 6, no. 1 (January 2009): 18–22. Available online at www.ncbi.nlm.nih.gov/pmc/articles/PMC2719447, accessed on February 6, 2010.

Suicide Prevention Resource Center. *Registry of Evidence-Based Suicide Prevention Programs: U.S. Air Force Program.* February 2005. Available online at www.sprc.org/featured_resources/bpr/ebpp_PDF/airforce.pdf, accessed on March 9, 2010.

Torre, D. M., N. Y. Wang, L. A. Meoni, J. H. Young, M. J. Klag, and D. E. Ford. "Suicide Compared to Other Causes of Mortality in Physicians." *Suicide & Life-Threatening Behavior* 35, no. 2 (April 2005): 146–153.

Yen, K., E. L. Shane, S. S. Pawar, N. D. Schwendel, R. J. Zimmanck, and M. H. Gorelick. "Time Motion Study in a Pediatric Emergency Department Before and After Computer Physician Order Entry." *Annals of Emergency Medicine* 53, no. 4 (April 2009): 462–468. Epub November 20, 2008, www.ncbi.nlm.nih.gov/pubmed/19026466 accessed on November 28, 2010.

CHAPTER 9: MIRACLE STUFF

Brown, R. S. "Live Donors in Liver Transplantation." *Gastroenterology* 134, no. 6 (May 2008): 1802–1813. Available online at www.ncbi.nlm.nih.gov/pmc/articles/PMC2654217/, accessed on February 1, 2010.

Dan Rather Reports. Episode 502, "Kidney Pirates." Aired on HDNet January 12, 2010. Transcript available online at www.hd.net/transcript.html?air_master_id=A6650, accessed on January 17, 2010.

Donate Life America Web site: www.donatelife.net.

Morgan, S. E., T. R. Harrison, L. Chewning, L. Davis, and M. DcCorcia. "Entertainment (Mis)Education: The Framing of Organ Donation in Entertainment Television." *Health Communication* 22, no. 2 (2007): 143–151.

Morgan, S. E. "The Intersection of Conversation, Cognitions, and Campaigns: The Social Representation of Organ Donation." *Communication Theory* 19 (2009): 29–48.

Morgan, S. E., L. Movius, and M. J. Cody. "The Power of Narratives: The Effect of Entertainment Television Organ Donation Storylines on the Attitudes, Knowledge, and Behaviors of Donors and Nondonors." *Journal of Communication* 59 (2009): 135–151.

Quick, B. L. "Coverage of the Organ Donation Process on *Grey's Anatomy:* the story of Denny Duquette." *Clinical Transplantation* 23, no. 6 (November/December 2009): 788–793.

Quick, B. L. "The Effects of Viewing *Grey's Anatomy* on Perceptions of Doctors and Patient Satisfaction." *Journal of Broadcasting & Electronic Media* 53, no. 1 (2009): 38–55.

Surman, O. S. "The Ethics of Partial-Liver Donation." *New England Journal of Medicine* 346, no. 14 (April 4, 2002): 1038.

CHAPTER 10: WHEN MIRACLES RUN DRY

"Living to the End." An Oregonian newspaper series about a former staff member, Lovelle Svart, who used the Oregon Death with Dignity Act. Available online at http://next.oregonianextra.com/lovelle/, accessed on March 16, 2010.

Bakker, J., T. C. Jansen, A. Lima, and E. J. Kompanje. "Why Opioids and Sedatives May Prolong Life Rather Than Hasten Death After Ventilator Withdrawal in Critically Ill Patients." *American Journal of Hospice and Palliative Care* 25, no. 2 (April-May 2008): 152–154. Abstract available online at www.ncbi.nlm.nih.gov/pubmed/18445866, accessed on March 10, 2010.

Bascom, P. B., and S. W. Tolle. "Responding to Requests for Physician-Assisted Suicide: 'These Are Uncharted Waters for Both of Us . . .' " *Journal of the American Medical Association* 288 (2002): 91–98. Abstract available online at http://jama.ama-assn.org/cgi/content/abstract/288/1/91, accessed on March 21, 2010.

Compassion & Choices. Advocacy group that offers information on "self-determined dying" and supports the physician-assisted suicide laws in Oregon and Washington. Website: http://compassionandchoices.org.

Ganzini, L., S. K. Dobscha, R. T. Heintz, and N. Press. "Oregon Physicians' Perceptions of Patients Who Request Assisted Suicide and Their Families." *Journal of Palliative Medicine* 6, no. 3 (June 2003): 381–390. Abstract available online at www.ncbi.nlm.nih.gov/pubmed/14509483, accessed on March 16, 2010.

Lee, M. A., and S. W. Tolle. "Oregon's Assisted Suicide Vote: The Silver Lining." *Annals of Internal Medicine* 124, no. 2 (January 15, 1996): 267–269. Available online at www.annals.org/content/124/2/267.long, accessed on March 15, 2010.

Lee, M. A., H. D. Nelson, V. P. Tilden, L. Ganzini, T. A. Schmidt, and S. W. Tolle. "Legalizing Assisted Suicide—Views of Physicians in Oregon." *New England Journal of Medicine* 334, no. 5 (February 1, 1996): 310–315. Available online at http://content.nejm.org/cgi/content/abstract/334/5/310, accessed on March 20, 2010.

Links to other resources and organizations are posted at www.oregonhospice.org/links.htm, accessed on April 1, 2010.

Oregon Hospice Association Web site: www.oregonhospice.org

Physicians for Compassionate Care. Advocacy group that believes "Medicine and physicians are not to intentionally cause death" and opposes legalizing physician-assisted suicide. Website: www.pccef.org.

State of Oregon. Death with Dignity Act—records and reports. Available online at www.oregon.gov/DHS/ph/pas/index.shtml, accessed on March 10, 2010. This Web site includes reports on all cases in which prescriptions were written and/or people ended their lives using the provisions of the law. Other documents including the act's history and requirements as well as studies are also available here.

Syllabus for Controversy in Modern Medicine: Physician Assisted Suicide. This medical education session was jointly presented by a supporter and an opponent of Oregon's Death with Dignity law. Available online at www.ohsu.edu/pcmonline/syllabus/session.cfm?sessionId=1109, accessed on March 16, 2010.

Washington Death with Dignity Act Web site: www.doh.wa.gov/dwda/.

CHAPTER 11: MISTAKES AND PUNISHMENT

Oh, No

Accreditation Council for Graduate Medical Education. ACGME Outcome Project. Common Program Requirements: General Competencies. Approved by the ACGME Board February 13, 2007. Available online at www.acgme.org/outcome/comp/GeneralCompetenciesStandards21307.pdf, accessed on February 16, 2010.

Baile, W. F., R. Buckman, R. Lenzi, G. Glober, E. A. Beale, and A. P. Kudelka. "SPIKES—A Six-Step Protocol for Delivering Bad News: Application to the Patient with Cancer." *The Oncologist* 5, no. 4 (2000): 302–311. Available online at http://theoncologist.alphamedpress.org/cgi/content/full/5/4/302, accessed on March 23, 2010.

Institute of Medicine. *Crossing the Quality Chasm.* Washington, D.C.: National Academies Press, 2001. Available online at http://books.nap.edu/openbook.php?record_id=10027, accessed on March 23, 2010.

Institute of Medicine. *To Err Is Human.* Washington, D.C.: National Academies Press, 2000. Available online at http://books.nap.edu/openbook.php?record_id=9728, accessed on March 23, 2010.

Kamangar, N., and A. W. O'Regan. "Lymphomatoid Granulomatosis." EMedicine. Available online at http://emedicine.medscape.com/article/299751-overview, accessed on February 16, 2010.

Levinson W. "Disclosing Medical Errors to Patients: A Challenge for Health Care

Professionals and Institutions." *Patient Education and Counseling* 76, no. 3 (September 2009): 296–299. Epub August 14, 2009. Abstract available online at www.ncbi.nlm.nih.gov/pubmed/19683408, accessed on March 22, 2010.

Liebman, C. B., and C. S. Hyman. "A Mediation Skills Model to Manage Disclosure of Errors and Adverse Events to Patients." *Health Affairs* (Millwood) 23, no, 4 (July-August 2004): 22–32. Abstract available online at http://content.healthaffairs.org/cgi/content/abstract/23/4/22, accessed on September 12, 2010.

Mazor, K. M., S. R. Simon, and J. H. Gurwitz. "Communicating with Patients About Medical Errors: A Review of the Literature." *Archives of Internal Medicine* 164, no. 15 (August 9-23 2004): 1690–1697. Available online at http://archinte.ama-assn .org/cgi/content/full/164/15/1690, accessed on February 16, 2010.

Penson, R. T., S. S. Svendsen, B. A. Chabner, T. J. Lynch, Jr., and W. Levinson. "Medical Mistakes: A Workshop on Personal Perspectives." *The Oncologist* 6, no. 1 (2001): 92–99. Available online at http://theoncologist.alphamedpress.org/cgi/content/full/6/1/92, accessed on February 16, 2010.

Rosenbaum, M. E., K. J. Ferguson, J. G. Lobas. "Teaching Medical Students and Residents Skills for Delivering Bad News: A Review of Strategies." *Academic Medicine* 79, no. 2 (2004): 107–117. Available online at http://journals.lww.com/academicmedicine/Fulltext/2004/02000/Teaching_Medical_Students_and_Residents_Skills_for.2.aspx, accessed on February 16, 2010.

Vercler, C. J., and P. Angelos. "Communicating Errors." *Cancer Treatment and Research* 140 (2008): 195–213.

Wachter, R. M. "Patient Safety at Ten: Unmistakable Progress, Troubling Gaps." *Health Affairs* 29, no 1 (January/February 2010): 165–173. Abstract available online at http://content.healthaffairs.org/cgi/content/abstract/29/1/165, accessed on February 16, 2010.

Discipline

Aristeiguieta, C. A. "Medical Board of California vs. Gregory House, M.D." *Medical Board of California Newsletter* 104 (November 2007): 4. Available online at www.mbc.ca.gov/publications/newsletter_2007_11.pdf, accessed on March 31, 2010.

Weber, T., and C. Ornstein. "Dangerous Caregivers Missing from Federal Database." ProPublica.org, February 15, 2010. Available online at www.propublica.org/feature/federal-health-professional-disciplinary-database-remarkably-incomplete, accessed on April 1, 2010.

Wolfe, S., and A. Levine. "Hospitals Drop the Ball on Physician Oversight: Report on Under-Reporting to the National Practitioner Data Bank." Public Citizen, May 27, 2009. Available online at www.citizen.org/Page.aspx?pid=585, accessed on April 1, 2010.

INDEX

Discover more facts behind the addictive medical drama

Discover what House, M.D. is built on—fact or fiction…

- How can a teenager adopted as an infant nearly die because his birth mother didn't get a measles shot?
- How can a missed eye doctor appointment reveal a genetic disease?
- How can a husband's faith in his wife's fidelity determine whether radical treatment will cure her or kill her?

And more!
Available now from Berkley

penguin.com